THE HIDDEN WAR

The True Story of
War in Afghanistan

Artyom Borovik

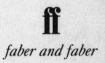

faber and faber

First published in the USSR in 1990 by International Relations Publishing House
Published simultaneously in Canada

Published in the United States of America in 1990 by the Atlantic Monthly Press

First published in Great Britain in 1991
by Faber and Faber Limited
3 Queen Square London WC1N 3AU
This paperback edition published in 2001

Printed in England by Mackays of Chatham plc, Chatham, Kent

A CIP record for this book is available from the British Library

ISBN 0-571-21544-0

10 9 8 7 6 5 4 3 2 1

Your name and your deeds were forgotten
before your bones were dry.
And the lie that flew you
is buried under a deeper lie . . .
*—*GEORGE ORWELL

CONTENTS

ILLUSTRATIONS

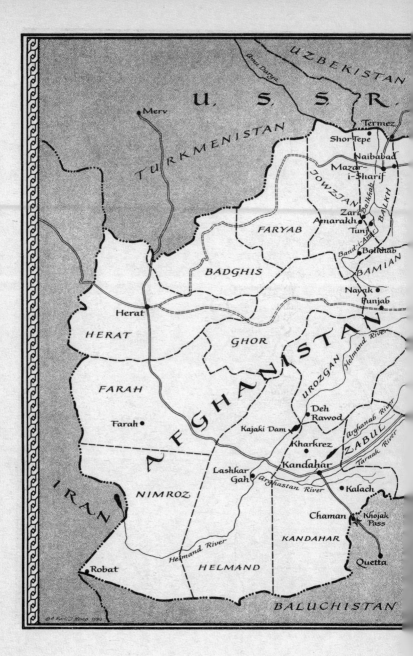

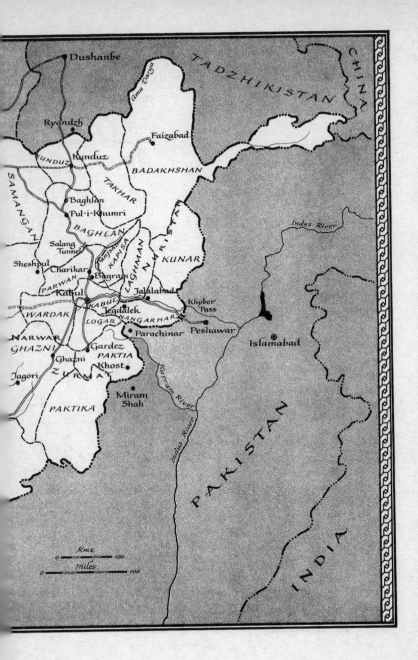

INTRODUCTION

Afghanistan isn't a country. And half a year has gone by since it's been a war. For those who were there, Afghanistan is more like a prayer.

Not only a prayer to God, but to oneself.

Whisper this prayer before you go to sleep—once for every person who died there. Spit out the word faster than machine-gun fire. If you are lucky, when you get to fifteen thousand you may perceive its hidden meaning.

Afghanistan became part of each person who fought there. And each of the half million soldiers who went through this war became part of Afghanistan—part of the land that could never absorb all the blood spilled on it.

Foolish men called Afghanistan "a school of courage." And were wise enough not to send their sons there. They spoke of "international duty," of "the battle against the hirelings of imperialism at the southern borders of our Motherland," of "the resolute rebuff of aggression from the reactionaries of the region." And on and on. They were trying to convince themselves, and the rest of the country, that Afghanistan "makes immature youths into staunch fighters for our communist faith."

But if Afghanistan served to inspire people to faith, it was a faith far different from the one promoted by our propaganda.

In April 1987, I met a sniper who'd inscribed a passage from the Ninety-first Psalm on the underside of his dirty collar: "He who dwells in the shelter of the Most High, who abides in the shadow of the Almighty, will say to the Lord, 'My refuge, and my fortress; my God in whom I trust.'"

Once I happened upon a huge sergeant of the Special Forces who was kneeling in the middle of a raving, passionate prayer. I could have sooner believed in a miracle—that the Soviet Union would win the war, for instance—than in what I saw with my own eyes. The sergeant embodied the indestructible power of the Special Forces; he was our hope of hopes, the larger-than-life idol of the Supreme General Headquarters.

What was he asking for?

The war gave ample reason to be either a cynic or a mystic. Month after month—and, in combat, day after day—it tormented you with the age-old questions: "Why him, Lord, and not me?" and "When will it be my turn—in five minutes or in fifty years?"

One day the soldier was offering prayers to God, the same God whom he cursed the very next day.

Four years ago, I think it was in Kandahar, a young soldier fresh out of boot camp was whispering quickly, as the bullets whizzed overhead, "Mommy, take me back inside of you. . . . Mommy, take me back inside of you." Another soldier, after losing his arms and his sight, wrote his father from the hospital to ask, "You old ass, what the hell did you have to do it for nineteen years ago?"

In one of our monasteries I talked with a sickly looking man who, at the end of our conversation, asked me, "You were in Afghanistan? When? Hmm. I was there, too." What a story he told me. He'd gone into the bushes to take a leak when his unit suddenly came under heavy enemy fire. He swore that if his life were somehow spared he'd join a monastery. At that very moment a mortar shell exploded nearby, killing all the other soldiers in his unit.

After finishing his story the man didn't utter another word. From force of habit I continued to throw questions at him. He clenched his teeth and abruptly turned away from me, army style. In a few moments, he was gone.

When the soldiers first went to war, Evil was a *dushman*. Then it became "the insurgents." A little later on "the rebels." Finally, it was known as "the armed resistance." But Evil also appeared in the guise of their own company commander or an ensign or a "grandfather" [an army old-timer] who had only two months to go before demobilization.

Their death on foreign soil was necessary to protect the Good. But where was the Good hiding? No one knew.

In June 1986, near Bagram, I spent twenty-four hours with Sasha Borodin, the political assistant to the commander of the company.

I was startled to see the stamp of death on his face. When you encounter something like that, it sends chills up and down your spine. That day there was a feeling of impending disaster in the air.

A little more than a week later, on June 24, Borodin's seventeen-year-old fiancée, who lived on the other side of the border in the village of Shelkino, was getting ready for prom night at her high school. She hadn't been able to find any white fabric in the local stores, so she'd made herself a black dress to wear to the prom. When Tamara Petrovna, Borodin's mother, found out about it, she gasped in horror, her legs giving out from under her. "Why black?" she screamed into the telephone at her son's fiancée. "Take the black off! For Christ's sake, take the black off!"

But it was too late. It was as if somebody—but who?—wanted this girl to become an unwed widow at seventeen.

Later that evening, just after his fiancée had arrived at her high-school prom, Borodin was gravely wounded. He passed away at ten-thirty the following morning. A Black Tulip [a military plane that transports casualties] flew his corpse to the Crimea in a cold zinc coffin.

Was this merely a bizarre coincidence? I don't know. But I do know that in Afghanistan people were often all too ready to grab on to exorbitant superstition, even though they might have denied it. People needed to see at least some measure of logic in the chaos of war.

To say that this war was a mistake is to say nothing at all. It's a lot easier to find a mistake than to find the truth.

"Franz Ferdinand is alive! World War I was a mistake."

"Leonid Brezhnev was wrong! The war in Afghanistan was a mistake."

The two phrases deserve one another.

But people, straining to explain something to themselves or to others, are often content with mere illusion or a meaningless phrase which, although comfortable, explains nothing.

Even if all the secret documents connected with the Soviet Union's decision to invade Afghanistan were made public tomorrow, I doubt that they would shed much light on the truth; quite possibly they might just add to the confusion.

It would be interesting to look through the secret telegrams that have been sent from Kabul to Moscow in 1979 by the functionaries of the MID, KGB, Minoborony, Puzanov, Ivanov, and Gorelov.

What did General Aleksei Yepishev, the chief of GLAVPUR [central political office of the Soviet armed forces], tell Moscow about his visit to Afghanistan after the rebellion in Herat, where he'd met with both Nur Mohammed Taraki and Hafizullah Amin? What impressions of Kabul were brought back by General Ivan Pavlovskiy, the commander in chief of the Soviet land forces? Why did Shelkov's assistant, General Poputin, having just returned from Afghanistan, shoot himself at the end of December 1979, shortly before the invasion? What sort of negotiations were held between Babrak Karmal and the Soviet leaders in the summer and fall of 1979? What gifts did Soviet leaders receive from Afghans who were offered high-ranking posts in their government immediately after the arrival of the Fortieth Army? And who ordered the assassination of Hafizullah Amin?

These questions are fairly easy to answer. There are some that are more difficult. The real issue, I believe, lies in the kind of socialism that we had been building for many decades.

There are all kinds of theories as to what actually triggered the fateful events of December 27, 1979.

Some researchers believe that Brezhnev, Ustinov, Andropov, and Gromyko were trying to kill two birds with one stone by sending Soviet troops into Afghanistan: to get rid of Amin and to crush the armed resistance as a means of bringing to power a coalition headed by Babrak Karmal. The international division of the Central Committee of the Communist Party of the Soviet Union, along with MID and KGB, hoped to bring about the reunification of the People's Democratic Party of Afghanistan, which had splintered into two factions—the Khalq and the Parcham. The Soviet Union would then offer to withdraw its troops in exchange for the termination of foreign military and financial aid to the rebels.

Others believed that Brezhnev himself was the chief cause of the war. Brezhnev, the theory goes, made the decision to invade Afghanistan because he was infuriated by blatant insolence on the part of Amin. During Taraki's brief stay in Moscow (on his way from Havana to Kabul), Brezhnev had hugged and kissed him. Only a few days later, Amin ousted Taraki from the post of president and ordered his assassination.

A. A. Gromyko, the former minister of foreign affairs of the USSR, recalled, "The assassination of the General Secretary of the Central Committee of the PDPA Taraki, whose government was asking us for help, brought the situation to a critical point. This brutal act was a terrible blow to the Soviet leaders. L. I. Brezhnev was especially shaken by his death."

The punishment was not long in coming. According to Amin's widow, a crack team of Soviet commandos stormed the palace and killed Amin after his cook, a Soviet agent, had tried unsuccessfully to poison him.

Babrak Karmal, who arrived in Kabul in a Soviet armored car after Amin's death, immediately declared himself the new ruler of Afghanistan and accused Amin of having been an agent of the CIA. He went so far as to demand that the U.S. government hand over secret documents that would confirm this. The Soviet press actively supported this version.

There is little question that KGB higher-ups were genuinely worried by Amin's activities. They were concerned about his extremist internal security policy, including the terrorization of clergy, intelligentsia, and party workers, as well as his increasing contact with representatives of the United States and Pakistan. Several times Amin had offered to meet with Brezhnev at any time and in any place, but Moscow remained silent. Indeed, it may have been the Soviet Union's failure to respond that led Amin to court alternately the United States and Pakistan. Moscow suspected Amin all the more because he had once studied at Columbia University in New York City.

I interviewed Karmal, who now lives in Moscow, in April 1989. "Did you really believe that Amin was a CIA agent?" I asked him.

"I could only judge him on the basis of his actions," Karmal replied. "Even if the Americans had spent a hundred billion dollars on the destabilization of Afghanistan, they couldn't have harmed it as much as Amin did."

"But if you follow that logic," I said, "Brezhnev, who really made a mess out of the USSR, must've been an agent of every Western intelligence agency at once."

As he had before, Karmal responded with a quotation from Lenin. "Tell me," he then asked with a cunning smile, "has it yet been made illegal to mention Lenin's name in the USSR?"

His own loud laughter was the answer.

To explain a nine-year-long tragedy as the consequence of Brezhnev's grudge against the obstinate Amin, however, is to explain nothing at all.

The academician Georgiy Arbatov, who knew Brezhnev well and frequently saw him even in his final days, once told me that toward the end of the 1970s Brezhnev was incapable of making any political decisions on his own and couldn't even sustain an intelligent conversation for more than twenty or thirty minutes; his attention span and intellectual capacities were fading by the moment.

"As they were making the decision, they didn't consult either the experts or their foreign policy advisers," Arbatov said. "I learned about it from the Voice of America. I immediately told Dobrynin. We were both in the hospital at that time."

"As far as I know, the Politburo, which was in session on December 13th, never even voted on it," another close associate of Brezhnev's told me. "As soon as Brezhnev announced the decision, [Defense Minister] Ustinov immediately turned to the military aspects of the situation."

Andrei Gromyko, on the other hand, maintained that the "Politburo of the Central Committee of the Communist Party of the Soviet Union reached a unanimous decision to send troops into Afghanistan."

"The decision to send troops into Afghanistan was being made by several top government leaders behind closed doors," said E. A. Shevardnadze, the Minister of Foreign Affairs of the Soviet Union, in an interview to *Izvestia*. "At that time I was a candidate to the

Politburo of the Central Committee and was simply informed of the fact, as were many of my comrades and colleagues."

Gromyko has a different recollection of that day.

"After the Politburo made this decision," he writes, "I stopped by Brezhnev's office and said, 'Shouldn't this decision be made official at the state level?' "

Brezhnev did not answer right away, Gromyko recalls. He picked up the telephone and said, "Mikhail Andreevich [Suslov], could you stop by here, please? I need your advice about something."

Suslov came. Brezhnev told him about the conversation with Gromyko. "It would appear that the current situation demands an immediate decision: we can either ignore Afghanistan's plea for help or save the people's government and act in accordance with the Soviet-Afghan treaty."

Suslov said, "We have a treaty with Afghanistan, and we must act at once to fulfill our obligations, if this is the decision that we've made. We'll discuss it at the Central Committee meeting later on."

According to Gromyko, the Assembly of the Central Committee, which met in June of 1980, unanimously approved the decision of the Politburo.

Although it's popular to fault the Soviet leaders for never discussing their decision to send troops into Afghanistan, I believe that this wouldn't have made much difference. Under the circumstances, and considering who its members were at that time, the Supreme Soviet would have surely voted unanimously in favor of the Politburo's decision.

As had happened so many other times in Russian history, a conspiracy of silence bound our country. And only one man dared raise his voice against the war. The society of "progressive socialism" scorned and violated one of the first laws of nature: sacrifice your own life, but save your offspring. It watched obediently as an entire generation of eighteen-year-olds perished in the Afghan bloodbath, together with the Afghans themselves. *

Nevertheless, many people blamed Brezhnev. Some asserted that he wanted to be remembered as a leader who extended the zone of Soviet influence in the East. Others argued that he got carried away by Peter the Great's drive to reach the warm seas.

---

*More than a million Afghans were killed during the nine years of the war.

One of our high-ranking MID functionaries argued that the military was to blame for everything. The military, he said, had instilled fear in Brezhnev by warning of the imminent landing of American troops in "our southern underbelly."

"Why else would they have brought in the antiaircraft units?" he asked. "The rebels didn't have an air force. The General Headquarters feared that the White House would react to the loss of Iran by invading Afghanistan. What's more, by the mid-seventies our military had reached a state of parity with America and, with Ustinov in the lead, they were anxious to try their strength somewhere. Afghanistan happened to be handy."

But Army General V. I. Varennikov, assistant to the minister of defense of the USSR and commander in chief of the Soviet land forces, who then served as the first deputy chief of the General Headquarters and chief of General Operations Office (GOU), flatly rejected such a notion.

"At first the General Headquarters was against the idea of sending troops into Afghanistan," he told me. "As an alternative, we suggested that Soviet divisions should be stationed there as garrisons, without getting involved in the fighting. It's now clear that the recommendation of the General Headquarters was correct in principle. We should have insisted on it until the bitter end, even though advocating such a course was fraught with grave consequences. Unfortunately, however, at one point we gave in to pressure from Babrak Karmal and allowed ourselves to be dragged into this drawn-out war."

Varennikov's words enraged Babrak Karmal.

"I declare with all responsibility that until 1980 I was not the leader of Afghanistan, either by law, or in practice, nor was I the man who invited Soviet troops into my country," he said. As he took another puff of a Kent cigarette I heard the wheezing in his lungs. "It must be said that the actions of Soviet troops in Afghanistan, especially during the first stages, caused the people great displeasure. I might mention the offensive tactics in the conduct of military activity, the testing of new types of weapons, and the bombings for the purpose of provocation, which happened against my will, the will of the Afghan people, and the will of a number of Soviet officers. It's well known that I've expressed the wish to resign more than once. If you want to know my opinion, more thought should have been given *before* the troops were sent in. It was necessary to know Afghanistan, to understand the Afghan people. If sending in the troops was a mistake, it was caused by a failure to understand Afghanistan—by a poor knowledge of the country and the Afghan character."

So who *did* invite Soviet troops to come to Afghanistan? Was it Karmal, who won't admit to it and claims he didn't have the authority to issue the invitation? Or Amin, who was killed by the troops that he had "invited," only several hours after the arrival?

Taraki did request a couple of Soviet battalions for his own security. But instead of two battalions, the entire Fortieth Army arrived.

Many servicemen and MID workers told me that the script for the events in Afghanistan was written by the KGB.

"The *osobists* must periodically justify their own existence, as well as their insane spending of funds, to the political leadership," one of them told me. "That's why from time to time they manufacture conspiracies that they can unveil and neutralize."

According to his close associates, Y. V. Andropov's actions seemed influenced by vestiges of the idea of world revolution. Initially, Andropov was against the idea of an invasion, but eventually he followed the same reflex that he'd learned some twenty years earlier in Hungary, where he served as an ambassador and where troops had to be sent in 1956. Many of the Kremlin leaders perceived life through the thick prism of ideological dogmas, which often played a decisive role in the process of political decision making on the highest level.

I've run into Trotskyists who claimed that Russia invaded Afghanistan to suppress the Afghan revolution. These claims were met with silent approval by some Khalqists, who were angry because Moscow had brought Karmal, a Parchamist, to power. "Why were you protecting private property and giving power to the middle class," they asked, "and not to the revolutionary peasantry?"

Alexander Haig, the former U.S. secretary of state, offered yet another explanation. The Soviet Union invaded Afghanistan, he told me in April of 1988, to undermine the strengthening of the Islamic fundamentalist belt at its southern borders.

"Between the Soviet Union and Afghanistan there is only the thin line of the Amu Darya," he said. "Because of this, any successful

Islamic movement at your southern borders will inevitably influence the Soviet Muslim republics. I can see Brezhnev's logic."

Haig's analysis of the situation has a great many adherents. Some go even further, claiming that the nine-year war represented the last crusade to the East, a preventive fight of Christians and Muslims before the Muslims' massive final attack.

I knew a few Islamic fanatics who saw the war as a struggle between Christ and Allah. I was reminded of them in Kabul when the local *dukhanshiki* [shop-owners] told me, "The Russian soldier always moved from north to south. Now for the first time he is moving from south to north. And he'll keep retreating farther and farther. Allah is our witness."

In May 1987, Gulbuddin Hekmatyar, a leader of the Afghan military opposition, said, "If the mujahedin persistently continue to fight, the day will soon come when the occupied lands of Soviet Central Asia will be liberated."

"The remote possibility that this might really happen at some point in the future is what forced the Soviet Army to enter Afghanistan in 1979," said Haig with a great deal of conviction.

On March 8, 1987, a detachment of rebels under Ortabulaki's command fired missiles on the Tajik town of Pyandzh (in the Soviet Union). The half-imagined danger of the growth of the Muslim Belt had suddenly become a nightmarish possibility.

But, eight years earlier, in the spring of 1979, the Kremlin was quite alarmed by American activity in Afghanistan. Moscow was convinced that after Washington lost Iran the United States was planning to turn Afghanistan into its anti-Soviet outpost in Central Asia.

In the meantime the Kremlin learned that Zbigniew Brzezinski, President Carter's national security adviser, had succeeded in convincing a dubious State Department that the strengthening of the alliance between Moscow and Kabul threatened U.S. security, and that the developing situation in Afghanistan could, if handled properly, prove politically profitable for the United States.

As the State Department noted in a communique, "the change of leadership in the DRA [Democratic Republic of Afghanistan] demonstrates to the entire world, and especially to Third World countries, that the Soviet's belief in the historic inevitability of socialism does not hold true in all cases."

In April 1979, under pressure from Brzezinski, U.S. foreign policy advisers began to meet regularly with the leaders of the Afghan armed opposition.

The Kremlin grew more and more nervous with each new communication from abroad.

General Mohammed Zia ul-Haq, who overthrew Bhutto's progressive government establishing a right-wing military regime, saw in the aggravation of the Afghan conflict a unique opportunity to obtain a sharp increase in U.S. military and financial aid to Pakistan. The Pakistani generals regarded the entrance of Soviet troops into Afghanistan as "Brezhnev's gift."

Peking viewed the events in Afghanistan as another Soviet manifestation of hegemony.

Egyptian President Anwar el-Sadat, who was called the "betrayer of the Arab cause" for signing a formal treaty with Israel in March 1979, was eager to be exonerated in the eyes of the world's Muslims. Supplying arms to the Afghan rebels provided him with just such an opportunity.

It is absolutely clear that without the help of the United States, Pakistan, China, and Egypt, the Afghan armed resistance would have had nothing to fight with. Andrei Gromyko used the entire foreign affairs apparatus in order to exert pressure on these four countries.

Gromyko, Ustinov, Andropov, Brezhnev, and Suslov are all dead. The mystery of the decision to send Soviet troops into Afghanistan accompanied them to their graves. They magnanimously left us with the opportunity to pile all the blame on them, saving those who are still alive. But should anyone take advantage of this "favor"?

There is another question that is even more important: What were the real origins of the fatal events in Afghanistan?

Perhaps it all started in 1978, when we called the military coup in Kabul the "April Revolution" and immediately became enslaved to the phrase. Or perhaps everything had gone haywire in 1968, when we proved to ourselves that Soviet military might could keep a regime like the one in Czechoslovakia in power. Or perhaps it had begun twelve years earlier, when we did the same thing in Hungary.

A few of us, arguing about this in Kabul, guessed that "Afghanistan" had actually begun in 1956. Besides the events in Hungary, that was also the year we began training the first group of Afghan officers in our military schools and academies, so that twenty-two years later they could attempt to put theory into practice.

What if everything started and ended in Afghanistan two years before the establishment of the Russian protectorate over Bukhara? As Colonel Glukhovsky of the General Headquarters, an expert on Central Asia, had written to his superior, General Kaufman, almost a century ago, "No amount of persuasion, advice, or threats is capable of rearranging the age-long mechanism of Muslim States."

Perhaps everything had gone to pieces when Russia ignored imperial England's unfortunate experience in Afghanistan.

Nearly a hundred years ago, Sir Roberts, one of the British military leaders in Afghanistan, wrote: "We must not be afraid of Afghanistan and would profit by letting it be the master of its own fate. Maybe it is not the most attractive solution for us, but I feel that I am right in asserting that the less they are able to see us, the less they are likely to hate us. Even if we suppose that Russia will attempt to invade Afghanistan, and through it to obtain control of India, we will have a much greater chance of getting the Afghans on our side if we abstain from any interference in their internal affairs whatsoever."

We were obsessed with our messianic mission and blinded by arrogance. How could we have possibly hoped to teach the Afghans anything when we ourselves never learned to manage our own economy properly? In reality we were exporting stagnation rather than revolution.

Sometimes we resembled the astronauts in Stanislav Lem's famous science-fiction story, "Solaris." Unable to gain insight into the nature of the conscious ocean, they decide to influence it by irradiating it with powerful x-rays.

But while the astronauts think that they are irradiating Solaris, in reality it is irradiating them.

"If you want to learn about a strange country," say experienced travelers, "disappear in it." But in Afghanistan we couldn't even manage to do that. During the nine years of war we were constantly separated from the country by eight millimeters of bulletproof glass through which we stared in fear from inside our armored carriers.

We thought that we were civilizing a backwards country by

exposing it to television, to modern bombers, to schools, to the latest models of tanks, to books, to long-range artillery, to newspapers, to new types of weapons, to economic aid, to AK-47s. But we rarely stopped to think how Afghanistan would influence us—despite the hundreds of thousands of Soviet soldiers and officers and the scores of diplomats, journalists, scholars, and military and political advisers who passed through it.

It's difficult to determine exactly what we managed to teach Afghanistan. It is relatively easy, however, to assess Afghanistan's effects on the Soviet people who worked and fought there. With a mere wave of Brezhnev's elderly hand they were thrown into a country where bribery, corruption, profiteering, and drugs were no less common than the long lines in Soviet stores. These diseases can be far more infectious and dangerous than hepatitis, particularly when they reach epidemic proportions.

The Soviet officers and advisers immediately split into two factions, the Khalqists and the Parchamists. And so the war that was taking place inside the PDPA soon spread to the members of the Communist Party of the Soviet Union who worked in Afghanistan. Toward the mid-1980s, in fact, the tail was wagging the dog.

With the passage of time we gradually began to see ourselves as Balaganov and Panikovsky in Ilf and Petrov's book *The Golden Calf.* Like Balaganov and Panikovsky, we long ago realized that there was no gold inside the weights, but nonetheless we continued to saw them in half all the more furiously.

The war in Afghanistan dragged on for nine long years—fully an eighth of Soviet history.

With each passing day, the war more and more resembled the sexual performance of an impotent.

In 1980, when I first arrived in Afghanistan, most of the soldiers were my age: they hadn't yet turned twenty. But in 1989, on my last trip to Afghanistan, I noticed with horror that the army was ten years younger than I.

One generation had entered Afghanistan. An entirely different generation was leaving it.

According to official statistics, during the war years we lost about fifteen thousand lives in our "southern underbelly." More than thirty thousand people were injured. More than three hundred soldiers are listed as missing in action.

Political voluntarism cost us about sixty billion rubles.

But how can these losses be compared with our moral losses?

It often seems to me that war and violence had crossed the border into our country.

In Afghanistan we bombed not only the detachments of rebels and their caravans, but our own ideals as well. With the war came the reevaluation of our moral and ethical values. In Afghanistan the policies of the government became utterly incompatible with the inherent morality of our nation. Things could not continue in the same vein. It is hardly coincidental that the ideas of *perestroika* took hold in 1985—the year the war reached its peak.

As a general to whom I became quite close in Afghanistan put it, "All of the wars that Russia lost led to social reforms, while all of the wars it won led to the strengthening of totalitarianism."

Over the years I've encountered many people who liked to look for the "positive aspects" of the war. "Every cloud has a silver lining," they say. "If Soviet troops hadn't gone to Afghanistan, they probably would've been sent into Poland. And that would've been an even greater disaster." Others maintain that the war in Afghanistan enabled us to test and perfect a wide array of arms and equipment.

But these were only a few thickheads, and hardly worth arguing with—they were as tough and stubborn as tanks.

The war itself wasn't the only thing that chipped away at our morality. The official lies about the war, in newspapers and on television, also took a heavy toll. I'm not blaming the journalists themselves. Even when one of us tried to report the truth the military censors masterfully made it into a lie.

Anyone who stayed in Afghanistan for a long period of time, or who was sent there on a regular basis, typically went through four phases.

The first stage (which would usually last up to three months) went something like this: "The war is proceeding on a normal course. If only we can add another twenty or thirty thousand men, everything will be fine."

Several months later, the second stage: "Since we've already gotten ourselves in this jam, we should get the fighting over with as quickly as possible. Adding another thirty thousand men isn't going to do it. We need at least one other army to shut off all the borders."

Five or six months later, the third stage: "There is something desperately wrong here. What a mess!"

Then, half a year or so later, the fourth and final stage: "We'd be wise to get the hell out of here—and the sooner the better."

I went through all of these stages, too. A reader who compares the two parts that make up *The Hidden War* will easily see that.

I wrote Part 1, Let Us Meet Under the Three Cranes, in the spring of 1987. Although I now have a very different outlook on a lot of the events covered in this section, I feel it would be dishonest of me to make any alterations.

For Part 2, The Hidden War, I worked from material that I gathered on an assignment to Afghanistan in January and February 1989, where I witnessed the final phase of the withdrawal of Soviet troops.

This book that I now submit to the reader's consideration is a subjective account. The author in no way claims to offer a complete account of the war in Afghanistan or any of the momentous events that are connected with it.

This story tells about what the author himself saw and experienced there.

A. BOROVIK
January 1990

LET US MEET UNDER THE THREE CRANES

E xactly how much time passes from the moment a man is wounded until he starts to feel the pain?

Sometimes it's a second.

Sometimes it's an hour.

Sometimes it's more than an eternity.

The commander of the mortar platoon, Lieutenant Slyunkov, has measured the interval exactly. By his calculation, it's "five seconds on the nose."

The *dukhi** had started firing their mortars. Slyunkov studied his watch to check how much time elapsed between the flash and the sound of the second mortar round. At that instant he felt something strike him in the shoulder. He felt the blow but no pain.

In the turmoil, Slyunkov paid no attention to the impact. He kept his eyes riveted on the sweep hand of his watch so he could multiply the seconds elapsed by 333 (the speed of sound in meters per second) to estimate the enemy's distance. But he never finished— the pain came hurtling at him like a locomotive roaring into a tunnel.

"I was lucky," he said later. "The shoulder wound is a romantic wound." To prove his point, he unbuttoned his collar and pulled open

*Literally, "ghosts"; Soviet slang for Afghan rebels.

his *telnyashka* [the Soviet sailor's striped tight-fitting undershirt]. Nothing about his wound looked romantic to me.

Sometimes the pain comes at the same time the shrapnel hits. And sometimes the pain doesn't come at all. It's like a storm that's far, far away—the lightning flashes but forgets to thunder.

But suddenly you'd feel a squish in your boots, as if you'd gotten your feet wet, or your *telnyashka* sticking to your body, as if you'd just broken into a sweat. Only the moisture is blood.

Lieutenant Maneev got a bullet in the belly. He noticed it only after another soldier said, "*Tovarich*, Lieutenant, it seems you have a little hole. . . ."

"A classic case of internal bleeding," Maneev says with a smile. "It's better that only pain follows the wound. Death would be far worse."

They say that you can't hear the bullet that kills you, but this, like so many other sayings, isn't so.

During the ferocious battles near the *kishlak* [Afghan village] of Malym-Gulym, which is close to Khanabad, the platoon was ordered to move out and surround a band of Afghan rebels. But the platoon's point men ran up against the *dukhi*'s base. There was nowhere to hide, no place to dig in—only flooded rice paddies spread all around. The commander of the platoon, Lieutenant Lobachevsky, was shot straight through his heart.

Major Novikov, who heard the lieutenant's last words, later told me, "Believe it or not, Lobachevsky told the command post by walkie-talkie, 'Allow me to break this connection . . . I've been killed.' "

I believed the story. It was too incredible not to believe.

In war, death is all too ordinary. As ordinary as the tinned meat in a soldier's rations or the blisters on his feet. The men talk about it casually, sometimes with a good deal of humor. ("What do you mean, life after death? Is there life before death?")

If Death had a mind, and such attributes of intelligence as pride and vanity, the old witch certainly would have been outraged that the soldiers had become so accustomed to her presence. War? It's nothing more than the tears of Death. One look inside a Soviet first-aid station is enough to convince you: Death is the heart-rending screams of the wounded, the silent moan in the eyes of those who can't scream anymore, the smell of alcohol, of antiseptic, of rotting flesh.

"Death is a bitch," Novikov would tell you. And he would be right.

Colonel Zalomin, squeezing his temples with his thumb and middle finger, is more specific. "Death," he says, "takes our best men."

"And still," Colonel Peshkov whispers almost to himself, "you must think about death. You mustn't set the question aside until worst comes to worst. The thought of death shouldn't catch you unawares, when you are exhausted and weak."

"But why should I be afraid of death?" Lieutenant Lukiyanov asks with a grin. As he speaks the cumbersome metal braces that hold his leg together rattle. "What happens will happen. For me, death is irrelevant. While I am, there is no death; when it comes, I won't be . . ."

Ensign Belous, who expresses his thoughts succinctly and dramatically, interrupts. "My death," he says, "will grieve everyone but me."

I couldn't help being amazed at how much thought and soul-searching these men had devoted to the subject of death. This habit had enabled them to develop such a calm and businesslike attitude. Then I finally came to understand that soldiers have no choice but to think about death. Death is natural, ordinary, and, in the final analysis, the one thing that's certain. The only way to conquer the fear of death, they've learned, is to confront it head-on.

It's very early in the morning, maybe a little after five o'clock. The Kunduz-Baghlan road winds around the hills like a snake, twisting upward, slithering down, disappearing from sight. Suddenly, somewhere far away, its wet back shines in the sun.

A mountain range rises on the horizon. The snow-covered peaks of the tallest mountains poke through thin, pancakelike clouds. It's almost like looking at a picture postcard from a resort in the Swiss Alps.

My road map, which was published thirty years ago in Kabul especially for tourists who were traveling by automobile, calls the province of Kunduz "Afghan's Switzerland." The map was given to me by an old British journalist who'd come to Kabul for a couple of weeks with a group of Western reporters. His mane of dark brown hair reminded me of the British lion. He and his family had used the map sometime in the 1950s to make their way around Afghanistan in a white Jaguar.

The map was worn through in places, particularly along the folds, and covered with reddish stains of either tea or whiskey. But to my eyes, it was only the better for the wear. It had some hidden, extra meaning—especially now, when nobody but me really needed it. It was a true relic. A ghost of a map.

I could only imagine my British colleague in his white Jaguar, with this very map spread on his knees, traveling from Kunduz to Baghlan on this very road.

At around seven o'clock, the sun becomes fierce. The clouds are covered with a faint golden crust, and the road, still wet, shines like a ribbon of foil. But like all the roads of Afghanistan, this one is wounded. Crippled by mines and mortar shells, it hobbles between the hills.

If roads could howl in pain, I would prefer to be deaf between Kunduz and Baghlan.

Our two armored personnel carriers (APCs) move along slowly, at a speed of no more than twenty-five kilometers per hour. We maneuver carefully around the shell holes, some of which resemble craters. The *dukhi* had been hard at work here. The heavy vehicles rock back and forth, like two ships in a raging storm at sea. It seems as if water could lap in at any minute from the twisting river to our right.

Our driver, weary from wrestling with the wheel, tries to turn the vehicle onto the left side of the road. Because the mines hadn't ripped up that side of the road so much, he could pick up some speed there. Nothing gets on the nerves of a Russian soldier more than crawling along at a snail's pace.

Lieutenant Colonel Artemenko puts his wide palm on the back of the driver's crew cut, which has turned red from the road dust, and turns the soldier's head to the right: the APC instantly taxis to the shoulder of the road. Apparently, it is safer here. While it's not an easy matter to shove a mine under asphalt, the *dukhi* have mastered the technique.

In Afghanistan, as nowhere else, your safety depends not so much on logic—the tactical rules of war—but on luck. Whether you want to or not, you quickly grow superstitious.

We sped by the camp of the 507th Regiment. Only a year ago its men had been fighting on the side of the rebels, but they'd recently joined the national army after extracting a number of concessions from the Afghan government: not to draft them into the regular army, to supply them with arms and ammunition, and to assign them a territory that they could defend from encroachment by the rebels. It was something of a calculated risk on the part of the government. After the regiment's arsenal had been replenished, might it turn against Afghan and Soviet forces? Such things had happened before.

By noon the road is dry and we are being trailed by a cloud of dust that stretches back for about thirty meters. The dust might as well be smoke; it's so thick that you can't see the APC following us. You can only hear the roar of its engine. Everyone seems to have a tan, but rub a handkerchief over your forehead and the "tan" comes off as reddish powder.

Donkeys, seemingly indifferent to everything around them, drag themselves along the sides of the road. They're loaded down so heavily—with huge sacks of rice, bundles of firewood, and incredible household goods—that you can see only their ears. Their owners follow them, thin switches in hand. As I look at these beasts of burden, I can't stop marveling at their contemplative, almost meditative, attitude toward life. A roar from a quartet of fighter planes over their heads, the growl of the APCs that crowd them to the sides of the road, the thunder of an exploding mine—nothing can jar them out of their silent calm. Maybe they know something that we don't. Maybe they have simply taken a vow of silence.

"Okay, here's Baghlan," Artemenko says. "Get inside the carrier."

No order was needed; I obey him instantly. For the fourth day in a row, Soviet forces in Baghlan are fighting alongside the Twentieth Division of the Afghan army and three strategic groups of the KHAD [the Afghan KGB]. They've tightly blockaded Gayur's detachment and what's left of the defeated rebel forces that recently fired across the border at Pyandzh, a town in Tadzhikistan. According to the intelligence data, three hundred and fifty rebels had turned South Baghlan into their base and equipped it with state-of-the-art fortifications.

The previous February, Gayur had returned from Pakistan with a few big caravans that carried an enormous shipment of arms and ammunition, which was delivered to the province of Kunduz, or rather to the city of South Baghlan. He's now armed with twenty antitank grenade launchers, eight mortars, machine guns, a 76-mm cannon, and a 122-mm howitzer.

Our second APC suddenly comes under machine-gun fire, but we don't even notice it. The constant asthmatic volleys of artillery drown out all other sounds.

Through the gun slits of our APC we can see ragged clouds of smoke hanging over the town. Soviet-made KamAZ vehicles and a few Afghan buses stand lifelessly along the road; they've been blown up by mines. It's an incongruous scene: the stooped figures of a few peasants who plow the grayish-yellow earth in the hollow between two hills, the explosive flashes and thunder of the artillery fire. A barber with a wooden comb and long razor in his old brown hands seems totally surreal. He sits on a rug under a scrawny eucalyptus tree, waiting for a customer. Even though the old barber seems frozen, he follows us with quiet, knowing eyes.

The moment we run into an obstruction on the road and stop, a brood of wiry, sinewy children, small and even smaller—*bachata*, in the slang of the soldiers—run to us, waving American gas masks and crying, "Commander! Gayur—gas! Gayur—gas!"

"This is their way of warning us that Gayur has chemical mines in his arsenal," Artemenko screams in my ear, trying to be heard over the low rumble of the engine. "Understand?"

As I shout something in reply, my eyes automatically search the cabin for even a single gas mask.

Artemenko leans even closer to me, so close that his stubble bristles against my ear. "It's also possible that Gayur bribed the *bachata* with toys to sow panic among the soldiers," he says. "Understand?"

We finally approach our command post, a clay-plastered brick house situated on a small hill. The governor of the province of

Kunduz once lived here, but he moved to a safer place. The road, which leads right up to the door of the house, twists in a spiral around the hill. The windowpanes, shattered by shock waves from explosions, have been replaced with smoky plastic. The ceiling and walls are finished with wicker and rough boards evidently salvaged from shell boxes. Every time a shell explodes nearby, dry dust sifts through cracks in the roof straight down into my collar. There's a wooden table with maps spread on it. The benches next to it are turning gray with age.

Colonel Shehovtsov, a strongly built man with prematurely gray hair, sits across the table from me. He already has considerable war experience behind him, and I can see it in his calm gray eyes. The subdivisions under his command have suffered minimal losses (although, of course, the loss of even a single human life can hardly be called minimal), and they recently encircled Gayur's gang and destroyed a group of Ortabulaki. He speaks quietly, evenly, rarely raising his husky voice. He issues orders over the radio the same way, never letting the burned-out cigarette slip from his pale lips.

A lieutenant sits in the corner. He wears the radio helmet of a helicopter pilot.

"Of all the local bands, Gayur's turned out to be the most bitterly opposed to national reconciliation," Shehovtsov says. "After the fifteenth of January, he sharply increased the shelling of Soviet and Afghan positions in the peaceful *kishlaks* of the Pul-i-Khumri region. That's why, immediately after we'd crushed the Ortabulaki group that had shelled Pyandzh, the decision was made to move farther south and blockade Gayur here, in South Baghlan. He has studied in the Soviet Union and knows our tactics inside and out. He is a formidable enemy."

Shehovtsov falls into thought for a minute and then adds, "Like any former friend who's turned into a traitor, Gayur had been on the side of the communist revolution. Later he deserted to the rebels, and since 1980 he's been masterminding much of their guerrilla warfare. He fights dirty—he forbids civilians to leave the blockade under penalty of death, keeping them as hostages. But all the same, our teams of Soviet and Afghan agitators keep at it. Under the cover of fire, we managed to rescue all of the women, infants, and old people. Then Gayur armed the children, starting with ten-year-olds, and forced them to fight. But the children believed us, not him, and in two nights they surrendered their weapons and left the blockade through our filtration posts."

The door suddenly bursts open and we hear the agonizing howl of an artillery shell, growing louder by the second. The shell passes the command post and lands somewhere behind us, a little to the left. Through the roar of the explosion I can hear the sounds of wood splintering and clods of dirt hitting the walls.

A major runs in, slightly hunched over. Stopping for a second to catch his breath, he speaks to Shehovtsov. "Zolotorenko urgently requests a tank with a mine sweeper," he says.

"Take it," Shehovtsov replies, "but not for more than an hour."

The major disappears and Shehovtsov asks the radio operator to connect him with Sonata.

"Sonata, Sonata, do you read me? You have too big a gap between the positions. Close up."

Shehovtsov then takes another telephone, squeezes it between his chin and shoulder, and says calmly into the mouthpiece: "Petrovich, figure out how we can use our artillery and mortars to keep the red and green zones under fire. Do you read me? Go for it!"

Suddenly I notice that I've smoked half a pack of cigarettes since arriving at the command post.

Shehovtsov comes out to see me off. Everyone else slouches slightly; only he stands straight, deeply inhaling the fresh air.

"Aren't you afraid of Gayur's snipers?" I ask him.

"The hell with them—I wouldn't lower myself!" he says, squinting in the sun. "Now the battles are moving from Tenth to Ninth Street and Third to Fourth; we're starting, little by little, to squeeze the pincers. At five P.M. we'll start attacking Fifth and Eighth streets. There are still two and a half kilometers between the jaws of the vise. We need to draw it together to one kilometer. Then Gayur will have nowhere to go."

At that moment, the radio chirps from inside the house. Shehovtsov disappears behind the door.

A whirlwind of dust and sand dances next to our APC. It spins faster and faster, lifting pebbles and dried branches from the ground. It dances on one leg, twirling around its axis like a prima ballerina, bewitching its audience and luring them with its giddy performance.

This is the *afganets* [fierce Afghan winds]. We hide inside the carrier. It will shelter us, if not from the antitank shells, at least from the wind.

Gayur has badly scarred Baghlan with his fire. All around us are stumps of houses, corpses of houses. I am shown the spot where a clay hut has vanished without a trace.

The sky hangs overhead like wet, dirty canvas. Two white eagles fight in frantic silence. Birds also get used to war.

A little boy, about seven years old, kneels near the ruins of a shack. He's praying fervently—no, furiously.

We arrive at one of the filtration posts that lead into the blockade. It consists of an armored carrier and a broadcasting station. As I get out of our APC to take a few photographs, I feel like a turtle who's been taken out of his shell.

One of the KHAD officers stationed here tells me that most of the civilians fleeing the blockaded zone pass through this post.

"We're checking documents very carefully and looking for concealed weapons," he says, twisting his thick mustache as he speaks. "But it's a complicated task. Gayur's bandits are trying to slip through disguised as peasants. These two over here," he says, pointing to a couple of red-haired youths sitting at the side of the road, "put on women's clothes and tried to sneak through."

The two young men are bearded and look to be about twenty years old. They seem rather harmless, I tell the officer.

"Harmless only until they start shooting at you," he replies. "While their disguise was cunning, it's a hackneyed method. They believed we wouldn't dare take off a woman's yashmak. We anticipated such trickery, however, and asked two girls from the local department of KHAD to assist us in delicate cases. But we saw through these guys ourselves—even very big women don't wear size-twelve shoes."

I spend nearly two hours at the filtration post. The Afghan security officers have next to nothing to do; virtually all of South Baghlan's civilian population has already left. I notice two soldiers yawn; they're guarding some unlucky *dukhi*. Three others begin to build a fire to keep bandits from sneaking up on the post after nightfall. Their kindling is still wet from last night's rain, and it takes some time to catch fire. Luckily, there's enough of a glow to keep us warm.

Forty minutes later, a flock of long-haired sheep begins to cross a road some five hundred meters away from us. The animals bleat incessantly. I count nine shepherds following them—a few too many for such a small flock.

With Major Said Ismail of KHAD in the lead, we approach them. Ismail, a man with sad but piercing eyes, is in charge of the filtration post. Because the shepherds are unarmed, we don't even bother to take our weapons. All of them are wearing red buttons that say XXVII Congress of the Communist Party of the Soviet Union. They smile and speak rapidly as Said carefully checks their papers. The major summons three soldiers and orders them to separate the shepherds from their flock. He quickly swings around and grabs one of the sheep, squeezing it between his knees.

"Do you want to check her documents, too?" I joke limply.

Said responds by taking his knife out of its sheath and cutting two thick pieces of rope that gird the sheep at front and back. Then he pulls a brand-new submachine gun out from under the beast's belly.

"Check that one!" he shouts to me, nodding toward a second sheep.

I'm not as adroit and catch the beast only on the second try. Hugging the sheep around its waist, I feel two machine guns without magazines, a bundle of three grenades tied underneath. My armory is somewhat richer, I think.

The rest of the sheep also turn out to be pregnant with weapons. The "shepherds" feign astonishment. One of them offers a particularly spirited performance, repeatedly declaring his outrage at the perfidy of the *dukhi*, who, he says, dare to exploit "the naiveté of peaceful shepherds for their criminal causes."

The road to Captain Zakharov's post is jammed with vehicles and people. It takes us thirty minutes to negotiate the five or six kilometers that separate it from the filtration post.

The sky, growing gloomier with every minute, threatens rain for the hundredth time today. Multicolored buses, packed with peasants, crawl by. People are tired now, as the end of the day nears, and the smiles have disappeared from their usually cheerful faces.

I desperately want to reach the post and see Zakharov before nightfall. His name is known in every *kishlak* in the province of Kunduz. Zakharov is a legend.

His post is situated at the intersection of several caravan routes, a place of immense strategic importance to the *dukhi*. By controlling this nerve center—and thus the shortest supply route for ammunition, arms, medicine, and provisions from Pakistan—Zakharov can squeeze Gayur's windpipe.

A year ago, Gayur proclaimed Zakharov to be his personal number-one enemy and put a price of one million afghani on his head. It didn't help. He then sent one of his agents to the post with this proposal: "Turn, Zakharov, to my side. I would load you and your wives with gold. Gayur."

Zakharov thanked the agent for the flattering proposal but sent this message back to Gayur: "Your gold is of a lower standard. Zakharov."

"Gayur flew into a rage," Zakharov says, laughing with uncontrolled glee. He scratches the round, crew-cut head that Gayur has been hunting so long and so unsuccessfully.

We're sitting in the camp's bakery, snacking on sour-sweet bread. The stove sends a gentle warmth through the cozy hut. In another moment, we'll be carried away to Zakharov's native village.

But a cannonade brings us back to South Baghlan and the command post.

Last month, it turns out, Gayur had tried to conquer Zakharov again. Since gold hadn't worked, he had tried sheer cunning.

A "well-wisher" arrived at the post and reported that a big caravan with weapons was due to pass just five kilometers from the post on the following day. If Zakharov cared about the civilians in the neighboring *kishlaks,* the messenger said, he should destroy it.

"I checked the information quickly through other channels," Zakharov says. "I have many friends among the local population, so there are people to ask. I get on well with the peasants who live in the *kishlaks* here. Never do I deceive them, and I share our provisions and fuel with them. If someone asks for protection so that peasants can plow in peace, I always oblige. In short, people devoted to me reported that the information about the caravan was false. Gayur's plan was clear. He wanted me to send my main forces out to ambush the caravan. In the meantime, he'd take me with his bare hands. No, I thought to myself, nothing doing. I generously thanked the 'well-wisher' and later that evening pretended our company was leaving to set up the ambush. But under the cover of darkness, all of our men came back. And I turned out to be right; my intuition hadn't let me down. That night, Gayur arrived with nearly six hundred bandits, armed to the teeth, and attacked the post from all directions. Well, I met him accordingly. Gayur turned on his heels and ran all the way to Baghlan without looking back.

"It is impossible to underestimate Gayur's cleverness. Next time, he decided to act by the rule of contraries. He sent yet another 'well-wisher,' who informed me: 'Zakharov, tomorrow at five in the afternoon Gayur will hit your post with all his forces. Be prepared.'

"As usual, I thanked the 'well-wisher' with all my heart and gave him money, flour, and firewood. And then I thought to myself, Aha! You, Gayur, want me to lock myself in my fortress, and in the meantime you'll lead a caravan through. No, fella, again nothing doing! The next day at five P.M. sharp—right on the nose—a caravan of a hundred or so pack animals and a dozen Toyota pickups moved by, carrying enough ammunition to keep Gayur's forces in active combat for two months. But my men were ready for them. So that's how Gayur and I fight with each other—the more cunning one wins."

Zakharov, who turned twenty-eight on May 27, came to Afghanistan a year ago. He spent the first four months exploring the territory and learning the customs and traditions of the local peasants. It's impossible to fight the *dukhi* successfully without such knowledge.

"I was in luck right from the beginning," Zakharov says. "The bandits were too busy—mostly bickering among themselves—to pay any attention to me. While they were occupied, I intercepted the caravans that carried their weapons. Gayur once again returned from Pakistan with an order to unite all of the quarreling bands and to persuade the peasants to cross the border. But nobody wanted to listen to him. Then the rascal thought of something else. As a way of forcing the peasants to leave Afghanistan, he began to fire at my positions straight from the neighboring *kishlaks* in an effort to draw our return fire. The provocations were repeated every day, but our guns remained silent. I refused to fire on peaceful civilians. Gayur also exploited our reluctance to mine the paths and caravan routes in the region, again for fear of wounding any peasants."

Zakharov steps out of the camp's bakery for ten minutes to have a look around. I sit as before, my back against a warm wall, smoking cigarettes. It is almost dark outside. The stove breathes a spicy warmth. Inhaling this pleasant aroma relaxes all the muscles in my body. Through a tiny window, I see the moon, which looks like the lone porthole of a faraway ship sailing slowly in the dark of night.

Zakharov suddenly returns, swearing as he slams the door behind him. "Sabotage on the pipe again, damn it."

One of Zakharov's platoons has been guarding a long section of the pipeline through which the Soviets pump fuel to Afghanistan. To punch a hole in it is no problem; a good swing with a sledgehammer is all it takes. The *dukhi* sometimes bribe little kids to do it, paying them a hundred afghani per hole. More often, though, they use explosives. Groups of rebels will approach the pipeline in different places, blowing up several sections at once and igniting raging fires. At the same time, they mine the approaches to the holes.

"Now it's been done, for sure," Zakharov says. "They hope to divert my forces into extinguishing the fires while they try to lead another caravan to Gayur. So let's postpone our talk until dawn."

The fire blazes at full force, illuminating the sleepy faces of soldiers from the repair brigade. The light is so bright that our sappers are able to work without flashlights. Clouds of smoke and soot speed into the night sky. We find no mines, and for this alone we could have thanked the *dukhi*.

One of the soldiers standing nearby gives me a few crisp crackers. I pour hot tea from my flask over the crackers so they won't crumble into dust.

"Do you have anything for a snack?" asks a squatting sapper.

I place one of my sodden crackers in his fuel-smeared hand. I look into his eyes and see reflections of the raging fire behind me.

Something thunders nearby, and weak convulsions run through the ground.

"It's a 122-mm howitzer," says a lieutenant colonel who emerges from the darkness, having just arrived from the regiment's command post. "Gayur is rushing around the blockade in search of an opening. We took Eighth and Fifth streets. The Afghans are combing the blockade now. There's not much distance between Gayur's forces and ours, so it's difficult to use our artillery—we might hit our own people."

The lieutenant colonel stretches out his arms and warms his hands on the fire. I take a swallow from my flask and pass it on to him. Suddenly something blazes up, as if someone had opened the door of a blast furnace. A few seconds later, we hear an explosion through the din of rain and fire. Evidently the howitzer has been fired, about seven hundred meters away.

The lieutenant colonel tells us that an hour or so ago another band of *dukhi* approached the blockade from the south. "The rebels tried to break open the blockade and lead out Gayur and his guards," he says. "They'd taken advantage of the fire to slip unnoticed very close to the blockade. Then they simultaneously attacked one of the junctions from the outside and the inside. Now the section has been strengthened by two platoons from the reserve. We captured many prisoners. During interrogation, one of them told us that Gayur had been killed."

I congratulate the lieutenant colonel.

"This is typical disinformation," he comments, taking another swallow from my flask. "Twice during the last three days they've spread the same rumor, hoping that we'd weaken the pressure. But even the devil himself can't fool Vanyka, because Vanyka knows his wily ways." (Vanyka is the diminutive for Ivan, the nickname for a Russian soldier.)

By three in the morning, the pipeline fire has been put out. Some time earlier the flow of the fuel through the pipeline had been cut off, and now its damaged section has to be replaced. I watch as the bulky piece of pipe is dragged to the road.

The lieutenant colonel gives me a lift to the command post. In farewell, he throws me a *bushlat* [pea jacket].

"Take this," he says, "so you won't freeze."

"To whom do I return it?" I ask.

With a wave of the hand, he replies, "Keep it. No one needs it anymore."

I climb inside an APC that's stuck in mud up to its chassis, closing the hatch to keep the rain out of the cabin. In a nearby seat, a gunner sleeps curled in the fetal position. A bright blue light illuminates the cabin, and the sleeping soldier has his green Panama over his eyes to shield them from the glare.

Before lying down I put on the *bushlat* and button it up to my chin even though it's warmer inside the carrier. The jacket has four little green stars on each epaulet.

From now on, I am a captain.

For a long time I can't fall asleep. I lie in bed listening to the calm breath of my accidental neighbor. My hands stubbornly refuse to get warm, so I push them into the deep pockets of my *bushlat*. I feel a little box in the right pocket and take it out. Inside are some British water-purification tablets. The neatly folded instructions that come with them say that each tablet can disinfect twenty-five liters of water. The erstwhile owner of my jacket evidently had to be in combat often, and for long periods. The same box holds five yellow pills for the prevention of hepatitis; those who've already had jaundice use them as a form of insurance. I also find a mixture of sand and tobacco at the bottom of the pocket and carry a pinch of it to my nose. It smells sweetly of Amphora, a British pipe tobacco that can't be confused with any other. You can easily buy a little red cellophane packet of Amphora anywhere in Afghanistan for three hundred afghani.

Who once wore the jacket that now keeps me warm? I gradually begin to form a mental image of this unknown captain. The picture is far from clear, but already I know certain things about him.

He was a calm, laconic man who liked to reflect on things in his leisure hours; people of different dispositions are rarely attracted to pipes. The sleeves of the jacket have been worn through at the elbows, and its rough fabric is embedded with dirt; the captain often lay in ambush. The back of the jacket is also quite shabby and torn in places; the captain spent a lot of time in armored carriers. The pockets are bulging out; he apparently preferred to keep his hands in them.

I imagine a man of about twenty-eight years, walking with his hands pushed deep into his pockets on a dank, freezing day—the kind of day that makes you pull up your collar. The jacket's collar, by the way, is greasy, worn through in the front and sides, and threadbare in the back; the captain obviously had a beard of coarse stubble.

The *bushlat* reminds me of an abandoned house. After wandering in by chance, you find the signs of recent life everywhere: traces of boiled-over milk on a burner or an open tin of still-moist shoe polish on the floor.

What is happening now to this man? Where is he? And why is it, when I think about him, that I use the past tense?

Although a lot of other questions pop into my head, the right pocket of the jacket holds no answers. I'm not ashamed of my curiosity. Curiosity is as essential to a reporter, after all, as the ability to type.

In the left pocket of the jacket I discover several dried wildflowers. Was the captain sentimental? I also retrieve a small piece of paper, covered with tiny script, from the very bottom of the pocket. Most of the handwriting is blurred, but I manage to make out two lines in the blue light: ". . . my position is pretty stupid, to be crazy in love with my own wife. Especially stupid if I take into account that we have known each other for more than fifteen years. Often I . . ." And, at the lower edge of the paper: "Stenunin is coming, so please send with him a tin of herring."

If only Sherlock Holmes and his buddy Dr. Watson were here in the APC. They could answer all my questions in a flash. Incidentally, Dr. Braiton, who was rumored to have been the model for Dr. Watson, once served in Afghanistan as a member of the British Expeditionary Corps. As I vainly try to remember the dates of the Anglo-Afghan wars, sleep embraces me in a bear hug.

For a while I hear the muffled sounds of explosions and shooting through the vehicle's armored walls; it is as if my ears have been plugged with wads of cotton. But soon the world outside loses its meaning. Thinking once more of the unknown captain, I drift into a deep sleep.

The gunner awakes me at six o'clock in the morning. I open the hatch and look outside. It is already light, although the heavy sky hanging low over South Baghlan only reluctantly lets the sun's rays shine through.

The artillery is silent, but the thick fire of automatic weapons sounds clearly behind us. The gunner brings a helmet filled to the rim with hot, rusty water, which he's drained from the APC's radiator. We wash our faces and warm them in the rising steam.

After eating a tin of ground sausage, I make my way to another APC, which is hidden behind an embankment under a sagging, rain-soaked camouflage net. Its engine is idling, and I warm myself in the sweet, damp exhaust. An officer with blue circles of soot under his eyes is sitting on top of the APC. In reply to my question, he says that we will be heading directly to Sixth Street. Last night it was still in enemy hands, but before daybreak the *dukhi* lost control; Afghan sappers are now sweeping the street for mines. We'll be leaving in a couple of minutes.

When we arrive at Sixth Street, there is nothing left but shell holes filled with gray water. On the side of the road are several burned-out antitank and antipersonnel mines, some Chinese submachine guns and British rifles, a few grenade launchers, and two machine guns.

South Baghlan resembles a half-destroyed labyrinth, something like one of those little mazes in children's magazines ("How can the bunny rabbit get out?"). It is as difficult to wind our way through the city as it is to understand the thoughts and moods of its recent inhabitants.

We enter one of the captured dugout shelters. Bowls of lamb pilaf, still steaming, rest on the dirt floor. Three corpses are slumped nearby. One of them clenches a spoon in his hand. Another grips a submachine gun in his frozen fingers.

In the corner we find a thermos. A trophy thermos. Even though it is empty, it seems unusually heavy. Valery Pavlovich Zalomin, who was one of the first to arrive on the scene, warns that we have to be careful with such a souvenir. He is right. I unscrew the bottom of the thermos and find a curious blob of black goo. It turns out to be a potent contact explosive from Pakistan.

"Tonight you would've learned your lesson," Zalomin tells me as he twiddles a small piece of the paste in his fingers. "After supper you would've poured some hot tea into your new thermos, expanding the paste and thus triggering an explosion from the increased pressure. It would've been the last time in your life you ever made tea."

The incident leaves me wondering about the sheer inventiveness of these bandits, about their rich and inexhaustible imaginations. Inside every fortification point—the bunkers, the pillboxes, the four-level underground dugouts—the soldiers find booby-trapped pens, watches, lighters, tape recorders, and the like. Hidden death has been camouflaged so masterfully that only someone with a practiced eye can see it.

This is the end of the four-day-old battle for South Baghlan. Although Gayur's capture has reportedly been one of the operation's main objectives, he can't be identified among the dead and wounded.

The office of Colonel Abdullah Fakirzad, the director of KHAD's Kunduz department, is austere. Nothing unnecessary: a desk, a few chairs, and a hard—maybe even too hard—couch.

The colonel himself is tall and stooping. His mustache reminds me of Budyonny, a famous Soviet military leader in the 1920s.

"According to my information," Fakirzad says, "Gayur left—dressed in female clothes—at three in the morning, right before our takeover of Sixth Street. I assume that he managed to bribe his way through one of our checkpoints. You see, anything is possible here, especially when you consider how many recruits come from the *kishlaks*. Many of them have little in the way of conscience."

I mention a few recent cases of desertion from the Afghan divisions in the province. The colonel already knows about them.

"Moreover," I add, "the moral and political spirit could be improved in many of the Afghan subdivisions that I've had the occasion to visit. Not every soldier can explain exactly what, in the end, he's fighting for."

The colonel shakes his big head of charcoal-black hair, which is combed smoothly backward. "It's a serious problem," he says. "There are a great many reasons, of course, but no excuses. I'll name just one. There isn't enough money. A soldier of fortune earns five times less than a rebel in the Ahmad Shah Massoud's band. And the sale of personal weapons? A single gun is going for eighty thousand afghani on the local black market. A kilo of meat—I'm giving this for comparison—costs two hundred and fifty afghani. For the price of that gun you could feed a family for a whole year. Recently, however, we have taken strict measures to suppress desertion."

"How do you envision Afghanistan after the withdrawal of Soviet troops?" I ask.

The colonel thinks for a moment, running a hand over his hair (the thought occurs to me that the hand might turn black, too). "Most of the rebel gangs, which are squabbling here for zones of influence, cover their banditry with a lot of talk about fighting *shuravi* [slang for 'Soviets']," he says. "It's all just a smoke screen that lets American politicians pour dollars into the furnace of the Afghan war with a clear conscience. When the Soviet troops leave, internecine war will break out all over the country. The rebel leaders, however, will no longer be able to disguise their terrorism with talk of 'holy war.' Many Afghans believe that *shuravi* shouldn't leave until all the bands have agreed among themselves to change a feudal ideology into a national ideology. The rebels, you see, are afraid of the Soviets, which is the only thing that's keeping them from unleashing their terrorism everywhere."

Colonel Fakirzad's constantly moving mouth is completely covered by his mustache. His powerful chin, which occupies a third of his face and has been shaved to a steely shine, barely moves during his tirade. The words seem to be flowing from his eyes, which are the color of a starless southern night.

After a short pause, he resumes his speech in a calm, muffled voice. "Now they will bring a captured mullah here, the one who functioned as a judge in the *kishlaks* around Emam Saheb and who became notorious for his rare cruelty toward sympathizers with the revolution. He'll show you his smooth hands with blue veins to prove that he never wielded a weapon and didn't kill. But don't believe him—he's up to his elbows in blood. He killed, executed, shot, and cut ears with his verdicts. Hey, bring in the prisoner."

Nobody, however, brings in a prisoner. The mullah in question opens the door himself and comes in.

The face of this puny, fifty-year-old man shines with all the human virtues. The sleeves of his loose coveralls are rolled nearly up to his shoulders. If I hadn't seen his face, I would've guessed that his hands belonged to a seventeen-year-old girl who'd been protected since birth from dirt, labor, and sun. Or to a musician whose hands had toiled only on the ivory keys of a grand piano.

The interrogation of the mullah, however, is as boring and

meaningless as all the interrogations I've witnessed in Afghanistan. I have the impression that all the *dukhi* have read the same carefully crafted script. I grow accustomed to seeing the same buttons on their clothing (most typically with Lenin's profile or the Red Banner). Because I've read and heard a lot about their religious fanaticism, I am always amazed at the ease with which they renounce Allah and swear their love for "nonbelievers." I remember how, the previous summer in Baghlan, we had given a little liquor to a captured Afghan rebel who was chilled to the bone. He emptied the glass and, grinning lustfully, asked for more. He was allowed to eat what we had on the table—canned pork.

"Are Allah's soldiers allowed to drink alcohol and eat pork?" I asked.

"We're under a roof," he replied, pointing to the ceiling. "Allah won't see."

The captured mullah zealously proclaims loyalty to the ideals of the revolution and swears that the only pain he ever inflicted on anyone was through the ceremony of circumcision. But that was holy pain.

According to intelligence reports, the mullah had vigorously pressed Ortabulaki to fire on Soviet territory in the region of Pyandzh. Naturally, he denies this.

"When the firing began," the mullah says, "I decided that the battle was between two hostile bands."

We also know that not long before the battle at Pyandzh, the mullah sentenced Kirghiz Abdullah and his four sons to death for joining the people's revolution. This is widely known in the region of Emam Saheb; the mullah can't deny it.

"I was against the execution," he says. "But Ortabulaki advised me to prepare a *kafan* [a white burial cloth] if I refused to sign a death warrant."

"If Ortabulaki ordered you to judge a Russian," I ask him, "what would you do?" I imagine for a moment that I am the prisoner and he my judge.

"Neither Ortabulaki nor Halif ever asked me to do it," he replies, spreading his smooth hands apart.

"You are old and wise," I say, nodding at his gray hair. "Tell me, what will happen here after the Soviet troops leave? Speak frankly, for no harm will come to you."

Even without my assurance, the mullah knows he is safe—maybe even safer than in his own *kishlak*. He attentively inspects his hands and arms, from the tips of his fingernails to his shoulders.

"After the departure of *shuravi*, the bands will start internecine war over the land," he says. "No one doubts this. It will be very difficult and a lot of innocent blood will be spilled."

The mullah is taken away. Colonel Fakirzad slams the door behind him and smiles, somewhat sadly, after the old man. He bites off the tip of a Cuban cigar and lights it, letting out a couple of thunderclouds of rancid smoke. "Kirghiz Abdullah and his four sons were shot at dawn," he says. "The youngest got a bullet in his shoulder. At night he got out from under the corpses of his father and brothers and by dawn of the next day reached here. That's who informed us that none other than the mullah had initiated the executions."

"Is it true that Gulbuddin was born in Kunduz?" I ask. (Gulbuddin Hekmatyar, a rebel leader, is now entrenched in Pakistan.) "As far as I know, that's exactly why he treats everything in this province with partiality."

"Put your question to Muhammed Yasin, the secretary of the province's Party committee," he replies. "Gulbuddin and Yasin studied together."

With this, our conversation ends. I say good-bye to the colonel, sincerely wishing him success.

"How was your conversation with KHAD?" Muhammed Yasin asks me as we meet in his tiny yard. He is a round, brisk man of about forty.

I tell him. Then I ask him about Gulbuddin.

"You see, I was studying with him in the same class," Yasin says. "He was later expelled for homosexuality."

"Really?"

"Even back then, Gulbuddin distinguished himself by different dirty tricks. He and his buddies would sprinkle acid on a woman's face if they saw her without a yashmak. That's how he was fighting for the purity of Islam. During his student years, Gulbuddin took up with Western teachers at local lycées; they were already laying the groundwork for counterrevolution. To this day, by the way, Afghanistan is swarming with American, West German, and British 'teachers.' They recruit new soldiers for themselves."

Yasin pauses briefly and then goes on.

"I studied in graduate school in Rumania for four years, where I took a great fancy to the history of World War II. Sometimes it seems to me that the leaders of the counterrevolution adopted a lot from Hitler. Their plan is to involve as many people as possible in their crime, which they call a holy war. If a crime takes on a mass character, you see, then it's as if it's not a crime, but rather the norm. At least Gulbuddin supposes so. Hitler was also striving to involve the maximum number of Germans in the crimes of the Wehrmacht.

"Well, once a soldier begins to muse over his deeds, he acquires something like a guilt complex. Then he fights as if he's possessed. He has nothing to lose. He's made his stake, his choice. But the members of the Seven aren't the ideological fathers of the counterrevolution. They are low-grade rogues."

He brings over a folder of newspaper clippings and begins to sort through it.

"You see, things got so bad that even American congressmen began to accuse the Seven of waste and corruption. Even Senator Gordon Humphrey, one of the main defenders of the interests of counterrevolution, recently admitted that the squandering of resources had reached . . ."

Yasin puts on his glasses and leans closer to the papers on his desk.

". . . a 'scandalous scale.' As a result of the swindling by my former schoolmate and his buddies, seventy percent of the aid given by the United States to the rebels doesn't reach its intended destination. Where, I ask you, did Gulbuddin get the money to open an antique shop in the center of London? I don't know either. Or rather, now I do."

My time is running out, but I have to ask one more question. "Tell me, how are things with national reconciliation in your province?"

Yasin doesn't beat around the bush. "Complicated. Not as good as we were counting on at the beginning. Right after January fifteenth, the rebels sharply increased—by four or five times—the number of attacks on Soviet and Afghan garrisons. So the military position intensified. Rebel bands even launched an attack on the territory of the Soviet Union, which earlier they wouldn't have dared to do. It was an act of propaganda. And yet we have some results of reconciliation. During the first three months, a hundred or so people turned to the side of people's power."

Again he refers to his file.

"Two hundred ninety out of four hundred and thirty-three *kishlaks* in this province are under our control. Local elections were held in one hundred forty-three *kishlaks*. In the district of Habbad, more than two hundred rebels are ready to form a tribal batallion. The Seven and Pakistan, however, are still preventing refugees from returning. Gulbuddin personally called upon people to remain on the other side of the border. When the threat of a mass crossing through the Durand Line materialized, Pakistan moved its Seventeenth Tank Division closer to this line. And Gulbuddin started a rumor that Najibullah was preparing to send any refugees who returned to concentration camps."

Yasin has grown noticeably gloomier. I have the uneasy feeling that our conversation has spoiled his mood.

We bid each other farewell.

As I wait near the airstrip for a pair of Mi-8 helicopters to arrive, I climb into a half-destroyed Czechoslovakian Albatross. Its propellers are turning reluctantly in the wind. A badly sunburned soldier is snoring in the cabin. I sit in the pilot's chair and light a cigarette.

It is chilly inside. If nothing else, the thick smoke seems to warm my soul. Later, I move to the airfield building. A few officers with cans of Sip, a fizzy orange drink, are sitting and watching television.

On the screen, Pastor Shlag* is trying on some skis in a businesslike manner. Then Shtirlitz strays around Berlin for a long time. A siren howls and people run for a bomb shelter. Then the artillery comes to life—not near Berlin, but to the north of Kunduz.

*A character in "Seventeen Moments of Spring," a popular Soviet TV show about a Soviet spy in Germany during World War II.

Fifteen minutes later, when Shtirlitz again is on the verge of failure, we can hear the roar of the landing helicopters.

Pyandzh, a tiny town in the Soviet republic of Tadzhikistan, is about three hundred meters from the Afghan border. Just three hundred meters from the war.

Never have I seen a border like this one. It isn't so much a geographic boundary as a border in time, a line between two social and economic systems, between two philosophies, between war and peace. The division is even more striking when you consider that people of the same nationality—the Tajik—live on either side of the border. On one side they live in the late 1980s under the socialist system, and on the other side they live in 1366 (by the Moslem calendar) under a feudal system with tribal vestiges. You don't need a time machine to experience the difference. Simply get into an Mi-8 helicopter and ask the pilot for a lift from Kunduz, Afghanistan, to Pyandzh, USSR. That's all you need to do.

From Pyandzh you can hear the war thundering like an angry sea, day and night, without pause. One day, the war rolled over the border and stole a young life from the town.

A band of Ortabulaki began shooting their mortars at Pyandzh on March 8, 1987, at 10:55 P.M. Just five minutes earlier, Zeinidin Norov, a cheerful twenty-five-year-old with a shock of coarse black hair across his forehead, had been sitting in his room.

"He sat and leafed through a magazine," Zeinidin's brother tells me. "Later he tossed it on the bed. I think that it must have been very boring. But he never stopped smiling; the entire evening he'd been out with his fiancée, Gulchehra. They were going to get married in May."

The thunder of the mortars shook the house to the basement. Zeinidin jumped up and raced into the street. Suddenly, he felt a strong blow between his shoulder blades, and he fell slowly, trying to throw his hands forward. His light, lean body hit the ground. He hugged the earth with his weakened arms and pressed his cheek to it, as if he wanted to hear a last farewell.

But he would never hear or see anything again.

It happened at 10:57 P.M. on a starless spring night.

"You know, he died right on the street," his father tells me. "Without suffering."

And then his father asks the saddest question in the world, the question that's so often heard in wartime: "Why him?"

It's a question that nobody can answer.

I can see Gulchehra and the tiny figure of Zeinidin's mother through the window. His mother's shoulders shake convulsively, but tears no longer stream down her face. In one night she was transformed into an old woman. She doesn't look at me. I've come from "there"—from the place that has brought death into her home.

Although I feel boundless guilt before her, my guilt doesn't strike me as strange. But still I try not to look her way. I avoid looking into her eyes, just as I avoid Gulchehra's. What is Gulchehra now? An unwed widow?

A helicopter is taking me back "there." Behind us, its shadow slides over the rust-colored swamps below. Ducks dash aside. We cross the border back into Afghanistan.

I look at the pilot, who is holding his breath, and think of how a swimmer inhales deeply before diving into the water. I remember every minute of those three warless hours in Pyandzh.

"Time here is limitless—you'll see for yourself," says Lieutenant Colonel Vladikin, who meets me at the airfield near Jalalabad. "Like a synthetic shirt from Hong Kong. Sometimes it shrinks. Before your mind manages to get a fix on a single week, another is rushing to take its place. And sometimes a single day seems as big as"—here he glances around, as if searching for a proper comparison—"as life."

Think of it. Thanks to a helicopter, you can visit several places that are hundreds of kilometers apart and meet dozens of people who were once total strangers—people who, for some reason, talk to you in such a way that their lives become part of yours. In time you begin to love their friends, children, and even wives, and you hate whatever they hate. Well, think about all this long enough and you'll come to agree with Vladikin.

"True, true, Yuri Ivanovich, just like synthetic shirts from Hong Kong," I tell him. "You should be writing. By any chance are you trying to be a writer between the combat flights?"

"I play with it sometimes," he replies. "Look at how much paper I've soiled."

Vladikin hands me a thick pocket notebook. Each grid-covered page is filled with his handwriting. The script is straight and neat. The lines have been penciled in with military precision. As I glance through the notebook, I think that Vladikin must be as straight, neat, and precise as his handwriting.

"Read it sometime when you're bored with the Moscow routine and want to remember Afghanistan," he tells me.

"Aren't you sorry to let it go?" I ask.

Vladikin waves his hand and says, "I would be sorry to die, and this . . ." He never completes the sentence.

We embrace and say good-bye. I watch him run along the airstrip, strapping on his shabby helmet as he goes. Soon he disappears through the door of his helicopter.

In Afghanistan, a reporter can't do without helicopters. They make you omnipresent. Helicopters are to a country at war what taxis are to Moscow—only there aren't any little black-and-white squares on the doors.

Otherwise, everything's pretty much the same. You stand near an airstrip, wait to flag down the next helicopter, and hope that it's heading your way. After each disappointment you cross your fingers again. Soon you have the eerie feeling that you're back in Moscow, trying to persuade a taxi driver to take you to Arbat, the city's oldest and most famous street. Over and over comes the same reply: "Can't you see that I'm off duty?"

Helicopters are the horses of the modern cavalry. They tirelessly carry me from one side of Afghanistan to the other. They land troops on the tiniest spaces between the sheerest slopes. They pick up our wounded and rocket to the skies from the gloom of the abyss. They fly past the maws of caves and ravines, where hidden machine guns spit fire at them. They speed, in single file or as a flock, through canyons so narrow that no more than three meters remain between the tips of the whirling blades and the rocks on either side. On these rides, everything inside of you suddenly dries up as you realize that a single, glancing encounter will smash the helicopter to smithereens and send you to your death.

you for a couple of hundred afghani. "Commander, *kaif!*" they will yell in perfect Russian. (*Kaif* is slang for "get high.") If you want something stronger, you visit the man who smiles so enticingly at you from a nearby yard. But remember: this time two hundred afghani won't be enough.

A camel stands on the side of the road. As he looks at me from above, he seems insultingly arrogant. Yet the camel has the eyes of a wise man, and wise men are forgiven for everything—or almost everything.

What can a lowly camel have to do with the poppy trade? Plenty. Two or three kilometers before the border, a trader will place a dozen or so small packets of white powder on the animal's tongue; the camel will swallow them without chewing. Forty minutes later, with the border far behind them, the camel will regurgitate the packets and the trader will slip them back into his bag. That's what I think of as I look into the camel's wet, violet eyes—eyes in which the earth and sky have traded places.

We soon reach the outskirts of the city, where the luxuriant crowns of Jalalabad's trees are turned toward the sky in an explosion of red, white, and green.

The flowering trees have buried the city in heady fragrances. We rush past a eucalyptus grove that our soldiers long ago nicknamed "the grove of nightingales." In the evenings, the *dukhi*'s bullets often fill the grove with the songs of death—the music of the Other World.

The winter residence of the former king of Afghanistan is wrapped in lilacs. Anyone who loves the color of lilacs, psychologists tell us, has a skeptical disposition. Inside the palace, there is a lot of marble: marble columns, marble walls, marble floors, marble bathrooms. Even the toilet bowl resembles a pedestal waiting to hold a sculpture. Marble never fails to remind me of museums and cemeteries.

Nobody lives here anymore. The *dukhi* have recently bombed the nearby post office, knocking out all of the palace's windows in the process, making the place even gloomier. A tomb for itself, I think. Gulyam Said, the mayor of the city, has begun the restoration of the royal palace. But who will live there?

Rebel sympathizers have recently unleashed a string of diversionary acts. Not long ago, the rebels stoned to death Mirza Inayatoll, the chairman of the commission for national reconciliation in the province of Nangarhar, and his ill son.

I come upon a hotel that has been restored from ruins by Soviet soldiers at a cost of eighty thousand rubles. The hotel, which has all the comforts of modern life, is intended to house the refugees who are streaming in from Pakistan. Never in their lives have Afghans seen such luxury. The rebels, however, have spread the rumor that it's actually a prison. Rumor is just one of the weapons the rebels use very skillfully.

The hotel is guarded by a youth who seems to be about fourteen years old. He is standing in the yard with a Tommy gun over his shoulder. His name is Mateolla. Before joining the army, he drove one of the motorized rickshaws that scurry about Jalalabad like ants. Childhood comes to an early end in Afghanistan—if laboring every day from dawn to sunset can even be considered childhood. And from childhood, the Afghan youth enter not adolescence but war. I wish Mateolla well. But I think to myself: God be with you. May you at least stay alive. You can't fight with children.

A woman in a yashmak is standing near the hotel, cradling an infant in her arms. The baby had died on the trip from Pakistan two days ago. But the mother still refuses to give up her child. His tiny body has stiffened and turned blue.

Of all the things I've seen in Afghanistan, this strikes me as the most horrible.

There is a light on in the officers' mess hall, drawing me in from the damp darkness of Jalalabad. People are getting ready to go to sleep, but I don't want to. I come inside and slowly take off my khaki cloak, which has turned black from the rain. I sit in the corner, at a table covered with a dazzlingly white tablecloth, and begin to rub my cold hands.

"Something hot?" asks the middle-aged woman who has appeared at the door. Without waiting for an answer, she pours me a glass of smoky, ruby-colored tea.

She disappears into the kitchen and soon returns with a plate of kasha and meatballs.

"Here," she says. "You must be hungry. Are you an inspector from Tashkent?"

"Correspondent."

Something is missing from the thin, classic features of her beautiful Russian face. Maybe time has washed it away. Or perhaps the Creator, while painting her portrait, has forgotten a couple of finishing touches.

"What's your name? Maybe I've read something by you."

I tell her my name.

"And my name is Olga Semenovna. Olya."

"What on earth is a woman like you doing in a wretched place like Jalalabad? Is the Soviet Union too small for you?"

"I have a son," Olya explains. "He was drafted into the army and was supposed to go to Afghanistan. I learned about it and also went to the military registration and enlistment office to ask to be sent here, so I could be with him in the same unit. But it happened that he was sent to Kishinev and I found myself here. Funny, eh?"

I push the plate away and wipe my lips with a sleeve. "Meatballs—death to the *dukhi!*" I say, joking for a moment. "No, seriously, they're very tasty. Have you been here a long time?" I ask.

"A considerable time."

"Is it tough here?"

She laughs. "For the first seventy years it's pretty tough," she says. "Then it gets easier."

"Seriously."

"Seriously, it's very hard here. In the beginning, there were no comforts at all. It's only now that they've installed air conditioners and refrigerators." She sits at the table and rests her chin on her palms. "We broke up the shell boxes and made beds and bookcases out of the boards. You'd work so hard each day that your legs would sprain at the ankles." She shows me how.

"Tell me, Olya, if it isn't a secret, how was your life turning out before Afghanistan?"

She smiles joylessly, with just her lips. "It's not a secret, but we'd better not talk about it. People's lives turn out differently here. One girl, a clerk, was seeing an officer. Such a big guy. Then they went to the consulate in Kabul to register their marriage. And on the way back they were blown up by a mine. She died. He was wounded, but he lived. So that's that."

Olya falls to thinking. About what?

"Or Vitya Kurnaus. He was turning twenty-five. Such a gaunt boy, just like a bicycle. He asked me to lay the table on the twelfth and went to the combat zone. The twelfth of the month arrived, and I laid the table. I sat and waited. Evening came, and he still hadn't arrived. I ran to the battalion, where they told me, 'Go back. Vitya will not come.' At first I felt hurt. I didn't understand what was the matter. It only struck me later—you know, nobody will tell you of death directly here."

We are silent for a while. Then I ask, "And when are you thinking of going home? Soon?"

"Not very soon." She draws her legs out from under the table and paces back and forth with her hands crossed on her chest. "Yes, you'd need health here. Not long ago, I went to donate some blood to a wounded soldier. I have a rare type of blood. And it was hard for the boy. His leg had been amputated. He was looking so pale. But he smiled up at me and said, 'Listen, Auntie, get out of here. Giving blood isn't women's work.' Then he saw me sobbing at the door and whispered, ever so softly, 'Thank you.' And I cried even more."

Olya comes and sits at the table again. Her hands are beautiful, with glossy, slightly pink nails.

"And in the Soviet Union we will meet with brothers in arms every year," she says suddenly, smiling and looking somewhere past me. "You come, too."

On my way out I think, No, my dear Olya, you don't have a rare type of blood. You have a rare type of soul.

Everyone is asleep in the officers' quarters. Night has silently crawled in through an open door. The only thing breaking the quiet is a muffled conversation from one room, where, over a late supper, colonels Evgeni Alexeevich Peshkov and Yuri Timofeevich Starov are reviewing the details of tomorrow's ambush.

Both Peshkov and Starov are about fifty years old. If not for a few wrinkles on their faces and some slight touches of gray in their hair, they could easily be mistaken for a couple of young officers.

Peshkov is slightly stockier than Starov. His voice has turned husky from chain-smoking a particularly bitter brand of cigarettes. Where on earth does he get them? He apparently likes to slip the cigarettes into an ordinary pack of Yava, the most popular brand in the Soviet Union. Peshkov is economical in his movements, leaving the impression that he has thought each motion out in advance and is simply carrying out his prearranged plan.

Starov has a soft voice, but I've been told that it can turn into rolling thunder when he addresses soldiers—just as if he were speaking through a bullhorn.

"They say that you are a cruel man, Yuri Timofeevich," I say, trying to provoke Starov into a reaction. "Is it true?"

He looks at me and laughs.

I know that Starov isn't a cruel man. I know that he's done no more than to demand discipline from himself and from others. I tell him what I've heard.

"You can't do it any differently in war," Starov says. "Kindness is like a rubber band. Here it could be kindness, but over there, evil. You can't draw a distinct line."

That's true. In combat conditions, kindness often turns out to be a form of negligence at best, and hence ultimately evil.

"This, if you please, is the logic of war," Peshkov says.

"Or perhaps the antilogic of war," I say as I bum one of his cigarettes.

"Yes, it's senseless to make up rules in war," he says. "Especially in this war, where there's no front or rear. It's a sparrow war, that's what it is. The *dukhi* adopted this ancient tactic from the Chinese."

I recall a conversation between two close friends in Moscow. One was from MID [the Soviet Ministry of Foreign Affairs]; the other had recently returned from Afghanistan to study in the military academy.

I relate the conversation to Peshkov and Starov.

"Take all those fine sayings about war," Starov says as he unbuttons the collar of his shirt. "Like 'a shell won't hit the same spot twice.' Well, a shell *will* hit the same spot twice, or even three times. If the *dukhi* want it badly enough, they'll hit it a dozen times in a row. And if there's a shortage of shells, a rebel leader will kill his own sniper for simply firing a couple of inaccurate shots."

Nodding his head in a businesslike way and abruptly rising from the table, Starov says, "Time for me to go."

Peshkov and I are alone.

. . .

In Afghanistan, a successful ambush, perhaps more than any other operation, depends on chance. Because expectations can so often fool us, I decided from the beginning to brace myself for failure—one more hopeless attempt to outwit fate.

But what is a successful ambush? To spot the *dukhi* at night and fire on them, when it isn't even clear at first who is shooting at whom, let alone who is ultimately going to win? Or to wait all through the night without moving anything but your jaws and without shooting anything but a scorpion? Soldiers—most of them, anyway—prefer the former.

The early morning promises hellish heat for the rest of the day. Everyone who is slated to take part in the evening's ambush greedily soaks up the cool freshness of dawn, which already has begun to dissolve in the sun's rusty rays. We line up on the parade ground, where dust and empty ration cans chase the wind. We are like a pack of hounds before the hunt. We face a six-kilometer run in full gear— merely a warmup exercise.

After the first hundred meters, sweat starts to pour down my face. (Is Afghanistan just getting back at me for my easy life in Moscow?) Earlier, the sappers swept a one-kilometer stretch of the road; now, to guard against grenades and sniper fire, the road is blocked by several infantry fighting vehicles.

As I run, my heavy backpack eats mercilessly against my sweaty spine. A flask flutters at my side. The barrel of my Kalashnikov assault rifle repeatedly tries to knock my teeth out.

All fifty airborne troopers and one reporter cover six thousand meters in thirty-two minutes.

We begin preparing for the ambush immediately after breakfast: checking the communications gear and other equipment, distributing the ammunition, cleaning the weapons. That night, each of our backs will have to bear as much as sixty kilos: an assault rifle, cartridges, a bulletproof vest, a sleeping bag, a cotton-padded *bushlat*, a rocket-launcher, food rations, two canteens, an ammunition belt with six magazines, flare and signal rockets . . . there is too much to even list, but all of it has to fit in.

The weather seems unpredictable in the extreme. Outside the

windows of the barracks, the rain and wind are changing as quickly as the mood of a neurasthenic.

I stuff a packet of bandages into the metal butt of my gun and wind a rubber band around it. Then I manage to squeeze an ampule of Promedol* and three batteries for night-vision binoculars into my backpack.

During all these weeks in Afghanistan, my equipment has become incredibly varied and is by now something of an international hodgepodge. My backpack was captured from the *dukhi* but bears a U.S. Army stamp. My eiderdown sleeping bag is English; according to the label inside, "This sleeping bag is intended for the use of British soldiers serving in arctic conditions." It was made in 1949. What soldier carried it on his back thirty-seven years ago, and where are his bones now? My thermos is apparently without kith or kin; it has no stamp of any kind. Its vacuum bottle may not keep anything warm, but at least it doesn't leak. I use it as a canteen. My khaki jacket, which is lined with thick artificial fur, was produced in Pakistan; that's why they call it a *pakistanka*. Only the lightest and most comfortable items wind up going with you on a march.

We are united—apart, of course, from our equipment and up-coming mission—by Kimri's shoe factory. All of us march in its virtually indestructible sneakers, which we call *kimri* for short. They are far more reliable than even the best running shoes made by Adidas, which invariably fall apart after the first hundred kilometers on the stony paths that wind through the deserts and mountains. The soldiers have to pay for *kimri* out of their own pockets; a pair costs twenty-four rubles and a few kopecks in the commissary. Only in the movies do soldiers fight in blue berets and shiny boots.

It is silent and dark in the little barracks. The rain and wind continue to fight outside the window. The sun is camouflaged behind a storm cloud. Vladik Dzhabarov comes in humming, almost to himself, "You don't have to shine with brains, but your boots must shine . . ."

"Right?" he asks Kirillov, who is dozing on top of the bunk bed.

Dzhabarov takes some cartridges from a box and begins to stuff

---

*The painkiller most often used by the army.

them into magazines. A shaggy-haired fellow with a red beard glides past the window.

"Don't worry," Dzhabarov reassures me. "It's the electrician. He's a civilian."

Dzhabarov and Kirillov* are also "civilians" in the slang of the local soldiers; in a couple of weeks they will be going home.

Kirillov is sound asleep, but from time to time he begins to argue aloud about something—so convincingly, in fact, that I want to tell whomever he is arguing with, "Don't contradict Kirillov. He knows what he's talking about."

All fifty men who will soon face a twenty-kilometer march through the desert to ambush a rebel convoy are resting. Their commander has allotted an hour and a half for sleep, and I try to use as much of it as possible for journalistic purposes. There will be no chance to talk tonight.

Each soldier speaks differently about himself. One speaks at such length that I have to keep turning to new pages in my notebook. Another gives me a stilted account of his past in army language, almost as if he were reciting military regulations. A third limits himself to short words and gestures, but they are so expressive as to be worth more than an exhaustive interview. Yet another speaks so vividly that I involuntarily become one of the characters in his narrative.

Some of the soldiers I meet can accurately reproduce all the nuances of their experiences. But others will lay out only the most naked sort of information, saying, "Emotions you can add yourself." And Vladikin, the helicopter pilot, simply gives me his diary.

I spend the entire hour and a half talking with Dzhabarov and others in the company. Pounding hard-rock music blasts out of a powerful Sharp cassette player. It has always seemed to me that rock and war, like rock and patriotism and rock and international duty, are concepts from completely different universes. But in this tiny room, as in dozens of others scattered across Afghanistan, somehow, in some striking way, these divergent concepts are in harmony.

---

*In the first Russian edition of this book I used the name Skylar throughout. A. V. Kirillov (Alexander) had asked me to avoid using his real name because he was hiding from his mother the fact that he was serving in Afghanistan.

A month will pass, and Dzhabarov and Kirillov will demobilize. And then, for years to come, the music they hear so rarely now will be dear to them—songs about Afghanistan. And about war.

"Rock and the war—I don't see anything incompatible in that," says Kolya Zubkov, a young lieutenant, with a grin. "You simply need to switch off from the fire and explosions, and rock can drown out everything."

The Sharp strains itself to reproduce the gravelly voice of Rod Stewart. Zubkov sits on the bed, nudging Kirillov aside. "Some people spend all their lives in search of life's meaning," he says. "Others give it up as hopeless in their youth and decide to take life as it is. But here I came to a very curious conclusion: Meaning should be introduced into life. It's that simple."

"Here nothing remains from your previous aims and ideas," says an awakened Kirillov as he gets up and begins to wash his pinkish face. "After your first outing in the combat zone, trying to unite these ideas again is unreal, as impossible as collecting together a head, a leg, and a body torn apart by a shell. When I was saying good-bye to my wife back in the Soviet Union, I understood right away that I was saying good-bye not only to her but also to myself—the myself I can never be again."

Kirillov places his toothbrush and toothpaste neatly back in his night table. It turns into a strange farewell: they are all sending me off, not vice versa.

To understand the stages of a soldier's life in Afghanistan, you must also look back on the changes in his state of mind. A soldier will shed his old habits, old fears, and old memories much as a turtle sheds his shell. But it seems to me that even the chemical composition of my cells has changed. I have the feeling that when I return home and have my blood analyzed, it will turn out to be different from the sample that was drawn two years ago.

Today's military maneuver is the last for Kirillov and Dzhabarov. Both of them have dozens of combat operations behind them—raids on arms convoys, assaults from helicopters and armored vehicles, ambushes. The commander doesn't let the "civilians" take part in combat operations; if you've served in Afghanistan for two years, you are spared and protected during the last twenty or thirty days before demobilization. Risk is like radiation; at some point the dose becomes critical. But by what unit of measure can the level of risk be assessed? A device for this purpose remains to be invented.

Ahead, the operation waits—an ambush that can separate you from the rest of your life. It is like the last five inches on the ledge of a skyscraper: you know that the distance ahead is insignificant compared with what is behind, but everything depends on those five inches.

Actually, it seems likely that I am the only one who is worrying. The soldiers are as calm as the mountains visible through the window. They pack their knapsacks silently.

It is also the last outing in the combat zone for Slava Sorokin. He has only fifteen days left before demob, even less than Dzhabarov and Kirillov. Not five inches but two. He sits with his arms around the waist of a guitar, humming something to himself.

Sorokin interrupts his song for a moment. "At the beginning it was hard because I didn't know or understand anything, and now it's hard because I know and understand everything," he says. "I look at these mountains and the deserts around us. A lot of strength was left there. You feel yourself not just matured but grown old. At the very end of the last ambush, everybody was exhausted, soaked, and freezing; I was only shooting so it would end sooner. But it feels bitter to leave Afghanistan. Life here, this low sky—everything becomes native, everything flows in here." Sorokin traces a vein on his left arm with his finger.

He slowly and tenderly runs his fingers over the guitar's strings, as he once must have touched the hair of the girl whose photograph he carries with him. In Afghanistan, a guitar is the only thing a soldier can hold in his embrace for two long years.

Evening smooths the colors of the distant mountains into a single shade of dull gray. The ground beneath us quivers. A long column of roaring APCs from a neighboring military unit stretches along the road, returning from combat. The big vehicles raise plenty of dust, which later settles slowly on the faces of the soldiers and the leaves of the trees. In the low murmur of the engines I can still hear the rough voice of Rod Stewart. For a long time we watch the procession of APCs from under our Panamas, which protect our eyes from the gusting clouds of exhaust, dust, and sand.

The APCs pass by ever so slowly, following one another nose to tail at precise intervals of fifteen meters. The drivers keep their heads poked out of the hatches in front. Their faces reflect the dashboard lights and seem to glow in the dark. It is impossible, though, to see the faces of the soldiers who are riding inside. They are just hunch-backed silhouettes. The antennas of the APCs are swinging back and forth, beating against the boughs of the trees as they brush against them. The column finally passes, its clang and roar disappearing behind the mountains.

"Hey, kid, are you in your place?" Kolya Zherelin, a twenty-five-year-old senior lieutenant, shouts into the microphone on the side of his helmet. "Get going, kid!" Zherelin's face is brown from tan and dust.

As the kid puts the pedal to the metal, our APC, along with eight others, rolls onto the road. After all fifty troopers have "saddled up," we head southeast on the road to Peshawar. Only thirty kilometers separate us from the border with Pakistan. Soon, under the cover of night, we will leave the APCs and turn sharply to the south along the Durand Line; then, after covering twenty kilometers more, we will set up an ambush near the *kishlaks* of Singir and Biru. According to our intelligence data, a band of rebels will pass by there tonight on its way to fortify its positions in the region of Jamali and, with the break of dawn, to shoot at our helicopters.

An Afghan scout accompanies our detachment. He is a lean man of about forty, with a coarse beard and protruding eyes. He was born in the *kishlak* of Biru, so he knows the local paths and caravan routes like the back of his hand.

As Zherelin talks back and forth on the radio with Captain Kozlov, he pats the cannon of his APC as if it were a faithful dog. It is pitch dark. About fifteen meters ahead, two bright red dots break the blackness—the taillights of the APC rumbling along in front of us. Cold dry air chills my face; I am almost thankful for the waves of hot exhaust fumes that hit me between gusts of wind. A couple of stars twinkle weakly in the sky; when I peer through my night-vision binoculars, I see a rash of them shining above.

An Afghan truck suddenly appears out of nowhere. It rushes toward us, bathing our column in the yellow glare of its headlights. "We're already clanking loud enough for half of Afghanistan to hear us," Zherelin says, swearing under his breath. "We might as well announce, 'Look, *dukhi*, Soviet troops are going to ambush!' "

It takes about five minutes for all of the APCs to turn off the road. Our column then heads due north over the rocky terrain. Our jolting journey ends after three or four hundred meters. We jump off the moving APCs, form a long line, and begin to walk in the opposite direction along a dried-up riverbed. The dull roar of the APCs behind us gradually grows fainter. They are still heading north; we are heading south. One by one, we crouch low to the ground and dash across the road on which our APCs were rolling smoothly just a short time ago.

The moon breaks from behind the clouds, illuminating the sweeping plain that lies ahead of us. The little stones that blanket the ground glitter in the moonlight as if they've been wrapped in aluminum foil. The pebbles do their best to work their way into the rubber soles of our *kimri*. Three kilometers later, however, we are no longer walking on gravel. We are up to our ankles in warm sand, which stretches out in front of us as far as the eye can see. We have reached the desert.

Sweat pours out from under my helmet—which I am wearing only as insurance—and covers my eyes like a sheet of caustic cellophane. Eventually, we stop for a brief rest. We sink to the ground in unison, lean against our backpacks, and stretch our legs. Sun Sunich, a sanitary instructor, is the only one among us who sits cross-legged, Turkish style. He's taken off his Panama, and his sweaty, smooth-shaven skull shines like polished silver.

"The night, brothers, is moonlit," Sunich says. "Moonlit." He tosses his head back and opens his mouth slightly, as if he were gargling the evening air. "And we're just sitting ducks."

That, in fact, is precisely the reason a team of scouts from our detachment is continuing on its way while we take a breather.

The desert is still ridding itself of the heat it soaked up during the day. It isn't as humid as a *banya* [a Russian steam bath], perhaps, but it is every bit as hot.

By now our throats are thoroughly parched. To a man, however, our canteens remain untouched. No one yet knows how long we'll be in the desert's wretched heat, but this much is certain: with every passing minute, each drop of water becomes more precious. Indeed, in just half an hour everything but water will have lost its meaning, and then there will be no greater curse than an empty canteen. In Afghanistan, thirst can actually make you stoop to drink from a puddle of camel urine. (Every Soviet soldier, in fact, carries a miniature water-purification device for just such an eventuality.) The only thing to worry about—and here I borrow from the lesson of Brother Ivanushka in a famous Russian fairy tale—is that you might turn into a camel afterward.

Time to get up. I tear myself from the ground as if I've been glued to it. Soon we are on the move again. We blend seamlessly into the background; even a chameleon couldn't camouflage himself so well. On the plain, we turn into grains of sand; on the mountains, into stones.

The moon paces the sky. It walks with us, illuminating our looping route between the hills and *kishlaks*. Fatigue follows like a shadow, sometimes catching up, sometimes falling behind. Here on the plain, exhaustion, thirst, and sand are all rolled into one. At first glance the plain seems lifeless and silent, but in reality it is littered with the telltale signs of man's presence: the sharp, rotten odor of a nearby *kishlak*; the muffled bark of a dog; the piercing howl and glowing eyes of a jackal rummaging for dinner somewhere in the dark.

The long march has taken its toll on my brain as well as my bones. My thoughts splinter into tiny fragments, mix with scraps of memory, and rattle around in my head like coins in a piggy bank. My mind jumps from here to there so quickly, in fact, that it is all but impossible for me to concentrate on the here and now. My mouth is filled with a metallic, rusty taste; my nose and throat feel a first wisp of blood, much as if I've just finished a long-distance run.

Up ahead, in the mountains, I notice some tiny red and yellow lights speeding in opposite directions. There must be a highway over there, I think. Then the absurdity of it strikes me. A highway? No, I am really watching two bands of *dukhi* locked in a ferocious battle. They are so far away that I can't hear the shots, but I can see the flashes of light. Summer lightning? No, rocket launchers. They are painting the sky with thousands of long, threadlike tracers—the slanting rain of a bloody storm.

Dzhabarov, who is marching in front of me, passes some crackers back along the line of soldiers. I take a bite from the one that finally reaches me, but the crumbs stick in my dried-out throat.

Soon we are crunching crackers loudly enough for the whole desert to hear. In the dry air of the night, even the slightest sound carries for kilometers. For safety's sake, I decide to nibble the rest of my cracker as noiselessly as possible.

Dzhabarov carries his heavy backpack with ease, just as if he were on a camping trip. The long marches every week have left him in very good shape, both mentally and physically. What's more, before Dzhabarov joined the army he was a world-class bicyclist, racing around Sverdlovsk on his duralumin-frame Start-Shosse [the Rolls-Royce of Soviet bicycles]. He still exchanges postcards with his trainer, who recently wrote: "Go for it, Vladik. Push on the pedals. There's only a little way left to go. After Afghanistan, any hardship will seem like a mosquito bite."

I gradually get my second wind and manage to line up my thoughts—not in as straight a line as we've been marching across the plain, but in some order nonetheless.

From behind me I could hear Kirillov's rhythmic breathing: in-out, in-out. He is a kind and amiable fellow. He likes to relate the story of how he and his wife first met, as fifteen-year-olds, at a school dance. As Kirillov tells it, they happened to find themselves standing awkwardly close to each other. Suddenly she broke the silence by turning to him and saying, in utter seriousness, "What a fool you are!"

"And why is that?" Kirillov asked, dumbfounded.

"Because no matter how many times you invite me to dance, I won't dance with you," she said, turning away from him.

"Where did you get the idea that I would even ask you?" Kirillov asked. He was used to putting boys who went too far in their place, but as for girls—well, this was something new. "I wasn't even thinking of asking you to dance," he blurted clumsily. "Understand?"

"And that's exactly why," she said, turning back to him, "you are a fool."

Her name was Elyka. And before Kirillov's departure for Afghanistan, she became Elyka Kirillov.

* * *

Again I smell a *kishlak*. We've been marching past the villages in a winding route to make sure that the wind keeps blowing from them to us, not vice versa. Otherwise the dogs in the *kishlaks* will smell our strange scents and begin to bark. We are guided only by a compass. Our maps are totally useless here: the plain lacks landmarks just as it lacks water. The only distinguishing feature of the landscape is lots and lots of camel burrs. Too bad I'm not a camel.

Once more my head is filled with dancing thoughts, most of them having to do with water. I'd just as soon kill myself, I think, as suffer from thirst any longer. So I pull out my canteen and take a long-awaited gulp of water, half expecting it to sizzle on my scorching teeth. Indeed, the water evaporates before it hits my stomach. (Or is it absorbed by all the dust and sand that I've inhaled?) The second swallow reaches its destination. As I drink from the canteen, head thrown back, I am looking directly into the black sky above. I spot Berenice's Hair and, a little to the side, seven other stars. There is Mizar, along with its heavenly neighbor Alcor. And, over there, the Big Dipper. *Dipper*, I think. *A big dipperful of water.* My mind has come, full circle, back to water. Once I took the freedom to drink water—as much water as I wanted—for granted, but now I realize that no such freedom exists in the desert. To build a democracy here, right on the sand, you would only need to bring in some water a couple of times a month. That would do it.

The *dukhi* are still fighting among themselves in the mountains. We have already covered about seventeen kilometers as the crow flies; take into account all of our zigzagging and we have probably covered somewhere between twenty and twenty-three kilometers. The sound of shooting and explosions still rumble from afar. The moon is now so bright that I can see the shadows of the clouds crawling across the plain. The butterflies are circling frantically as they try in vain to reach the moon.

A short rest. We plop down to take a moonbath, as Sun Sunich, our sanitary instructor, likes to call it. The five or six men who've stepped aside to answer the call of nature stand like statues in the distance. A few minutes later we are all back on our feet, marching exactly as soldiers marched three thousand years ago. The only difference is that we are wearing *kimri* instead of sandals and carrying assault rifles instead of swords and shields. Three thousand years from now, I wonder to myself, will soldiers still be marching as we do now?

We come upon a horseshoe-shaped chain of hills. Splitting into small groups, we climb upward until we occupy all the prime firing positions. (One of the first lessons of war: whoever climbs higher wins.) We immediately begin to erect stone fortifications on the hilltops, although to do so we have to run back down to the greenie, the area of lush vegetation, where there are plenty of big rocks in the shriveled riverbed. Twenty-five to thirty boulders are needed to build each pillbox.

The left flank of our lookout group is situated, according to our map, on hill 642; the right flank is on hill 685. My group is right in the middle. Captain Kozlov and his group are covering the greenie under us. The band of rebels is expected to move directly along the empty bed of the Hvar River, which separates the hills from the vegetation. Through our night-vision binoculars we can make out several of the *dukhi*'s stone fortifications, but we don't get close to them. Usually, the approaches to such strategic positions have been mined.

Dzhabarov and I line the bottom of our pillbox with ponchos. The ground is cold by one in the morning, and it's not getting any warmer. We crouch down and fix our guns in firing position. Now we can finally take off our sweaty backpacks, which are heavier than ever. Zherelin and a radioman settle down in the neighboring pillbox. In a quiet but clear voice, Zherelin is talking to Kozlov over the radio: "Dispute, Dispute, I am Comet. Do you read me? Do you read me?"

We shiver in the mountain's gusting winds. My sweat-soaked *bushlat* has frozen stiff, so I pull my *pakistanka* over it. Not that it helps much; my teeth are still chattering, and my helmet shakes as if I had a jackhammer in my hands. For safety's sake—the occasional clinking of my helmet might give away our ambush—I take the "frying pan" off my head. My bulletproof vest is the only thing that saves me from the bone-chilling cold; during our march, its titanium plates absorbed so much body heat that I now feel as if I'm inside a warm thermos.

With the sharp drop in temperature, my throat begins to tickle. Now another freedom has been taken away from me: the freedom to cough. Everywhere I turn, it seems, I run into dictatorship of one kind or another.

We communicate with gestures and whispers. Speaking in a normal voice is forbidden, and so is smoking. Even if you cup the cigarette in your hands, the *dukhi* can still see its weak glow through their night-vision binoculars. We have seven pairs of them in our group. In combat they are the next best thing to clairvoyance, even though they have to be used sparingly lest the batteries die out. Under orders from Zherelin, however, I peer through mine every minute or so. Through the binoculars everything looks pale green: the riverbed, the moon, Kirillov's face, even the *kishlak* in the distance. The magnification is so powerful that I can make out a couple of human figures on one of the *kishlak*'s streets. I mention this to Dzhabarov.

"The band that's heading toward us has an ammunition depot in the *kishlak*," Dzhabarov tells me. "After spending the night there, the *dukhi* will disguise themselves as local peasants. Tomorrow night they'll set out on some diversionary operation. By day the *kishlaks* are ours, but by night they are theirs. That's the thing."

Dzhabarov pauses for a moment before waving his hand in the direction of the two green figures, who don't even suspect that four kilometers away two sets of eyes—mine and Dzhabarov's—are staring at them through the thickness of the pitch-dark night. "Over there," Dzhabarov says, "they already know."

"Know what?" I ask in a whisper.

"They know that the band is on its way," he wheezes, "and they're waiting for it."

Suddenly all sound disappears, as completely as if someone had just turned the volume off. In a concert hall, you can hear a trace of reverberating sound even after a violinist takes his bow off the strings. But in Afghanistan the last ringing note fades inside of you rather than around you—a feeble echo of the war-torn day.

For the moment, at least, the war has forgotten you.

As you lie there, however, you feel in your gut that the silence is deceptive and foreboding. You know that a band of rebels, which about an hour ago dropped out of the bloody battle in the mountains, is silently moving toward you. You know that other rebel bands are lurking in ambushes or mining the paths through the mountains and the approaches to their emplacements.

You ride the devil's merry-go-round: you believe that you are pursuing the enemy ahead, but the enemy assumes that he is following you. The silence is neither relaxing nor restful; it is more exhausting, in fact, than combat. It goes about its work so patiently and persistently that your eyelids, rubbed sore by the eyepieces of the night-vision binoculars, grow heavy and try to close. As you struggle with every remaining ounce of will power to stay awake, you realize that, at the very moment your eyelids drop and sleep captures you in its tender embrace, the silence is sure to explode with machine-gun fire. Everything around you will erupt, but for several seconds you won't quite comprehend what's going on.

Waiting in the pillbox, I shut off the outside world entirely and let my conscious mind gently collapse into nothingness. Indistinct memories of the day are roaming around in my head, but suddenly they become sleep, then a short dream, filled with soldiers and armored carriers but virtually devoid of dialogue.

In a dream, just as in war, actions speak louder than words. You're flying in a jet and suddenly have to bail out. You throw open the hatch only to realize in horror that you have no parachute. Panic strikes, immobilizes you, and then rescues you from your nightmare, leaving tiny beads of cold sweat on your forehead.

Tomorrow night the APC that is carrying you through your dream abruptly loses power and coasts to a standstill. Its single engine sputters but refuses to turn over. Suddenly the *dukhi* are shooting at you, point-blank.

From now on you'll do your best to travel only in the double-engine BTR-70 armored carriers. Your life, after all, may well depend on it—whether you're sound asleep or wide awake.

I hear a familiar tune through my fitful doze. I open my eyes; Kirillov's electronic watch is beeping. After a short struggle he succeeds in silencing it. It's exactly the same kind of watch I saw on the wrist of Peter Arnett, the Moscow correspondent for Cable News Network. An interesting coincidence.

The second coincidence is that Arnett has just recently walked past the same riverbed that I'm now carefully examining through my binoculars. He wasn't with a detachment of Afghan or Soviet airborne troops, naturally, but with a band of rebels. They'd crossed the plain, which stretches behind my back, and had reached Jalalabad.

Later they'd returned to Pakistan. I recall how I'd met Arnett in his Moscow office and had asked him to tell me in detail about his illegal travels in Afghanistan. His story is indelibly imprinted on my memory.

Arnett is at least fifty years old. As I followed him into his office, which was strewn with newspapers, I marveled that he'd managed to get through such a long march on foot in the Afghan mountains and plain. Even though I'm a little more than half his age, the night march in the plain has by no means come as easily to me as I supposed it would. The hardiness Arnett gained during his years as a war correspondent in Vietnam, Lebanon, and El Salvador apparently helped a lot.

"Have you been to any countries in Central America besides El Salvador?" I asked when we sat down at the coffee table.

"Nicaragua as well." He took a sip of mineral water. "In the winter of 1985."

"It's strange that we missed each other. I was there at the same time."

I take another look at the riverbed and imagine how the water roars when the rain falls in torrents or the snow melts in the mountains. Tonight, the river twists silently between the hills.

Nicaragua, I think, is the third coincidence.

"Were you there with the Contras or the Sandinistas?"

"Both," he answered. "As American journalists, we can peep behind both sides of the barricade. Those positions ensure our freedom of thought."

"Listen, Peter, we have so little time, let's move from the Contras to the *dukhi*," I said. "How did they meet you? Did the pernicious spirit of the West you embody defile the primitive innocence of the Moslem East? I bet you at least taught them how to drink whiskey."

Arnett laughed and began his tale.

"There were two of us: Ed Healy, a photographer from Dallas, and me, a correspondent for *Parade* magazine. We were moving with a group of rebels along a moonlit path. Our robes were flapping in the wind. I was wearing a robe and a turban so that my alien Western appearance wouldn't attract attention. But it was difficult to walk in those clothes. We secretly crossed the border into Afghanistan and continued moving over stony mountain paths, which seemed to lead to the clouds. Sometimes we had to climb sheer rocks.

"Later we had to climb down into a dried-out riverbed, and once I almost dislocated my knee. A half-dozen rebels were serving as our guides, and they were leading us to a detachment based in the mountains near Jalalabad. They ignored our complaints about the fast pace; we were in danger of finding ourselves in the open at daybreak. None of us had any particular desire to let teams of your combat helicopters spot us."

Arnett picked up a napkin and wiped the sweat from his bald spot. He reached into his pocket, took out a notepad, and wrote something down. Then he took another sip of water and went on with his story.

"Next we entered a little *kishlak*. I asked our guides whether we risked running up against a Soviet military patrol. They laughed and said that during the night the village belonged to the rebels. My years in Vietnam came to my mind. There, the villages always belonged to the Vietcong at night.

"We came to a picturesque valley. The sun had already risen, and Soviet helicopters had begun to circle in the sky. Frankly speaking, Ed and I came to Afghanistan to find out whether you would win your first real war since 1945; I knew that the West preferred not to notice what was happening there. Soon we reached our destination. It turned out to be a mountain camp with about fifty rebels, all of whom had been born in neighboring villages. There we had sort of an observation post—a window on the war."

"Weren't you afraid to cross the border illegally?" I asked.

"Sure, somebody might say that we violated the law by crossing the border. But such a violation hardly means anything in a country where war is raging. As Western correspondents who wanted to write about the rebels, we were traveling down a truly risky road. First we had to find the headquarters of the *dukhi* in the region of the Pakistan border, and then we had to obtain their permission for the long march inside Afghanistan."

"Whom do you meet in Pakistan? And where? Or is it top secret?"

"It is top secret," he said with a smile. "I knew that the outcome of the war in Afghanistan would influence the fate of our world, and that's why I went there. You see, I wanted to find out the truth—and that's quite a precious commodity, especially since the world knows nothing about the events there. It's one more unknown war. The rebels don't even have radios to send out information about themselves. Many of them were armed with ancient weapons: bolt-action Enfield rifles and rusty copies of the Kalashnikov. And there was a complete collection of Soviet fighting strength in Afghanistan. When Soviet fighters fly over the mountains looking for a target, the rebels can only hide behind the boulders or melt into the background with the help of their coarse robes."

As Arnett raised a cup of hot coffee to his mouth, his face was fogged by aromatic steam.

"Traveling around Afghanistan, I always remembered the Vietnam War, which was so disastrous for America, and looked for common features. I covered Vietnam for ten years, and the analogies with Afghanistan were obvious. My status in Afghanistan, however, was completely different. Now I was with the rebels—with those who were being pursued. The guerrillas, though, denied any comparisons with Vietnam. 'We draw our strength from faith in Allah,' they told me. In Afghanistan, when a guerrilla is wounded in the head, chest, or abdomen, it means almost certain death. A wound in the extremities means gangrene and, in the end, amputation."

Arnett finished his coffee, turned the cup upside down on the saucer, and waited for the grounds to trickle down and tell his fortune.

"Do you want to hazard a guess," I asked, "as to what other war you'll be thrown into by fate?"

"No," Arnett replied. "I would be much more interested to find out whether *Ogonyok* magazine will publish our conversation. If you'll take the risk, that'll be my contribution to your campaign of *glasnost.*"

In reply, I asked, "So, anyway, how did your Afghan adventure end?"

"One day we left our hosts and crossed the Kunar on rubber floats," Arnett said. "Ed Healy fell into the stream and got all his cameras wet, but he heroically managed to save the film. And that's it."

• • •

"What are you thinking about?" Dzhabarov asks me.

"It's already three in the morning," I reply, "and there's still no sign of the rebels."

We suddenly notice a scorpion clambering persistently, like a tractor, over the stones of our pillbox. "Don't be afraid," Dzhabarov says, reading my thoughts. "They're not too poisonous at this time of the year." Just in case, however, he neutralizes the scorpion with the butt of his gun.

Far away, almost at the horizon, we can see the snow-covered peaks of the mountains. Dzhabarov is daydreaming aloud. "Someday, after the war," he says, "they'll build a ski resort over there, and we'll come back to ski across these battle sites. . . . Not a bad idea, eh?"

Kirillov, who's wedged between us, speaks without unclenching his teeth. "Let them build as many ski lifts as they want over there," he says. "I never want to set foot here again. We'd be better off meeting at the sculpture of the Three Cranes in Tashkent. Okay?"

"*Dukhi!*" Zherelin suddenly croaks.

A drop of sweat rolls down the hollow of my spine. I look through the binoculars and see about twenty rebels moving swiftly along the riverbed in the distance. All of them are armed, but I can't make out exactly what kind of weapons they're carrying.

We're so quiet that you could hear a pin drop in the pillbox. Zherelin hisses something to Kozlov through the walkie-talkie.

We let the band of rebels draw as close to us as possible, our nerves near the breaking point. Kozlov has blocked the riverbed behind the *dukhi* and is closing a noose around them. If the *dukhi* dash to the greenie, they'll run up against our troops; if they try to slip between the hills, they'll also get a proper reception.

Desperate shooting starts down below. The dark is pierced by intermittent flashes of gunfire. About a dozen rebels flee toward the right bank of the river. Several fall to the ground; five or six others drop behind boulders. A few moments later they open fire to cover the rebels who are trying to break through between us and the neighboring hill. There's thunder on my left and right: Dzhabarov and Kirillov are firing their machine guns at three *dukhi* who are trying to outflank us on the left.

Then the fireworks begin. Tracers cut the darkness into stripes. Several incendiary bullets land to the left of Zherelin's pillbox, instantly igniting a camel burr. The radioman is now alone; Zherelin is rushing about between our firing positions.

Suddenly the shooting from below us stops. Kozlov has taken out all of the weapon emplacements near the riverbed.

Three *dukhi* are still returning fire from the greenie. It looks as if someone had stretched red and yellow wires across the night sky. But soon the glowing wires fade into the blackness. There are no *dukhi* left.

The battle has lasted for ten minutes.

The assault rifles are scorchingly hot. Tiny drops of sweat sizzle as they fall on the metal. Everything is as it has been, except for the moon in the sky, which has grown paler.

Shooting suddenly breaks out again to our left. Two *dukhi* lie in hiding on the far side of the hill. From the top of the hill the left flank of Zherelin's group leads the return fire. Someone sticks himself out of a pillbox for a second; a hand hurls something downward. There's a powerful flash and an explosion. Shrapnel flies. The shooting stops. A moment later another grenade explodes in the same place. This one, apparently, is just to make sure.

For a minute we lie silently in our horseshoe-shaped stone fortification.

Evidently it's over. This time it's final.

Strange thoughts pulse through my head. Was I shooting at the *dukhi* with an assault rifle to attack or to defend? Did I want to destroy them or protect my own life? If I'd been able to ask the *dukhi* about it, it's doubtful that I would've gotten an answer—even if the *dukhi* were still alive.

Dzhabarov sends another long burst of assault rifle fire into the darkness, as if to ask, "Hey, anyone there?" A strong rolling echo answers him. But it comes so late that it could be taken for return fire.

In the center of the riverbed lies one of the twenty *dukhi* who had been planning, at dawn tomorrow, to attack our airfield with mortar fire. His knees are pulled to his chin. For some reason Vladikin comes to mind. The way he gently jogged to his chopper along the scorching airstrip, how he would have been killed tomorrow by this man, who's now lying helplessly at my *kimri*-shod feet, if we hadn't killed him first. The Afghan's eyes are wide open and stare with astonishment into the sky, as if he wants to ask about something. His narrow, dark-skinned forehead is still covered by tiny drops of sweat. Each of them shines in the moonlight, which now suggests the fluorescent light in a morgue. The dead man's chest is delicately tattooed with the forty-eighth chapter of the Koran. He'd apparently thought that it would make him invulnerable. Through his torn shirt I can see the chapter's opening lines. I later learned what they meant.

> In the name of merciful Allah! We granted you a manifest victory, so Allah will forgive you for those of your sins that precede it and those to follow. And so he will crown his mercy to you and lead you by the straight way, and so he will help you with his greatest help.
>
> He is the one who brought down evil in the hearts of the believers to make greater room for faith. It is to Allah the war between sky and earth belongs. Allah is wise and knowledgeable!

Allah didn't help him, I think.

He has a huge canteen tucked in his shirt. Quite a convenient thing, I think: the canteen has a valve mounted in its lid so that you can heat tea over a fire. What's more, it can hold five mugs of water. The Afghan won't need it now. I take the canteen and hang it on my belt.

Whenever a mujahedin dies with his face to the ground, they say that he's sinned a lot. The face of the third *dushman* [rebel] is buried in the pebbles. He'd fallen awkwardly to the ground and had broken his right hand under his body. He seems very uncomfortable in this pose. He is holding a machine gun in his left hand; to pull it out, we have to unclench his fingers. The bullet has passed right through his Adam's apple, and a thin rivulet of blood trickles slowly down the dry riverbed. In the right pocket of his *pakistanka* is a cellophane packet of raisins and walnuts.

We shoulder the captured weapons and climb back up the hill. After taking positions in the stone fortifications, we pull some dry rations out of our backpacks. Dzhabarov and I join Kirillov, who's already opened two tins of ground sausage.

Only now do I realize how hungry I am. Dzhabarov skillfully spreads some sweetened condensed milk on crackers and eats them one by one. I take several swallows from the captured canteen, which is filled up to the neck with a strong, slightly salty tea.

Fifteen minutes later we are walking along the plain toward our APCs. For nearly an hour I march on autopilot, thinking of nothing. Sometimes it seems as if I were sleepwalking in the endless womb of the night. Later, as I begin to feel the birth of the new day, my mind begins to work again. If we'd run into a bigger band of *dukhi*, I think, we could have been caught in a drawn-out battle. Another stroke of luck: the band we'd encountered had become engaged in combat with a rival gang. How many people, I wonder, had they left in the mountains?

I remember Arnett. What if he'd been traveling in Afghanistan now instead of then? Had we met not in his Moscow office but here on the plain, our conversation would have been played in a totally different key.

For eleven o'clock in the evening, the airfield is unusually crowded. A troop carrier with twenty or so military personnel has just landed. All of them are jammed, along with their luggage, under the wing of the jet. A big man, his long legs spread far apart and his beefy arms crossed on his chest, stands out from the mass. Although it's pitch-dark, he's gazing into the distance. His eyes sparkle in the glare of a searchlight, and his chin, which is pulled far forward, shines like a chrome-plated bumper. If he hadn't been wearing jeans and a shirt labeled COMMANDO, he easily could have passed for the commander of the army. I walk up to him with Starov. They weren't acquainted.

"I am Leshchinsky," he says as he stretches out his hand. *

"Comrade Leshchinsky—I know that you are Leshchinsky," Starov replies, introducing himself in turn.

A new cameraman—Boris has been hospitalized in Kabul for three months with hepatitis—bustles around Leshchinsky. He moves in circles, as if the huge video camera on his shoulder were a grenade launcher. Evidently the cameraman still hasn't come to terms with the fact that he is no longer in Washington, D.C., where he's worked until recently. He is still entirely civilian. I exchange news with

---

*Mikhail Leshchinsky is a special correspondent for Gosteleradio, the Soviet TV and radio network.

Leshchinsky. Ten minutes later, after embracing Starov, I take off into the starless sky over Jalalabad.

In my breast pocket is the rolled-up notebook I'd gotten at this very airfield just a few days ago: the diary of Y. I. Vladikin, the helicopter pilot. So as not to waste any time, I decide to read it during my flight to Kabul. The light in the An-12 has been turned off, and its portholes covered with dark fabric. I have to move to the very tail of the plane, where I settle under its only blue lamp.

The diary is the literature of war—or, more precisely, literature that has been written by war itself. I open it to the first page.

October 25. After the four-hour flight in an armored helmet, my head itself becomes armored.

November 3. All main concepts of the war have been firmly embedded in every one of us. They don't even cause splashes of emotions anymore. An exhausted man has a weak reaction to everything except the letters from home. November separated two seasons of the year in our work; it also became a kind of milepost. On November 1, Senior Lieutenant Sergei Shinnikov, the commander of a Mi-8, perished on a landing ground at a high altitude in the mountains. My commander landed me there later, and for the first time in my life I saw how creepily scorched skulls grin. Serioga and two soldiers hadn't managed to jump out of the burning plane. To the side, the front wheel, engine block, and pods are a puddle of melted metal. We wanted to pull the bodies out right away, but as we approached a grenade exploded five meters from us. We were spattered with charred remains. For two or three days my flying suit smelled of fried meat. I write about it not to forget, and that means to save other guys. Not that such things are possible to forget.

November 7. The preparations for the parade on Red Square are shown on TV, but we have no time to watch: Valera Savchenko is covering his leading plane under strong fire near the Black Mountain. Tutov was put out of action by a rocket. He is a cool and calm fellow. The aircraft crew jumped with parachutes from an altitude of 150–200 meters. Kiselevich and Tutov had a normal landing, but Golovkov didn't have enough altitude, by only some ten meters. They landed right in the *dukhi*'s nest. Tutov saw one of the *dukhi* at a distance of five meters. Tutov managed to shoot first. He was picked up under fire. I thought he'd be shot down. It turned out OK.

November 15. Landing troops—to the Black Mountain, where Tutov fell yesterday. For thirty minutes everything was quiet, but then even the stones began to shoot—that's how many emplacements there were. The bees [Mi-8 helicopters] are underneath; we are up above. Those in the bees need real courage: the landing grounds are difficult to negotiate, and there are thousands of troops to land. Enemy fire comes from every cliff. I'm already circling the landing ground for a second hour. Very little ammunition is left. We use our resources sparingly and shoot only at large-caliber machine guns. Several times we smashed servants [gun detachments], but every time a new one would hurry to take its place. Vitya Buyashkin is passing over the peak where just a short while ago we wrecked a welding [soldier's slang for a large machine gun]. Right in front of my eyes, point-blank at Buyashkin—several bursts of machine-gun fire. The jet's right side was heavily damaged; its cigar [engine pod] was blasted away. Nikulin, the pilot, went for a forced landing without radio communication. He was covered by Matveev. Gergel and I stayed over the landing ground. Nikulin landed normally. I shouted to him, "Throw the blocks overboard." He did not hear. Everybody is alive, but two of us are broken. Fedorich, most likely, will not fly again. Pilots can fly without legs but not without arms. Vitya Buyashkin took off the same day but didn't return to the airfield. We picked him up in the evening. . . .

Peshkov taps me on the shoulder and tosses me a parachute. It seems as if I'm somewhere far away from him, however, still taking a turn with Vladikin in his bumblebee [helicopter gunship].

"Put it on," Peshkov shouts in my ear. "If you have to jump, it's easier with your back first."

I hitch my parachute to the plane's suspension system. It dangles on my stomach. Everyone sitting on the hard benches along both sides of the cabin has their parachutes on. We all look like pregnant women.

Then the clear voice of a lieutenant on my right rings out: "At least we're lucky to be with such tummies for only an hour. A woman has nine months to go!"

Thunderous laughter fills the cabin.
I go on reading.

April 12. March has passed. I was at home from the fourteenth to the eighteenth. It's impossible to put into words what it was—a meeting after a long separation. And now I am in Afghanistan again. Over the centuries the wind has evened up many of the peaks in the old mountains here. Then again, the wind has sharpened the peaks of the tallest mountains. The wind has cut through ravines and chiseled holes through the steep slopes. Evidently the same wind, raising sand and salty dust, has stripped people of their surface husk and mold, leaving them the way they were initially created. Weak and strong—those are arguable concepts. But no doubt there exists some minimum of human qualities without which a man cannot count on the trust of his comrades on earth. There are some people who, from their first flight, prove trustworthy—like cartridges of high quality. But there are some people who are like the clouds over the mountains—clean, light, soaring high above the ground. And yet these people are not built for something big and important. There are also the averagers. At first glance they are hardly noticeable. They are last to be recommended for rewards. But they are perhaps the most reliable. These fellows could be compared with good soil. When looking at roses we rarely admire the soil, which nurtured their beauty.

Today is the Day of Cosmonauts. Wonderful, necessary, and important—cosmonauts. But still, a Day of Internationalists could have been established. . . .

"That's it," Peshkov says, more to himself than to me. "We are landing. Kabul."

I slam closed the diary of Lieutenant Colonel Vladikin. I still haven't read it to the end. With our meeting my Jalalabad story began. With the fifteenth page of his diary it ends.

By day Kabul is dull and prosaic; by night it is full of mysterious fascination. The danger only intensifies the feeling. You can get a bullet in your belly without any special effort. As a veteran of Kabul's press corps once told me, "Just land in Kabul and you are already at risk." He was right.

Another colleague warned me against using public transportation in Kabul and told me the story of how he once got from one end of the city to the other by taxi. "After the car took off, I realized that I hadn't taken along a gun," he said. "There have been cases of taxi drivers taking unsuspecting passengers straight into the *dukhi*'s den to make some extra money on the head of *shuravi*. So I decide, just in case, to put some fear into my driver. I thrust my hand into the inside pocket of my coat and began to click the cap of a ballpoint pen, hinting that I had a Makarov concealed in a shoulder holster. The Afghan, however, didn't even seem to be curious about what I was amusing myself with."

I peered at Kabul from the backseat of a Vazik, which rushes me from the airport to our trade delegation's hotel. Next to me sits a man in civilian clothes. His face is covered by a net of red vessels and framed by a coarse gray beard, and his high forehead is cut into equal parts by several deep horizontal furrows. I had gotten acquainted with him a week ago on a flight from Kabul to Kunduz. A man of rare intellect, he heads a department in one of Moscow's institutions of higher education. With his elbows perched on his knees, he looks straight ahead through the windshield.

The electric lights of Kabul's shops rush by us to the left and right. They have an abundance of goods from practically everywhere in the world, and they accept any currency, except perhaps the Mongol tugrik. You can buy anything in these stores. Sometimes it seems that if you jokingly ask a shopkeeper for a Boeing 747, he'll smile shyly and pull this two-story monster out of his pocket. Then he'll wink at you and say, "Only for you, Commander, there is a big, big discount."

During the day, Kabul's merchants hide from the heat in the depths of their shops. Dozens of pairs of green and blue eyes sparkle from the gloom, like so many coyotes in the night. Old-timers can recite a whole catalog of heart-rending stories about how a watermelon from one of Kabul's shops, or a bottle of vodka or a tin of canned food, turned out to be poisoned, and how the incubation period of the fatal illness was more than a month. Then you try to remember exactly where you've done your shopping. It's just another kind of guerrilla warfare. As the Russian rhyme goes: "Afghanistan / A wonderland./ Just drop into a store / And you'll be seen no more."

When our car stops at an intersection to let other vehicles pass, I notice a new Sharp stereo in the yellow floodlights of a shop window. I silently marvel at the way modern business techniques and patriarchal/tribal customs can coexist so peacefully in these small shops, some of them only two or three square meters in size. I suppose it's possible to wear a liquid-crystal Seiko watch on your wrist while you wear a prefeudal outlook on your sleeve. I recall how Nimatula, an Afghan pilot at Bagram, once grinned and told me, "Yeah, I am flying supersonic, but my wife wears yashmak."

"Do you remember," my companion suddenly asks, "a verse titled 'Night'?"

"My sin," I admit. "I know the Koran very poorly."

" 'In the name of merciful Allah! I swear on the night, when it covers . . .' With this I am trying to say that some things can be understood only at night."

It is a strange thing to hear from him. During the day he is always hiding behind the armor of his cool cheerfulness. But now no trace of it remains.

"Yes," I say. "At night, as strange as it may be, you can see farther and deeper."

"The human mind isn't suited for understanding too much," he replies. "Or for looking ahead too far. Clairvoyance is a tragedy, not a gift. Even the wisest of the wise loses the feel of real time. He sees only the future, not the present."

As our Vazik makes a sharp turn to the right, my neighbor is pressed against the left door. I ask, "If you were in the shoes of this wisest of the wise man—who, let's suppose, thoroughly and correctly understands the perspective of society's development but also sees thousands of people living in misery, backwardness, even barbarism—wouldn't you have a desire to help those people and bring culture within their reach?"

My interlocutor answers without delay. "I'm deeply convinced," he says, "that barbarism is the opposite of culture only within a society whose views and attitudes have grown out of its culture. Outside such a society, however, backwardness and barbarism mean something quite different, not at all the opposite of culture."

Taking a little time out from the argument, I begin to unseal a pack of cigarettes.

"But if life is so nasty and unfair, isn't it quite natural to try to change it?" I ask. "Isn't it so?"

He cracks open the window. "I'm not inclined, you see, to be outraged over the objective course of things in the world," he says. "It's silly. It wouldn't occur to you to be outraged over the way the Volga is flowing, would it? I've never been a supporter of the idea of relativity. It leads to inactivity and paralysis of will power, which is worse than paralysis of the body. By the way, have you ever noticed in the morning how the vigils of the previous night always seem something like the work of an alchemist?"

He grins with a corner of his mouth.

"All right, let all this philosophy go to the devil," he says. "Tell me, which of the things that you've seen in Afghanistan has had the strongest effect on you?"

I recall the ambush. The night. The tiny drops of sweat on the forehead of the slain *dushman*. The strange and heavy feeling that overwhelmed me then has oppressed me since. A feeling that I want to destroy, to forget. But with every night it grows even stronger. And I can't get away from it.

My companion falls silent. A curfew is in effect throughout the city, and at several intersections we run into Afghan checkpoints. A pass on the windshield of our Vazik, however, frees us of the necessity of stopping.

At one o'clock in the morning we finally reach the hotel where the Soviet trade delegation is staying. I bid my companion farewell, climb out of the car, and head toward the hotel's guarded entrance gate.

I have no documents. My appearance—dirty *kimri*, crumpled military uniform, tousled and sweat-hardened hair—is in such contrast with the classic image of a trade representative that for a long time the sentry on duty refuses to open the door. Finally I get tired of trying to prove that I am a correspondent for *Ogonyok*, not a *dushman*. So I sit down on the bench and say, "Let me in. I'm falling asleep on my feet."

Psychology is a strange thing, particularly when you're dealing with guards at entrance posts. You never know what words—if any—

will do the trick. Fortunately, however, mine must be convincing enough. The guard opens the door, muttering after me, "Brown devil, gray devil—same demon."

After taking a shower in my suite, I climb into bed and put out the light. From the window a floor above me comes the voice of Alla Pugachova, the Soviet rock singer: "I know, darling, I know what it is with you. / You have lost yourself, you have lost. / You have left your native shore, / But never have you pulled to the other."

In time a mullah replaces Pugachova, shouting something in the loudspeaker for all of Kabul to hear. Two universes, side by side in one city. A fantastic juxtaposition.

The Supreme General Headquarters of the People's Voluntary Army of Afghanistan, which is headed by Dr. Najibullah, the general secretary of the Central Committee of the People's Democratic Party of Afghanistan [PDPA], was formed in November 1986 by a decision of the Politburo of the Central Committee of the Communist Party of the Soviet Union. Today's meeting is scheduled for eight o'clock in the morning at a private residence in the center of Kabul. I arrive thirty minutes before the meeting is to start. The house has been built recently, and its fresh paint shines in the morning sun. Security personnel stroll along a little path in the garden. The residence's massive wooden doors are wide open, and a slight wind stirs in the hall. A steep spiral staircase leads to the second floor.

The members of the General Headquarters, which include all of the country's top political and military leaders, begin to assemble at around ten minutes to eight. Soon almost everyone is present. Ghulam Faruq Yaqubi, the minister of state security, is holding a conversation in whispers with Sayed Mohammed Gulabzoy, the minister of the interior. Lieutenant General Shahnawaz Tanay, the commander of the armed forces staff, is evidently saying something funny to Olumi, the head of the Department of Justice and Defense of the Central Committee. The minister of defense is standing alone, examining his watch.

Dr. Najibullah arrives at five minutes to eight. Under the supervision of the security service, he heads for the doors of the residence, pausing along the way to greet the members of the General Headquarters.

All of us then proceed to a J-shaped hall, which is decorated with carved wood and imitation marble tile. A door slides out of the wall and silently closes behind us. The wide windows are curtained with brown fabric. Everyone takes seats around a massive table, which has been covered with green cloth. Tanay unfolds a map and begins his briefing.

According to intelligence data, he reports, the leadership of the counterrevolution is planning to carry out combat operations to the north in the immediate proximity of Kabul. He tells of continuing armed conflicts near Jalalabad, where casualties on both sides over the last twenty-four hours have amounted to four killed and seventeen wounded. Pakistan has moved its Twelfth Infantry Division closer to the Afghanistan border. Rebels have fired at the Eighth Border Detachment; nobody killed. Two Afghan MiG-23s have collided during a training flight; both pilots survived, but an investigation has already begun. During the last twenty-four hours, military vehicles in Afghanistan have carried 638 people and 138 tons of cargo. In the region of Rabatak, a local inhabitant has been blown up by a mine. In the province of Kunduz, five rebels and five rifles have been captured. Near the border, a Pakistan fighter has violated the air space of Afghanistan by flying fourteen kilometers into its territory.

Najibullah interrupts the report. "If this could be confirmed," he says, tapping his pen on the map, "it is necessary to inform the Ministry of Internal Affairs so that it can take corresponding measures."

Tanay nods in agreement. After finishing his operations report, he describes some problems that, in his opinion, demand urgent consideration and action.

Then Najibullah's soft but confident voice fills the room.

"I share your anxiety over the fact that we have few resources and a lot of unsolved problems," he says. "We should not, however, make a tragedy of it. There are means to take care of the named problems."

He proceeds to list his recommendations, among them more effective use of the territorial troops and increased call-ups to the army. Soon he moves on to an examination of a joint Soviet-Afghan airborne operation, planned for the next day, to the north of Kabul, where many *dukhi* formations have gathered after leaving Panjshir.

At around ten o'clock the meeting ends. The government cars depart as quickly as they had appeared, leaving behind bluish puffs of foul exhaust fumes. I climb into the Vazik that is waiting to shuttle me to the airborne unit scheduled to attack the *dukhi* north of Kabul tomorrow. On the way, I mull over the meeting's detailed discussion of the military and political situation in Afghanistan. These people have no illusions.

Lieutenant Colonel Borisov outlines the problem quickly and laconically. He stands next to the large map that is on the wall of his light, spacious office. Although his lips barely move, Borisov speaks in a rolling bass. From time to time he lapses into deep thought and silence. Then his mouth becomes as straight as the horizon, with the deep cleft in his chin pointing sharply downward. His cheeks, shaved to a blue color, resemble sheets of steel that have been coated with a thin layer of light-brown enamel. One after another, the officers in charge of various aspects of the next day's operation approach the map.

Having fully laid out the task, Borisov addresses the officers. "I remind you once again of the necessity for evacuating the wounded in the allotted time, of the need for retransmission in the event of breakdowns in radio communications. I remind detachments not to mark themselves with smoke simultaneously, or else the helicopters will get confused. All unnecessary talk on the radio should be eliminated; go on the air with a minimum of words. Remember the principles of working with fire at night and the dangers inherent in reciprocal exchanges of fire. Remember that all approaches to depots are mined. I am finished. Any questions?"

There are none. After a brief pause, Borisov thunders, "Comrade officers!"

Everyone leaps up and stands at attention.

Borisov's epilogue to the briefing isn't an afterthought. His reminders and warnings may have struck some as banal truisms. In the heat of combat, however, they invariably mean the difference between success and failure, between life and death.

The *dukhi*, after being caught in the grip of a block [part of a blockade], generally try to slip out of the trap under the cover of night. They typically fire at the entire block in the hope of inducing the opposing troops to answer at once and therefore disclose all of their emplacements. I ask Borisov about possible countermeasures.

"In such cases you must keep silent and not fall for a provocation," he replies. "And only one weapon emplacement should be working on the enemy."

The *dushmani* often attempt to trigger reciprocal exchanges of fire between enemy units. If two Soviet platoons are moving along parallel routes, for example, the *dukhi* trapped between them will frequently open fire on one platoon in an effort to get the other caught in the return fire.

"In general, the *dukhi* fight competently," Borisov says. "Not for nothing are there so many Western advisers here. The rebels, just like our own troops, have clear zones of responsibility for the alignment of forces, resources, and matériel reserves—both on their front and in the rear. What's more, their base depots are well guarded and situated in inaccessible regions. So are their headquarters, along with the advisory apparatus, means of communication, and pack animals on which weapons and ammunition can be carried away in case of danger."

Borisov has fought in Afghanistan for nearly two years.

He's become thoroughly familiar with the *dukhi*'s tactics. That's why there hasn't been a single casualty in his detachment during the previous year. A unique case.

To talk about the *dukhi*'s tactics, however, is to overgeneralize. Each band of rebels has its own style of fighting. And despite a common headquarters, each has its own interests and views on conducting combat operations.

During the years of war, the *dukhi* have learned our tactics thoroughly as well. They regularly exchange information about the commanders of Soviet and Afghan troops.

"They know by heart all the peculiarities of how we use airborne troops and conduct combat operations in the mountains," Borisov says, nodding in the direction of the window, through which we can see several ashy peaks. "While planning their operations, they take into account all of the factors that complicate our work: the minimal number of landing fields for helicopters; the complexity of delivering ammunition to the mountains and evacuating the sick and wounded;

our assignment of armored groups and artillery to particular regions; our inability to support airborne troops with the firepower of the armored vehicles; our limited supplies of water and provisions; the limited capacity of our generators for radio communications. The *dukhi* stay away from open conflict, but by repeatedly ambushing us they interfere with our ability—and the ability of the Afghan forces—to maneuver quickly. In this way they often gain time to move their main forces, weapons, and ammunition out of the danger zone. Very recently we captured one of their depots and discovered some pamphlets, written in Dari, that summarized how we conducted the guerrilla war in Byelorussia more than forty years ago. In short, they are cunning rogues."

Borisov himself was born in Mogilev, a city in Byelorussia. During World War II his grandmother was a messenger in one of the guerrilla detachments. To this day he remembers her many stories. He remembers how he lived with his parents, until the 1950s, in a mud dugout. He remembers how he raced with other boys around the wounded woods of Byelorussia.

"You'd find a grenade and throw it fifteen meters away, knowing all the time that the splinters wouldn't fly more than ten meters," he says with a grin. "The girls would squeal with delight.

"I don't compare this war and that one, of course," Borisov says as he fills our glasses with tea. "But it's difficult here, too. In these extreme conditions the psychological and physical reserves of the human organism come to the rescue. During a month of combat you sleep for only two or three hours a day. You sweat profusely during the day and shiver with cold at night—and it's all nothing to you. Here, back at the unit's camp, you sit in a draft for a short while and you've already caught a cold."

Borisov gets up and closes a window, just to be on the safe side.

"For me, personally, the moral burden is a hundred times more difficult than the physical burden. It's easy to answer just for yourself. But to answer for the soldiers entrusted to you—that's more complicated. I know for sure that it's easier to carry a grenade launcher, bulletproof vest, and backpack—which weigh sixty kilos—on your back than to be responsible for dozens of nineteen-year-old lives."

Borisov nods at the tall, slender lieutenant colonel who's just entered the office. The soldier has a lean face with sharply chiseled features and looks to be in his late thirties. "You haven't met yet?" Borisov asks me. "This is Kazantzev, my political deputy officer. I still have my hands full, so he'll take care of you. And don't forget: the time for Operation Ch has been moved one hour ahead."

From the first glance, Kazantzev doesn't seem like an affable man. Screwing up his left eye and aiming the right one at me, he asks: "Fresh meat?"

I don't understand him. "What do you mean?"

"First time in our detachment?"

I nod.

"Why didn't you choose a different one? If, during the landing operation, something would happen to you, off with our stars!"

He glares at me the way the coach of a championship sports team might eye a rookie.

I decide to calm Kazantzev, who, with only one month to go before demobilization, doesn't want any trouble. "Don't worry," I say. "Nothing will happen to me."

Kazantzev shifts his cigarette to the left side of his mouth and grins with the right. "Did a gypsy tell your fortune?"

"No, it's just that my assignment is coming to an end the day after tomorrow."

Five minutes later I realize that this was the most ridiculous of all possible answers. But at the time it seemed convincing to me and to him.

Kazantzev's words didn't strike me as strange, nor, for that matter, did they offend me. Had I been in his boots, I'm sure that I would have greeted a newly arrived reporter with the same scowling look. It is only natural. To Borisov I am an unnecessary bother, and to Kazantzev I am an uninvited guest (which is even worse, they say, than a *dushman*). But to the ordinary soldiers I am a sign of attention. They receive me with open hearts, treating me to tasty tea and stories. I've followed the chain: from Borisov to Kazantzev and further down until, finally, I find myself in the barracks with two airborne troopers, Simonov and Okhotnikov. They hand me a brand-new flying suit. "You'll be less noticeable to the *dukhi* in this one," Simonov tells me, "since its muted colors blend in better with the color of the mountains."

Simonov and I instantly find a theme for conversation. He also was born in Moscow. His reservoir of questions seems inexhaustible. I fire answers back as best I can.

Simonov has forty-three "wars" under his belt. (In the slang of the soldiers, a war is a combat operation.) In a week and a half he will be demobilized, so tomorrow's airborne operation is to be the final episode of a long epic. Maybe that's why a kind and weak smile doesn't leave his face, which has been coarsened by the sun and the wind. The glance of his light eyes is clear and straight, like Simonov's twenty-year-old life itself. But if you look deep enough into his eyes you'll see such an endless abyss that it will send a chill down your spine.

Okhotnikov is a little stockier than Simonov. His hair is coarse and stubborn—just like its owner, perhaps—and his eyes look out at you from beneath a prominent forehead.

"Muscovites are not loved here in general," Simonov says. "Many of them began to 'squint'—to shirk combat. It's easy to report yourself sick. Put some sand or pebbles in your boots, walk around for a day, and by evening your feet are rubbed sore and bloody. Or sit in a draft for a minute right after a steam bath, and an hour later you've got a fever. When I arrived here nobody expected anything good from me. So from day one I had to fight not only the *dukhi* but also the attitude of others toward me. But from that battle I came out a winner."

Simonov pauses, takes out a threaded needle, and begins to skillfully mend a hole in his backpack.

"At first the 'wars' were gloomy. Along with the sweat out came Mom's stewed fruits, laziness, and even your old attitude toward life. I remember how, on the tenth kilometer of a march along a mountain path, I began to 'die.' We had to climb from zero up forty-five hundred meters—there was little oxygen. I was working my lungs like a fish on the shore works its gills. But I didn't stop repeating to myself, No, fellow, you will not fall, you will not fall, period! And I didn't fall, even though it often happens with new guys. If I had given up, someone else would have had to carry me, my machine gun, and my backpack. So my conscience didn't allow me to 'die.' And conscience, by the way, is the principle of a man."

Then Okhotnikov, who's been scratching the bridge of his nose with a fingernail, speaks. "War trains you to think of others more than yourself. You have no right even to be killed. Four other guys would have to carry your corpse, and they have enough to carry without you. When you march in the mountains, you must be careful not to step on a mine or fall down. If you're blown up by a mine, those ahead of you and behind you will also be wounded. Simonov, by the way, is the only one of our young call-ups who marched his first 'war' two years ago from beginning to end. All of the others 'died'—left the march—and were later picked up by choppers. Morozov toiled along with us that time. Before Afghanistan he was a weightlifter, such a robust fellow. But he began to 'die' on the fifth kilometer."

"This Morozov was a real goofball," Simonov interjects. "At night, when everybody was asleep, he drank all of the water from our canteens. It's hard to imagine such meanness under these conditions."

"In war a loner isn't worth a damn," Okhotnikov says, putting out his cigarette against the sole of his shoe. "To give an example, one man will never be able to climb a sheer cliff. Several people, in the manner of mountain climbers, must bind a rope around their waists to safeguard the person who climbs upward."

Simonov, his mending job finished, bites off the strong thread with his teeth and checks his backpack for strength. "The mountains teach you to make a sensible estimate of your abilities," he says. "If you feel that you can't cope with a march, you'd better think of your comrades and stay home. For the same reason, reckless bravery doesn't stand high in our esteem. Great, if the weather is clear and the choppers can pick up the wounded and dead. But in the case of fog and low clouds, they must be carried by others."

Okhotnikov tosses me a little can of shoe polish.

"This is for your boots. Shine them."

I open the can. The shoe polish has turned almost liquid in the heat. Okhotnikov watches as I polish my boots.

"Sometimes it seems that besides Afghanistan, mountains, and war, there's nothing else in my life. No childhood, no parents, no school. It's as if you were born here twenty years ago, complete with a backpack, a gun, and a dry ration."

* * *

I walk out onto the parade ground, where my boots shine gloomily under the moonlight. Nearly a hundred and fifty stuffed backpacks—BPs—sit close to one another between the barracks. How many BPs have I seen during this time? BPs gone with a wind to the ravines; BPs torn by eagles; BPs covered with frost and fused into a frozen mass in the high-mountain snows; BPs reduced to ashes by the sun; BPs with their guts turned inside out; BPs shredded by bullets . . .

But now, safe and sound, the backpacks humbly wait until five o'clock in the morning, when airborne troopers will shoulder them and drag them to the mountains. Tomorrow's route is well traveled; the guys have gone through this routine many times. Thinking about it, I tie my "armored vest" to my BP and throw the pack onto the heap. Till tomorrow.

We're awakened at four-thirty A.M. by a plaintive meowing. A deputy technician, swearing loudly, goes to reconnoiter. It turns out that during the night a cat stole into one of our built-in closets and gave birth to a whole company of kittens. The technician reconstitutes some powdered milk in a saucer and offers it to the new mother.

"Well, old girl, some work you've done here!"

He ducks out of the closet and turns on the radio. "If you haven't had time to drink a cup of coffee before your workday," an announcer's happy voice says, instantly destroying our last traces of sleep, "we are hoping that our radio show gave you a supply of energy."

"A cup of co-oo-ffee! A cup of co-oo-ffee!" The technician pulls the plug on the announcer. "Would you like it Turkish style? No thank you," he says, responding to his own mocking question. "I prefer exclusively Afghan style."

It's easy to understand. It's so early that they haven't yet started pumping water, so not only can't we drink a cup of "co-oo-ffee," there's nothing even to wet our throats. From the faucet comes a gastric sound that destroys any hope of shaving. For the sake of appearances I scrape my bristle with a safety razor.

Five minutes later our entire detachment lines up on the parade ground. The warm morning wind is playing with a sheet of newspaper that has been fastened like a poster to the wall; it bears a red-marker drawing of two fat-bellied troopers—"food destroyers"—consuming three dry rations apiece. The caption in one corner reads "Rodionov and Lokshin, special correspondents of the *Afghan Times*."

We move, in formation, to the airfield. A tractor that's been fitted with a turbojet engine from a junked Il-76 and a gigantic fuel tank is moving slowly toward us along the takeoff strip. The engine works with all its might, blowing sand off the runway—and our Panama hats off our heads.

"This is a turbojet yard keeper," Simonov shouts to me. "The poor must be cunning with inventions."

"Some poor!" I shout back.

We throw off our backpacks, stack our guns, and sit down on the ground, squeezed between the runways. Nearly everyone lights cigarettes. Five minutes later the airborne troops are shrouded in a thick cloud of tobacco smoke. One hundred and ninety-two men, 192 BPs, 384 eyes, 192 Panamas, and 192 lives sink in the smoke.

I sit near Simonov and Okhotnikov. Simonov maintains that Kalashnikov invented his assault rifle in a hospital, where he found himself after being wounded.

"His first model of the pistol machine gun wasn't accepted," Okhotnikov argues, "but when it did happen and the AK-47 was approved, Kalashnikov wasn't even thirty years old." Gradually the conversation turns to celebrities who managed to earn fame before they were thirty. Two more soldiers take seats near us. Soon we are firing jokes at one another.

"A soldier comes to an army commander and asks to be put in charge for only one minute," says a fellow whose face is thickly splashed with freckles. Even before he starts, he is convulsed with laughter. "The army commander loves democracy, and for that reason agrees. He tears out all the telephone wires and lets the soldier sit in his place. After the soldier settles down in the chair, he orders the general to stand at attention and says, 'Starting this minute I am off on vacation for a month. You will fill in for me.' "

Okhotnikov tells us a joke about an ensign whose teeth were all metal, so that every time he took a steam bath he scorched his tongue. As he finishes a sergeant from another company comes up to us.

"Hey, infantry, got any matches?" he asks.

"We have everything but conscience and money," says the freckled fellow. He offers the sergeant a matchbox.

"Petruk, you joke all the time," the sergeant says as he lights his cigarette. "It's okay. In the mountains your humor will be sweated out of you, that's for sure."

Not far from us, a scarecrow with a rusty helmet for a head is swinging in the wind. It's his job to frighten away birds, a flock of which are calmly lined up on his outstretched metal arms. The birds here are slow-witted to the point of mockery.

Okhotnikov places a cartridge shell in his breast pocket. This is his *deathnik,* an empty shell containing a piece of paper that gives only the requisite vital statistics: the numbers of his military card and army unit; his family name, first name, and patronymic; and the dates of his birth and call-up.

Simonov looks at his watch. "Artillery preparation is over," he says. "Now it's aviation."

Even though we haven't heard a single explosion, we know that rocket artillery has finished its work along with the mortars and howitzers. Now the fighter-bombers rise into the air, but our ears still can't even catch a rumble of the powerful high-explosive bombs. They are too far away.

"Reconnaissance!" shouts a round, notebook-toting man who's wearing a summer flying suit and a long-peaked cap. "Reconnaissance! Let's go-o-o-o!"

We get up slowly, strap on our BPs, pick up our guns, and, after breaking into eight-man groups, ramble to six waiting Mi-8s. The bees are squeezed from front and back by four bumblebees—the helicopter gunships of the airborne troops.

Each group lines up opposite its helicopter. The commander of our helicopter's crew, Lieutenant Colonel Plastkov, pulls on his helmet, which is equipped with a microphone, and disappears into the cockpit. Gorshkov, the air mechanic, and Streltzov, the pilot-navigator, follow him.

Gorshkov turns on the generators, feeding the aircraft with electricity. The left and right engines start to murmur. The rotors slowly start turning, gaining revolutions. Another minute passes, and the engines reach working speed, switching from low to high gear. We're already sitting inside—vibrating inside the bee. Tuned to the same radio frequency, all six bees, escorted by four bumblebees, lift off from the airstrip.

The flight to the landing region takes seventeen minutes. Our wave of aircraft is moving at the low limit of altitude—five to seven meters above the ground—and raising puffs of thick yellow dust. With each minute the airfield grows smaller, and the huge fuel tanks seem to turn into tiny insects covering the runway. We cross a ridge of mountains. Plains, *kishlaks*, and the ragged posts of high-voltage lines rush past us at a speed of 250 kilometers per hour. The posts resemble crosses in a cemetery, every empty grave of which could become yours.

The plains suddenly come to an end. Now mountains jump under us, becoming steeper and sharper. We pass a yawning ravine. At this moment I feel like the circus performer who sticks his head between a lion's jaws and feels the beast's stinking breath with every fiber of his being.

Our helicopter is the second to descend. The landing area is tiny—only seven to nine meters square—and covered with pits and bumps. Even though there's no vertical turbulence yet, Plastkov has some difficulty keeping the aircraft steady in the hot—and therefore even thinner—mountain air. Gorshkov flops himself down on the bottom of the chopper, opens a hatch, and, sticking his head outside, shouts into his mouthpiece, "Altitude—two meters, three meters forward! Altitude is one meter—half a meter to the left! Land!"

Plastkov fixes the helicopter over the spot. Keeping his eyes focused on the crew-cut brush, he continues to descend, all the while stealing glances at the drift gauges.

A strong blow. Plastkov slows the engine. A second blow.

"Front is touching!" Gorshkov says, turning his head in all directions.

They fail, however, to put one rear wheel on the ground; there's a steep slope to the left and a dangerously strong wind beating at the helicopter's right side. Gorshkov jumps to his feet, freeing the exit. We jump out one after another, and, fanning out, run away from the hovering helicopter, bending down, pulling our heads even with our shoulders so that the rear rotor won't chop them off.

Our Mi-8 abruptly soars into the sky, and another one lands in its place. We hide behind boulders and scan the tops of the mountains. The empty pillboxes of the *dukhi* stare back at us. The small stones underneath me stick into my elbows and knees. The wind, swirled by the helicopters, tries to tear off our Panamas and backpacks and showers us with dust and small rocks.

"Watch out so it won't knock your head off!" someone shouts to me from behind.

A hundred meters away, our helicopter gunships form a circle. Their roar has a calming effect, like a strong tranquilizer.

The last bee has fifty meters to go. Slowing down, it begins its approach to the landing ground. Suddenly there's an unexpected jerk to the left, a flash under its rotor, and an explosion. Its commander apparently doesn't yet understand what's happened. He takes the helicopter down along the slope to pick up speed and go in again for a landing. But with the second turn it strikes the slope; slowly it turns to the left, careening onto its side and simultaneously dropping its nose. A second—even stronger—hit on the left side. The rotors hit the ground in a rolling crash, flying in all directions and slashing the cliffs. The craft, clutching at the rocks, continues to slip downward, and the airborne troopers jump off as it slides. The beats of my pounding heart alternate with the blows of the helicopter against the boulders. A second later the pilots drop through the hatch. I feel as if I've just been shot down, that it is me rolling down the slope, clutching at the rocks with weakening fingers.

In Jalalabad I'd met a woman with a dead infant in her arms. It was, I'd thought, the most frightening thing I'd seen in Afghanistan. But this fresh sight has a far more depressing and tragic effect on me, maybe because the flaming, disintegrating helicopter—abandoned by people in a hurry—seems to me to be a symbol of our most precious hopes now collapsed.

All four bumblebees have turned around to work a nearby cliff from which the *dukhi* have put our Mi-8 out of action. Their gunfire sends splinters of rock flying, enveloping the top of the mountain in a cloud of dust.

For ten minutes more my chest throbs as the gunships, their glass sparkling in the sun, shoot at this and three other nearby cliffs.

"Better than the mountains only mountains can be," Kazantzev says through clenched teeth, reciting a line from a famous song by Vladimir Vysotsky.

"The *dukhi* hold fireworks in honor of our arrival," Simonov wheezes from my right.

One of the guys from the downed bee is examining with astonishment a hole in his canteen; a *dukhi* bullet, after piercing the side of the chopper, had sliced through the canteen as well. No more water. But life remains.

"This is the third close call for me," he jokes gloomily.

Soon we shoulder our backpacks and weapons, form a line, and begin to march. We're facing a long trek to a hill that's marked on Kazantzev's map with the number 1945. With the help of a laser scouting device, our spotter calculates the distance. Referring to a tiny spot of green light, the spotter reports, without the slightest degree of sympathy, that we have 15,700 meters to go. This distance, however, has been measured as the crow flies. In fact we will march at least twenty kilometers.

"Do you know what an airborne trooper is?" Simonov asks me. Humor is as essential to Simonov as his backpack, Panama, and mountain boots. "An airborne trooper is an eagle for all of a minute, and for the next five days he is a horse. You turn into a horse the minute you jump off the helicopter. So in reality we aren't 'the reindeer of the airborne troops,' but the workhorses."

In front of us are the commander of the platoon, a radioman, and a particularly puny guy who somehow manages to carry a "cliff" (a heavy antiaircraft machine gun), a BP, and a whole pile of God knows what—including firewood—on his back. They're followed by the weak, who will be the first to "die." Then come the stronger men, prepared to shoulder the backpacks and weapons of the exhausted ones. Behind me are Simonov, Okhotnikov, and Kazantzev.

"Old mountains are good mountains," Simonov says. "They have no steep slopes. But young mountains you can't cross without a 'cat' (a mountain-climbing tool). In Panjshir the mountains are just wonderful—"

"Stone!" Okhotnikov suddenly shouts, interrupting Simonov in midsentence. A heavy rock leaps out from under his boots and rushes headlong down the path. Everyone in front dashes aside.

We reach the bottom of the ravine and begin our climb up the next slope. Making your way uphill is considerably easier than moving down. You just plant one foot firmly on the ground ahead and straighten it. Put down and straighten. During a descent, however, your knees are shaking after just a few minutes, like after a nightmare. What's more, you have to carefully and constantly choose a place between the stones where you can place your boot. If your attention wavers a little you could fall, bringing down an avalanche of cobble-stone-sized rocks.

"It's better not to stop in the mountains," Okhotnikov says as he fixes the straps of his BP. "After a rest it's impossible to tear your bottom from the ground. Once you pause you get the feeling that the pull of gravity has increased at least tenfold."

We now tramp along the tactical crest of the mountain, which is ten meters lower than its ridge. This reduces the chance that we'll be spotted by the *dukhi*'s scouts. While I can't get rid of the feeling that I am being aimed at, it's best not to think about it.

"What are you going to do after the army?" I ask the breathing and footsteps behind me.

"I'll go to college." The breathing and footsteps are now accompanied by Simonov's bass.

"Which one?"

"To journalism school. I want to write about Afghanistan myself. Such nonsense in print—sometimes it's sickening."

"Let's do without insults."

"It's just that you write one thing and we see something totally different. If I hadn't read the papers, I'd never have known that here we have a reconciliation in full swing."

The rhythm of my breathing gradually merges with the marching footsteps and tinkling assault rifles.

Kazantzev wheezes something, but the wind muffles his words. I want to look back, into Kazantzev's face, but I haven't the strength to turn my head. My sweat-soaked collar has hardened in the wind and scrapes my sore neck like sandpaper with each turn of my head.

We halt for a short while. Kazantzev offers me his canteen. After taking a big mouthful of cold tea, I return the canteen to this man of rare courage who has been rewarded with medals more than once.

We move again. Over our heads, somewhere in the endless blue sky, cruises a patrolling fighter-bomber plane. The bomber utters a low-pitched, drawn-out wail—like someone running a bow for an agonizingly long time over the string of a double bass. The mournful music from above blends in my mind with the words of Kazantzev, which I'm still digesting.

"Simonov!" Kazantzev shouts from behind me. "Let off a red rocket. Otherwise they'll take us for a *dukhi* caravan and drop bombs on the head of our correspondent."

Simonov carries out the order instantly.

"Live stone—be careful!" shouts Okhotnikov, jumping in front of me. I manage to place my boot on another boulder. Ibragimov, a round fellow with short black hair, doesn't catch Okhotnikov's warning. He makes an unfortunate step and twists his right ankle. As it turns out, he'd sprained the ankle three hours earlier when he jumped from the helicopter.

We make an emergency stop. Ibragimov unwinds a bandage and massages his ankle. Someone turns on a portable radio.

Ibragimov laces up his boot and takes a testing step, a second step, a third step. He can walk. Kazantzev takes Ibragimov's BP and AK-47 and slings them over his shoulder.

"Well, Ibragimov, Ibragimov," Kazantzev says in a singsong voice, "you found your Sancho Panza. You are an ill-bred person, Ibragimov."

Ibragimov, smiling guiltily, hobbles slowly in front.

"It's okay, Ibragimov. When we come back to the camp you'll bring me as many bottles of lemonade as you can fit in your BP. And if you don't, you'll cover your name with eternal shame, Ibragimov, and your brothers in arms will scowl at you. Right, Simonov?"

"Sure thing," Simonov replies.

But soon all the conversation dies. Our strength is ebbing and yet we still have an eternity to march. In the saddles of land between the mountains, we pass the *dukhi*'s shooting positions and masonry-faced peaked gabions.

Somewhere along the way we apparently get our second wind. No more than seven thousand meters separate us from hill 1945. But Ibragimov can't walk any farther. He sits down on the side of the path. This time it's final.

"Well, Ibragimov," Kazantzev says as he throws Ibragimov's BP and AK off his back, "you'll have to be picked up by a chopper."

Fifty minutes later there are four of us who can't cope with the remaining distance. We gather together to sit and wait for the promised Mi-8. The strap on someone's backpack tears off, and his BP plummets into the ravine.

"Bad timing for your automatic unhooker to work," Simonov says wryly.

Weary laughter.

Oleg Gontzov takes a seat next to me. As he looks down at his feet, he asks, "When are you going back to Moscow?"

"In a week."

"Want to?"

"Not yet," I say, feeling that there's still something about Afghanistan I haven't captured.

"Me too."

Oleg's first tour of duty in Afghanistan began in 1980. Two years later he was demobilized, and he returned to the Soviet Union—a move he eventually came to regret. So he went to a military enlistment office and asked to be sent back to Afghanistan, which is how he found himself here for a second time. Last October he was married—in Kabul.

"I have a lot of friends here—some serve, some lie at rest," he says, patting the ground with his wide palm. "You see, I can't go back to the world. I tried. It doesn't work."

We can see several dots on the horizon, which soon turn into one bee and two helicopter gunships.

"Lay out the smokes!" Kazantzev shouts.

As we clamber up the slope to clear a landing ground for the Mi-8, one man stays below. In a matter of moments thick orange smoke is pouring out of his hand, winding its way upward. The helicopter lands while the bumblebees lay down a barrage from overhead. Kazantzev and I help Ibragimov and three other airborne troopers to climb inside.

The helicopter, escorted by the two bumblebees, lifts off and heads for Kabul.

That's how the first of the operation's five days passes. Each day is unlike every other. During this time the detachment of airborne troops covers more than one hundred kilometers. The soldiers' faces turn darker and darker from the dust and the sun. After fighting two battles, capturing lots of weapons, and crossing a nameless mountain river, the airborne troops return home—to Kabul.

Before my departure from the unit's camp, Slava Belous comes to me and says, "If you have a spare hour, try to drop by the hospital to see Andrei Makarenko. Tell him hello from us. Okay?"

They say the same person can't be killed twice, but Ensign Andrei Makarenko was killed three times in the same day.

On November 30, 1986, a Soviet cargo plane on its way from Kabul to Jalalabad was blown up by the enemy. "Our unit was sent to search for the remains of people and the burned plane," Makarenko is saying over the rattling from the complex metal apparatus that's attached to his legs. "There were many young soldiers in my platoon who had just arrived in Afghanistan. So I was the first to go on that path."

Makarenko went first so that he would enter any mine fields before the new recruits. Because they hadn't brought along combat engineers, he took the ramrod from his gun and tested the soil himself.

"My guardian angel, who is generally an idle fellow, was performing his sentry duties wretchedly. An explosion tossed me up, and when I fell to the ground my left leg was gone below the knee. All of a sudden my face grew cold, but my brain was working like a clock."

I imagine Andrei sitting on a stony, dusty path, a puddle of his blood soaking into the ground. I see a ghostly pallor cover his face like a veil. I feel a sharp pain in my left leg.

"I never lost consciousness, and I ordered the soldiers to remain in their places and not to move. It was quite clear: I was sitting on the mine field."

They threw a rubber cord to him. He wrapped it tightly around his leg, bandaged it, and gave himself a double shot of painkiller. A long time passed before the combat engineers arrived. They cleared a corridor to the spot where Makarenko lay, and four airborne troopers put him on a makeshift canvas stretcher and carried him out.

"Well, I thought, the danger is behind me. One can't die twice. Thank God, things are settled now, one way or another. The shell splinters could have hurt others."

But at that moment one of the soldiers took a false step. An explosion followed, this one even more powerful than the first. The blast broke Makarenko's right leg, twisting it around below the knee. Seven men fell, all of them seriously wounded.

"My brain kept working—it just wouldn't switch off. Yes, I think, it would have been easier for a weaker person. The loss of consciousness is sort of a narcotic, allowing you to lapse into oblivion, to hide from pain.

"Soon we were all put aboard the chopper. I was connected to an IV made from a plastic bag. We were lying not on stretchers but on the floor of the copter. More comfortable. We took off. Gained altitude."

Suddenly the chopper twitched; slowly it began to fall. It had run out of fuel.

Death attacked Makarenko for the third time.

"At that moment the pilot-navigator came out of the cockpit. I called out to him, 'What's happening out there? We're falling!' Instead of answering me he fastened a parachute to the overhead rigging and calmly said, 'No reason to worry, comrades. The flight is proceeding in a normal way.' In a businesslike manner, he readjusted his helmet, opened the door, and jumped out."

Makarenko looked out the window. The ground was rushing toward the helicopter with open arms, promising an instant release from pain. The mechanic jumped out after the navigator—silently, without casting a look at the wounded.

The soldiers moaned softly. Makarenko reached for the overhead rigging and tried to grasp a parachute, and the IV tore out of his leg. Blood oozed through his bandages and trickled down toward the nose of the descending helicopter. A parachute slipped off a seat and sped across the floor, splashing blood on the soldiers' faces. Makarenko followed the parachute with his eyes until he remembered that you can't jump without two legs.

"This understood, I lay on my back not caring a bit. Suddenly I became completely indifferent as to what awaited me. Some kind of calm entered my body. I even read an inscription that had been scribbled by someone on the left side of the door."

One of the wounded soldiers loosened his collar and said in a low voice, "Now the third pilot will take to his heels, and that'll be the end." But the commander of the team, Captain Smirnov, didn't jump. He turned on the accumulators, which were somehow continuing to turn the helicopter's rotors.

A paratrooper quickly learns how to lessen the blow of landing by pulling on the shrouds of his parachute just before he touches the ground. Smirnov used the same technique: a second before the helicopter would have crashed into a knoll, he applied the brakes and reduced the impact.

Makarenko turns his face and looks to the left, behind me. I turn, too. Seeing nothing but the naked wall of the hospital ward, I understand: he is looking back to November 30.

I want to ask him about the navigator and the mechanic. They'd saved themselves but lost the army, which kicked them out. But I can't bring myself to ask. Some wounds of the heart cause more pain than wounds of the body. The betrayal of the two helicopter crewmen still bleeds in Makarenko's memory like the wound of a person whose blood cannot coagulate. But then again, if war consisted entirely of heroes, heroism would not exist.

"Do you think I'll be able to return to the airborne troops?" Andrei asks. "Will I be able to jump?" He traces a fingertip over the metal brace on his right leg.

"Certainly," I answer. But he doesn't believe me, and I don't believe myself.

Soon I say farewell to the man who'd been killed three times. I shake his icy hand firmly and head for the door.

I leave Kabul the next morning. It is hot and stifling. The white sun has begun to fry the city early that day. By the time I reach the airport, the air is shimmering over the scorching runways. I drop my suitcase near a ladder whose stairs, for the moment, lead only to the sky. On the other side of the ladder, Major Novikov and Lieutenant Colonel Leonov are talking. I met both of them a week ago near South Baghlan.

Novikov offers me a thermos of coffee. Before taking a drink, I examine it suspiciously, trying to unscrew the bottom.

"Why such a precaution?" Leonov asks me.

I tell them the story of the booby-trapped thermos that had been found in a dugout near South Baghlan. We all laugh.

Leonov had served in Byelorussia before coming to Afghanistan, and last summer he returned there on leave to see his family. Even though he is supposed to make the trip home in a single day, he has been stuck in Dushanbe for nearly three days. As usual, there are no airplane tickets available.

"I'm sitting in a restaurant with a deputy commander of the regiment," Leonov tells us as he fingers a cigarette. " 'Petrovich,' he asks me, 'why do you keep turning around?' And I say, 'Someone is sneaking up from behind.' He smiles and says, 'Oh, that's a waiter. You, brother, overfought.' I remember how I walked in Dushanbe, absentmindedly going around all the greenie areas. For the first two days after I came home I didn't get a wink of sleep, even though I knew I was awfully tired. But on the third day, when they began firing practice, I fell asleep instantly.

"Well, as usual, everyone had hundreds of questions for me. I even decided to write my answers on cards—'Yes, I think soon,' or 'No, I don't know him,' or 'Lousy,' or 'Leave me alone'—so I could simply show them and not chat unnecessarily. I had a good vacation, except that all sorts of little things poisoned my mood. Imagine— you're on native ground and want to kiss it, but because of some lousy airplane ticket you're so tired out that you want to send everything to fucking hell. A ticket to Moscow costs two hundred rubles on the black market in Dushanbe! Stuff the two hundred in your throat but let me see my wife sooner."

"It's no better in Tashkent," Novikov says. "My reservation for a ticket to Kharkov turned out to be no good. There was nothing left for me to do but to cry in the middle of the station. And there, behind the taxi dispatcher's office, stand a few civilians who are whispering to one another. I move closer and, cupping my hands, bark at them: 'Citizen profiteers! Who can offer a ticket to Kharkov?' In a second one of them rushes to me and whispers: 'Not so loud, Comrade Major. We are risking so much after that decree about unearned income.' I couldn't bear it any longer and shouted, 'You, son of a bitch, are *risking*?' He shrank into a clot. I took pity on him. What was the point in arguing with him about risk? I slipped him a hundred, and eight hours later he was knocking on my door."

At this point our conversation is interrupted by the murmur of a transport plane.

"Looks like it's for you," I say.

We shake hands. Soon Novikov and Leonov blend into the group of other army men who are waiting for the same flight. Ten minutes later the plane is high over Kabul. I sit on one of the stairs of the ladder and look at the little dot as it melts away in the sky.

I think about all of the subconscious associations you bring back with you from Afghanistan. In a store you look at the blades of a fan as they limply knead the sultry air over the meat counter, and it suddenly occurs to you that something's missing. Well, of course, it's the sound that's missing—the rolling murmur of a helicopter's engines.

Or the predawn silence is broken by a fierce burst of machine-gun fire. You awaken from your remote Afghan sleep, rub your eyes, and only then understand. Calm down, old man, it's simply a motorcyclist, damn him, racing around town without a muffler.

Afghanistan even steals language from you. War has taught Soviet soldiers to speak in a way that even their relatives can't understand: "greenie," for example, means a zone of lush vegetation in which the *dukhi* are likely to be lurking, and berries are people. A brief dictionary of slang: yogurt (diesel fuel), bee (an Mi-8 helicopter), bumblebee (a helicopter-gunship), marlet (Su-17), cheerful (MiG-21), elephant (tank), seagull (automobile), rook (Su-25), milk (kerosene), sour cream (gasoline), canned food (mines), and black tulip (a plane that transports bodies).

Afghanistan moves into your subconscious and haunts you day and night. Some utterly harmless incident can drag up a heap of unpleasant visions that only you can see.

A neighbor's son rings your doorbell.

"Look here," he says, offering you a small black tulip. "Our botany teacher told us to put a flower in an inkwell for a night, and look what happened!"

But the flower does not bring you any delight.

At times Afghanistan is reality, while everything around it is only an illusion, a dream. Before my assignment in Afghanistan, I met a pilot in Moscow who'd served there on a rook and had more than 150 combat flights under his belt. He'd been decorated with two Orders of the Red Star. As we walked along Moscow's boulevards he looked very attentively under his feet, as if he were searching for something. For a long time I couldn't understand what the problem was. My eyes searched the sidewalk, too, but they saw nothing but the puddles under our feet, discarded candy wrappers, and rotting leaves.

Soon, however, everything became clear. After fixing on some reference point—a cigarette butt, for example—he'd mentally calculate a point of entry for his diving fighter plane so that the rear sight of his gun would be under the cigarette butt. In this way he would be able to ascertain the correct angle of attack. Besides, he explained, the bombs had to be dropped at just the right moment. This preoccupation absorbed so much of his attention that it had gotten on the nerves of his wife and relatives.

In summer you go to the Crimea with your wife. But at the sight of the Kavadag your brain begins to calculate the most advantageous position for a machine gun.

And then one day, when you're hopelessly immersed in a good detective novel, as you were a while ago in the *kishlak* of Malym-Gulym, you begin to long—no kidding—for poetry. You pick a volume at random from your bookshelf. It turns out to be Pushkin. At bedtime you start reading from the middle:

> The horses dash off again;
> A little bell—ding-ding-ding . . .
> I see: the dukhi gathered
> Amid the whitening plains.

But as soon as you run into the word *dukhi* ["ghosts" in Russian], your imagination replaces the speeding horses with APCs, the little bell with the clank of their treads, and the white plains with yellow sands. You slam the book shut and toss it on the bed. You don't have Pushkin anymore either. At least not this poem.

You save some money, go to the store, and finally buy a brand-new Zenith camera. But the first time you click the shutter you're astonished that there's no recoil.

And at night you wake up with the feel of a trigger on your index finger. If you're lucky, you learn to take it easy five or six months later.

THE
HIDDEN
WAR

1

While much of the Fortieth Army had already left Afghanistan by the end of 1988, nearly fifty thousand troops remained behind, obediently waiting for orders to withdraw.

December turned into January, which dragged on at an unusually lazy pace, like a slow-moving freight train as it nears the end of the line. There were only short bursts of daylight in between the draining, hollow nights.

Toward the end of the first week in January, a strong northern wind blew in, bringing a bitter frost with it. More snow fell on the mountains, but not on Kabul. Dust and sand swirled in the streets of the city; rusty tin cans rolled back and forth in the wind's wake.

The evacuation of the central military hospital in Kabul had begun on December 19. By January 8, there were only three or four doctors left, rumor had it, and they were said to be leaving on the next morning's flight to Tashkent.

Because I still had one more month in Afghanistan ahead of me, I rushed to the hospital shortly after nightfall to try to get some essential medicine.

The hospital, once so crowded and noisy, seemed ominously empty; its doors and windows were flapping violently in the gusts of wind. Judging from the blinking red lights and low-pitched drone above me, there were more transport planes than stars in the sky. As

I approached the obelisk in front of the hospital, a soldier tried to sell me ten cans of sweetened condensed milk at an exorbitant price.

Then, as I had five years ago, I stopped to read the inscription on the obelisk: "Soviet-Afghan friendship was everlasting and inviolable."

I entered the hospital and nearly bumped into three Afghan officers in Soviet *bushlats* who were lugging rusty air conditioners on their bony backs; they'd apparently ripped them out of the windows of empty rooms. The wind whistled as I walked down the hall, and every now and then I could hear the eerie echo of bedsprings punching through the rotting mattresses. A door with a sign that said HOUSE NURSE creaked open and then closed. Two years ago, in this very room, I'd had my knee bandaged after a clumsy jump from a helicopter. They'd drawn a sample of my blood and, without ever bothering to wait for the test results, told me that I had nothing to worry about. As I limped out of the hospital I passed a soldier who'd lost both of his legs above the knee, which made him resemble one of the dwarfs from a painting by Velázquez. His tear-stained face, which could have pierced the heart of even the most war-hardened officer, had the look of a man who could see ahead into his future.

As I walked through the dark, empty corridors of the hospital, I felt as if the hundreds of sick and injured men who'd passed through the hospital—those who'd survived as well as those who'd died—were silently and invisibly following me.

Here, in July 1986, right next to the operating room, I'd seen a young soldier whose face—at least the lower half of it—had been all but obliterated by shrapnel. The boy never lost consciousness, and for three hours he silently endured the most excruciating pain imaginable. Someone finally thought to turn him over on his stomach, shoving what was left of his face into a pillow, so he wouldn't choke on his own blood.

I'd first visited the hospital soon after my arrival in Afghanistan, at the invitation of General Sherbakov, whom I'd naively asked for a lift to the combat zone in the Rukhi region. "Why don't you first go to the hospital, walk around there for a while, and see what war can do to a man," he'd told me. "It'll cool your enthusiasm a bit. Then we'll talk."

While the hospital hadn't cooled my enthusiasm, it had convinced me that the sight of someone else in severe pain makes your own problems evaporate, no matter how hopelessly desperate they may have seemed. As you look at a mortally wounded man, a vile and happy thought stirs at the very bottom of your subconscious: "Thank God I wasn't the one," you say to yourself. "This time I wasn't the one."

Now, making my evening rounds in search of at least one living soul, I ran into a middle-aged man who was methodically slicing a slab of meat on a bloody wooden stool. It was the hospital's chief internist.

"Lamb," he explained. "The chief of the psychiatric ward and I are preparing our farewell meal. Do join us."

Seeing a bloody piece of meat in a hospital ward did nothing for my appetite. I politely declined the dinner invitation and asked for the medicine, which I hoped I would never need. The huge cupboard contained mostly Seduksen, along with some obscure depressants and tranquilizers. For some reason—perhaps greed—I stuffed my pockets with them.

As it turned out, I never needed the pills. I exchanged them for some canned pork offered by an airborne trooper at the Forty-second Post who wore a look of otherworldly melancholia. Tossing a couple of whites into his mouth, the guy promised to "make the high last till the border." He not only knew the names of all the drugs by heart (Relanium, Elenium, Aminreptilin, and so on), but he also had his own savory slang name for each one. Seduksen, for example, was *perpetuum kaif*, a comical mixture of Latin and Russian slang that meant "perpetual high."

"Whatever happened to the vice consul?" I asked the internist. (Last year the vice consul had been brought to the hospital after someone had thoroughly and cruelly beat him at his villa. He had had many injuries, including a fractured skull, and news of the incident had echoed throughout Afghanistan.)

"The consul's roof started slipping," the internist replied. "All of a sudden he asked for a rifle. 'What do you need an AK for?' he was asked. 'The AK is essential for killing whales,' he said. And then, out of the blue, he asked to be sent to the Far East."

"Why?"

"That way, he said, he would be closer to the Americans. In other words, his subconscious thoughts were busting out."

"Did you send the vice consul back to the Soviet Union?"

"There was no alternative. We had so much trouble with him that we thought we'd let somebody else have a turn."

During my last trip to Afghanistan I'd met a guy in the hospital's psychiatric ward who was concerned that he had no shadow. He proved to me, by means of excellent logic, that a man without a shadow cannot—and must not—live. He tried to commit suicide several times. I was reminded of this incident in Moscow, when Zhenya Raevsky, an *afghantsi* and student at Moscow State University, shared with me his idea for a screenplay; his main characters were going to be Afghanistan veterans who'd returned home from the war. What makes them different from all other people, Raevsky told me, is that they have no shadows. Some hideous meaning was buried there, inaccessible to a sober mind. That's when I realized that what happened in Afghanistan *outside* the psychiatric wards was the true insanity. The psych ward, in fact, was only a way out of the insanity called war.

The Soviet airborne troopers in Afghanistan, who typically took on the most dangerous assignments and fought the most selflessly, were often among the first to lose their minds. I knew one of these men—"Ramboviks," they'd been dubbed—who was on his second tour of duty. I once watched him drop a pill of dry alcohol and five spoonfuls of instant coffee into a glass that contained some sort of yellowish liquid. After finishing his cocktail he looked at me and said: "Vodka is water. Alcohol is fuel. The same thing happens to a man's head, you see, that happens to a woman during an abortion— all logical links are severed. Would you like a drink?"

I hesitated. Just one look at his drink had been enough to tie my stomach into a sailor's knot. Besides, he probably figured that I was a moron who wasn't worth talking to, much less drinking with.

Colonel Frolov, the chief of the hospital's psychiatric service, arrived to join his colleague for the farewell supper.

"Are you afraid?" I asked him.

"Should a man who sees a puddle in front of him and steps around it be called a coward?" he replied. "I am fifty years old. I am a colonel. Why should I ruin my own life?"

His logic was bulletproof.

I went back out into the courtyard, where the soldier once again offered to sell me some condensed milk. This time the price was lower, but he was still asking more than a journalist on assignment in Afghanistan could afford.

Leaning against the obelisk, a woman in a military uniform was sobbing, her tiny body convulsing as if she were in an electric chair. The tears kept streaming out of her eyes, leaving whitish traces of salt that resembled the lines on the sweaty rump of a horse after a quick blow of the crop.

"By any chance are you from the relocation office?" she asked me, barely able to hold back the spasms that choked her throat.

"No, I'm just a reporter." The woman burst into tears again, and I immediately felt sorry that I wasn't from the relocation office. Her lips were quivering. Her eyebrows puckered over the bridge of her nose.

"Can I do anything for you?" I asked.

"How could you in this madhouse?" she replied, rubbing her eyes with her tiny fists like a child. "I was sent here from Mazar-i-Sharif to do an abortion on a *blatnaya* [a well-connected woman]. They promised to send me back—all my things are still there—but then forgot about me. This morning I went to the airfield, and all of us were loaded into a transport plane. We were supposed to be taking off any minute, but then"—here she let out another sob—"they kicked us out and started to load some army archives. I'll bet all my things are stolen by now."

Suddenly I heard a harsh male voice from behind me. "Stop your hysterics! I've got much too much work without you here."

It was the major, who'd run outside in just a *telnyashka.*

"Who are you?" he asked me.

"A reporter," I replied.

Then, giving me a wink, he barked at the woman again. "Stop this bawling! See, this is a reporter, you little so-and-so. Stop it, I'm telling you!"

"All I need is a stamp right here, Comrade Major," she wailed plaintively. "A stamp and a signature to be transported."

The major turned to me and said, "Don't pay any attention to this woman, Comrade Reporter. She's messed up, like all women. It's just a nervous breakdown. An extraordinary situation. The people are very tired. Come back tomorrow."

"But tomorrow there won't be anyone here, right?" I asked.

"Then *don't* come tomorrow," he said. "Best of luck." He gave me a strained smile. His teeth were as yellow as an old man's dominos.

The major took the woman by the arm and led her toward the building. She flashed a thin, pathetic smile of farewell at me.

I took her smile with me on my trip, as a souvenir.

2

With each day there were fewer and fewer troops in Afghanistan. The Fortieth Army was retreating to the north, like a sea approaching low tide. When I stopped by the defenseless Soviet embassy during the day I felt, along with the bevy of diplomats, like a hare in a forest full of wolves—a hare who, laying its ears back, frantically holds up a gigantic sign that says "Guys, let's all live together in peace!" Now we were actively making peace with the whole forest and officially calling the wolves the "armed resistance."

Quite often I would recall a little song that the regiment's Party secretary used to like to sing:

Down the road, along the valley, a regiment rode in a car.
Suddenly a gray wolf came out, but then we persuaded him:
'Don't be afraid of us, old wolf, don't gnash your teeth.
We're only a regiment on paper and we're afraid of you ourselves.'

The army was leaving Afghanistan, and at some point the journalists had to give back the weapons that had been distributed to them a long time ago—the Makarov pistols.

Underneath the empty holster, my heart started to beat a bit faster.

Leshchinsky, a veteran of the Soviet press corps in Kabul,

encouraged everybody by saying that the only use for a Makarov was to shoot a bullet through your head in case things got bad; it could never save your life.

Then he'd say, "But it's all right—I still have my fangs." Leshchinsky displayed an impressive scowl, yellowish from the local water and Marlboro cigarettes.

Every night, like a shrill call of a bat, came the voice of the mullah: *"Allah-o-Akbar! Allah-o-Akbar!"* He'd inevitably wake me up at least three times a night.

One time I woke from a nightmare in a cold sweat. In my dream I'd seen a field strewn with corpses. Even awake, I could smell the vivid violetlike odor of carrion. In the morning, I learned that my refrigerator was broken. It was shaking feverishly (it was afraid, too, the bastard) in a gigantic pool of blood. The blood was still oozing out of the freezer, which my predecessor had packed tight with meat. Despite all my efforts to scrape the linoleum clean, the large blood-stain had remained on the kitchen floor ever since.

Every time I saw the bloodstain it reminded me of the dream, as did the war itself—a running, real-life nightmare. To find out the meaning of my nightmare, I once borrowed a dictionary of dreams from an acquaintance, but apparently no one else had ever dreamed such vileness.

One of our old-timers in Kabul tried to reassure me. "Spooks, buddy, hallucinations!" he told me. "It'll only get worse."

Sometimes clouds would rush across the sky with the speed of a bomber, even though there was no sign of wind. And when the wind did come, crushing down on Kabul with all its might, the clouds would hang motionless in the sky like swollen white helicopters—the souls of all the Mi-8s and Mi-24s that had been shot down in the past nine years. We were booed by the wind more and more often. And not once since the day in the fall of 1988 when the trees shed their leaves did the wind sound anything like applause.

I woke up with headaches more frequently than ever before. Judging from the complaints of witnesses, I was grinding my teeth in my sleep.

With the rising of the sun, which would swiftly break through the shell of darkness, it would grow lighter in the city, and I would grow braver.

At the same time, I'd notice that my room had grown even smaller. The walls were closing in on me. Meter by meter, each new day would audaciously claim the remaining space. "There isn't an inch . . ." A ray of morning light would make its way through my small window, which was protected by iron bars, a Venetian blind, newspapers, a blanket, and a curtain.

I'd take a long time shaving and slowly sip some Good Spirits, a drink made from acorns. Then I'd head for a Soviet office to make telephone calls and arrange some interviews with local big shots. Each day I'd see the sign on the telephone that inevitably sent chills down my spine: "Attention! The enemy is listening!"

"There isn't an inch . . ." The major from Bagram was right.

During my first visit to Afghanistan I'd started collecting various signs and inscriptions for fun—official and unofficial, from helicopters and APCs, from the butts of AKMs and the undersides of helmets.

Here's what I read on the back of the door to the Kabul morgue: "Enjoy your youth. But remember—this, too, is vanity." I wouldn't have found anything like it here in 1980, 1981, or 1982. But nine years have passed since then. The signs have changed, and so have I.

3

Somewhere around January 10 I came to feel that I'd stayed in Kabul too long, so I started to get ready for a trip.

A large army operation apparently was being planned at the southern approaches to the Salang Tunnel. It was whispered about in the city. There were no official statements, but there was plenty of talk at General Headquarters, at the embassy, in the journalists' villas, and in the *dukhani* [shops] of Kabul.

The specter of upcoming military action hovered in the prickly air, gradually materializing in the form of a general nervousness at General Headquarters as well as various precautions in Kabul against terrorism, sabotage, and other rebel retaliation.

I took a night flight on an An-12 transport plane to get to Bagram and, hitching a ride on an armored carrier, headed north. Mines weren't a problem; it wasn't easy to bury them in frozen ground.

After passing the crossroads at Bagram (where Sasha Sekretarev, a photojournalist for *Izvestia*, had been killed the previous spring), we picked up speed.

Like a hooker, the road swung its curvaceous hips back and forth, winding between the cliffs, rising and falling.

An ensign with a stony face and grayish lips sat across from me in the armored carrier. His body was jerking rhythmically. He seemed to be listening to some music that only he could hear and dancing to it in his own mind. The dance began in his eyes, spread to his lips, and then traveled down his body in a wave. His shoulders were rock'n'rolling, and his right index finger, which was ringed with grease (he must have fired an AKM quite often), was tapping out a fast rhythm.

"Hey, Ensign!" I called out.

He didn't respond.

"Ensign, can you hear me?"

Only after I gave his shoulder a hard shake did he focus his roaming glance on me.

"What?" he asked.

"Are you feeling all right?"

"I don't feel anything at all, but you're getting on my nerves. Here, listen for a couple of minutes and then buzz off."

He produced a tiny set of earphones and handed them to me. The wire led back to the pocket of his *bushlat*, where a cheap Walkman was hiding.

I put on the earphones and was carried off to a "Concert in China" by Jean-Michel Jarre. For a few minutes I floated in the swells of electronic music. Then, pressing the stop button, I once again heard the roar of the armored carrier—the hard rock of war.

"Where did you buy it?" I asked him. "In Kabul?"

"A war trophy," he replied, smiling mysteriously.

For some reason the ensign found it necessary to tell me that he was serving his second tour of duty in Afghanistan.

"The first time wasn't enough for you?" I asked.

"You see, old man, I'm sick to hell of everything back there. Sometimes I even had a physical, almost lovelike, craving for this godforsaken land. At night I'd dream about Afghanistan. In the morning I'd laugh, during the day I'd cry, and in the evenings I'd get drunk to the gills. I remember once at some party this middle-aged woman sat down next to me and said, 'Tell me about the war.' 'What do you want to know?' I asked. 'Well, for instance,' she said, 'did you ever kill people? What did it feel like?' I lost it. I went crazy and yelled, 'Do you understand *what* you're asking me? No, I mean it, do you understand *what* you just asked me? You can't ask me just like that, the way you just did. You can't, do you understand?' The next morning I woke up with a definite decision to go back again. And that night I dreamed about Russian Orthodox churches in Moscow, but with Islamic symbols—crescents on top of the domes. Give me back the earphones."

The ensign kept his teeth clenched tight for the rest of the trip. His face shone like the moon in the hazy interior of the armored carrier.

The shimmering mountain air was dissolving into darkness. Day was turning into night. The hemorrhaging sun slowly slipped behind the horizon; somewhere in its lair it rested, licking the wounds it had received during the day. By morning it would peek out again and, looking around with caution, daringly head for its zenith, as if to a sacrifice. Every day was like this.

The sun had suffered in this war, too. Soldiers shot at it when they were bored and cursed it when it looked them straight in the eyes, blinding them and preventing them from answering enemy fire. The Muslims prayed for the sun to rise in the east, as did pilots trying to evade heat-seeking antiaircraft missiles. If they were lucky, the missiles would head for the sun.

I once figured that I'd spent half my time in Afghanistan traveling from one point to another, sometimes in the air but more often on the ground. The road could run through drilled-out tunnels in the cliffs or pass down through a valley. It could be dull or terrifying, white by day or black by night, covered with ice or sand, asphalt or blood. Hundreds of people kept me company during my countless journeys. Most of them I remember. Some I have forgotten.

Everything I saw and heard in Afghanistan, whether it could or couldn't be understood, whether it was experienced or merely imagined, conceived but never executed, promised but not carried out, dreamed but never realized—all of this in one way or another was connected to the road that came from and led to God knows where. So much wisdom has been unwittingly shared with me, revealed to me, or simply given to me free of charge by the people that I met along the way.

I remember a guy with a barely perceptible earring hole in the torn lobe of his right ear. He would put the earring on every night and take it off every morning. He had a strange last name: Pepel, which is the Russian word for "ashes." He couldn't have been older than twenty that summer.

A couple of days before demobilization and the flight back to the USSR, I slapped Pepel on the shoulder and said, "Well, buddy, now you've really got to do some living to the max." Although he was standing only a couple of meters away, he looked at me as if he were in some faraway place and said, with more than a trace of amazement, "Damn it, on the inside I feel like I've turned gray already."

I met a guy stationed in Jalalabad whose nickname was Momsy. Momsy was short; all of the energy that might have made him tall had apparently wound up in his eyes, which had a piercing glare. He was glad, he told me, that his girlfriend in Kharkov had left him. His masochism baffled me at first, but then he explained everything clearly and succinctly. "Now it will be easier to fight," he said. "It's simple to be in the war when you are miserable. You have a lot less to lose." When it was time to say good-bye, Momsy smiled and wished me good luck. But at the same time his eyes said, Scum, I hope you drop dead—you and your tranquil life in Moscow!

I heard about a guy in Kabul who'd nearly been sent to a mental ward because of abysmal manic depression caused by the war. The thought of suicide was slowly but steadily eating at his mind and quite possibly would have eaten right through had it not been for a lucky accident. After suffering a concussion, he developed total amnesia. The boys who served with him took turns telling him his life story, but he kept asking them the same question: "What are we doing in Afghanistan?" No one could give him a definite answer.

And how could I ever forget the lieutenant whom I met in Leningrad? We'd been sitting in the restaurant of the Pulkovsky Hotel, chatting about this and that. Although he was a superb storyteller, he had the annoying habit of making a sucking noise with his tongue every three minutes or so. I finally offered him a toothpick, and then he told me a story that made it impossible for either of us to touch our food. He and some other soldiers had been positioned for forty-eight hours in a blockade near Kunduz. Early in the morning, right at dawn, a sniper had begun firing into the block. He killed two people—the mortar man and the radio operator—with just three shots. At first the sniper's bullets landed a meter away from the lieutenant's head, then only a centimeter away. It was as if the sniper were toying with him, sending one bullet after another into the thin line between life and death. But every fourth or fifth bullet would thump into the dead bodies that lay near him.

"The sound of a bullet entering a dead body . . . my dear God, I wouldn't want my worst enemy to see or hear it," he said. As he finished the story he squeezed his temples with the tips of his fingers.

4

The ensign with the Walkman jumped off as we approached the Charikar green zone. We traveled onward but were forced to reduce our speed when we ran into the rear troops of the regiment. The road was jammed.

Night had left behind a thin blanket of frost. The road was covered with a crackling crust of ice, and I could see the reddening sky in the frozen puddles. We came upon an armored carrier sitting helplessly at the side of the road. Someone had stuck the tail of an unidentifiable animal onto its antenna; below it, a homemade paper flag fluttered in the wind. "We're going home," the flag said. "Don't shoot!" As we made our way along the road, inhabitants of the nearby *kishlaks* scurried between cars. Most of them were men, dressed in Soviet *bushlats* and armed with submachine guns.

"Nice outfits on these *dukhi*," observed our driver. As we stopped again, he nodded toward one of them and said: "He's from the band of Ahmad Shah. Well, since we haven't been in combat for a while, both our people and their people maintain an amicable neutrality."

A *bachonok* ran up to our armored carrier and, mischievously flashing his eyes, shouted to me, "Hey, Commander, go to fucking Moscow soon!"

I used to cringe whenever I heard Russian curses on the lips of Afghan boys. But eventually I learned to take them with a sense of humor. (As one of our advisers had jokingly put it, "At least we taught them to swear like us. That's something.")

"Hey, *bacha*, want to go to Moscow with me?" our dirty-faced driver yelled out the hatch. "Come on, get in."

"No, Commander, Moscow is . . ."

"Well, *bacha*, tell me what's better."

"Ahmad Shah—good! Your Moscow . . ."

"You're obnoxious, buddy," our driver said with a smile.

The *bachonok* yelled out something in his own language and ran away, his naked ankles flashing.

The Charikar green zone was now behind us, spreading across the horizon like a tranquil black sea. The air above it was gray and rancid from the smoke of hundreds of chimneys. The smoke drifted slowly upward, mingling with the day's other colors and turning the sky into an impressionist painting. The Afghans burnt everything they could find: rubber tires, kindling, diesel fuel from the pipeline, even old galoshes with the made in the USSR stamp.

Nearby a river thundered, occasionally breaking the thick layer of ice around its humpbacked boulders with a resounding crack.

The *komendachi** sat at the side of the road, warming their hands over a bucket of burning diesel fuel. Their sheepskin coats had once been white but were now gray. A disabled tank was lying on its belly not too far from them, its right tread buried in a soot-specked snowdrift. The tank's charred turret lay twenty or so meters away, the mangled cannon pointing at the sky. I joined the soldiers who were huddled around the fire and drank some steaming tea from a hot flask (pieces of ice rattled inside mine). Soon I was off to the division's command post.

The division's forces were spread out along the road. While the rear column had gone north, two motorized infantry regiments and one artillery regiment remained in Kabul. Two more motorized infantry regiments were stationed near the town of Jabal os Siraj. The remainder of the division was scheduled to march from Kabul to Jabal (as our soldiers sometimes referred to the town). Nearly five thousand troops were to fly to Tashkent on Il-76 transport planes.

Nine years of war had nearly devastated the division. Its heaviest

*Soldiers who serve in the subdivisions of the commandant's office.

losses—596 soldiers killed—came in 1984 during the excruciatingly long Panjshir operation.

As they fought against the rebel forces of Ahmad Shah Massoud, many soldiers froze to death in the alpine snows; others were blown up by Soviet mines that had been laid in Panjshir during a similar campaign in 1982.

The 1984 Panjshir operation seemed cursed. There were many instances of miscommunication that needlessly cost many Soviet soldiers their lives. One day in late April, a single battalion in the division lost seventy soldiers.

Two Soviet companies and one Afghan company had been moving along the left bank of the river in Panjshir; two Afghan companies and one Soviet company had been moving along the other bank. The zone of combat was to their right, and the enemy was nowhere in sight. As it turned out, the decision to march along the river instead of along the strategically important ridges above them had been based on false information. The regiment's command post had been erroneously told that Soviet troops already controlled much of the high ground.

The men had quickly grown tired in the stifling heat. The commander of the battalion ordered them to stop for a cigarette break. They sank to the hot ground, propping themselves up against their backpacks. The silence was punctuated only by the clanging of submachine guns and the striking of matches. The aroma of cigarette smoke spread through the air.

Suddenly the *dukhi* attacked from three different directions. They showered the battalion with bullets, pressing the soldiers to the ground and lacerating their bodies. The commander of the battalion barely had time to scream "R-a-a-a-i-d!" before a bullet hit him in the forehead. He fell back-first into the river. The strong current swung his body around and carried reddish ribbons of blood downstream.

April's fatal misfortunes came like machine-gun fire: one burst after another. A few days earlier some of the Soviet bombers stationed at the Bagram air base had flown to Panjshir. The gorge was closed, however, and the planes were ordered to drop their payloads on secondary targets. A division of Soviet airborne troopers was fighting in one of these areas. The Soviet pilots, failing to look carefully at who and what was below them, dropped bombs on their own soldiers.

Then there was the case of the Soviet helicopter pilots who, responding to a call for help, mistook the soldiers in a motorized brigade for a band of rebels and almost completely wiped them out with NURSs [heat-seeking missiles]. An officer from the headquarters of TURKVO [the Turkestan Military District] tried to save the helicopter pilots by blaming the Afghans in the Sixty-sixth Motorized Infantry Regiment of the Eleventh Division. But the lie didn't work. An official investigation established that all the wounds had been caused by shells, not bullets.

In short, all kinds of things went wrong in Afghanistan. The reality of the war often wasn't part of the victorious reports that dominated the media coverage at home, particularly from 1986 on.

"Want some tea? Are you freezing?" Without waiting for an answer, Lieutenant Colonel Nikolai Vasylievich Ivanov, the chief of the division's political department, dumped a spoonful of fragrant Georgian tea leaves in my mug. "Take off your *bushlat* and put your gun down already. The war is canceled this evening. Do you take sugar?"

I'd heard a lot about Ivanov, but I'd never before had the chance to meet him. The soldiers who'd lived and fought alongside Ivanov told me that he was a remarkably decent, utterly incorruptible man who could see the big picture but distinguish between the halftones.

I was amazed by Ivanov's delicacy. Although such a word may seem out of place in a military context, I couldn't think of a better one. Everything about Ivanov—his calm, soft voice, his use of language, his mannerisms—strongly suggested that he was, as military men go, a breed apart. It was widely known that he'd declined a promotion to the rank of colonel because he felt that he was not yet worthy—an unusual but admirable decision, I thought. Some of Ivanov's higher-ups, however, resented him. "This truth-seeker is really missed at the nuthouse," a colonel in his division, who'd stained his hands in needless bloodshed, had told me. (Ivanov apparently had interfered with this colonel's dashing ascent to the military Olympus.)

"Does your delicacy get in your way?" I asked Ivanov. "Doesn't the army look at it as a character flaw rather than an asset?"

"I happen to think that courtesy and respect are precisely what the army lacks," he replied. "Rudeness and harshness won't improve discipline. A soldier will respond to kindness sooner than he'll respond to mean or callous treatment. Still, some of our people have grown accustomed to thinking of callousness as asceticism and heartlessness as maintaining order. I'm talking here not only about the army, but about society—you can't separate one from the other. If you look at many of the army's biggest problems, it's easy to see that they're rooted not only in irresponsibility and a lack of professionalism, but quite often in a shortage of kindness. Including the suicides."

I listened raptly as Ivanov continued to talk, but my mind somehow clung to that one word: *suicides*.

The war was full of mindless suicides: two nations, dozens of Soviet soldiers and officers. I wasn't sure which was more absurd, nor was I privy to instances of suicide among the rebels. But even these three cases, I thought, were three too many:

A young soldier received a letter from his girlfriend. In it she told him that she'd finally found the man of her dreams, the man she'd been searching for all her life. After reading the letter, the soldier put it in his breast pocket. Then he picked up his submachine gun, stuck the barrel in his mouth, pointed it toward the sky, and pulled the trigger. With one shot his brains and blood were all over the wall.

A senior lieutenant noticed that a soldier's hair was too long, so he straddled him like a horse and gave him a haircut. He dismounted, made sure that the length of the soldier's hair met military regulations, and shook his index finger at him. The senior lieutenant headed back to his quarters. The soldier took one look at himself in the mirror. Then he took his gun, caught up with the senior lieutenant, and shot him. He felt his pulse to make sure that he was dead. Only then did the soldier kill himself.

A senior lieutenant made a harsh comment to a "grandfather" [army slang for an old-timer] during physical training and assigned him an extra detail. The old-timer took it as an insult. After the training session he went into the officers' building, where he found the senior lieutenant with his buddies. He paused at the doorstep, unclenched his fist, pulled the pin out of a grenade, and threw it at the senior lieutenant. (By now the other officers had all jumped out of the room.) The grenade missed him and exploded above a cot; shrapnel cut up the walls. Realizing that his quarry was still alive, the old-timer threw another grenade at the senior lieutenant, who had just enough time to hurl himself into the hallway with a giant leap. The old-timer decided not to give chase. He went to his room, took out a Makarov pistol, and, pulling the trigger, blew his brains out. As he fell down, the pistol slipped from his hand. For a few seconds he heard the stampede of soldiers' boots. The screen of light in front of him narrowed to a single point, and then flickered out.

"Missing in action?" Ivanov asked me. "Naturally, we've had that, too. And more than once, as a matter of fact. Here, take a look at these lists."

Ivanov handed me a file that contained a pile of papers. I read one after another: surnames, names, patronymics, unit numbers, dates of birth, brief notations. After five minutes my eyes came to a halt, like a stake driven into hard ground, in the middle of the fifth page:

"Private Derevlianiy, Taras Yurievich. Military unit P/P 518884. Gunner. Born 2/9/68, city of Khodorov, Lvov region. Drafted 14th of November at the Yavorov enlistment office of the Lvov region. Ukrainian. Member of VLKSM [Komsomol]. Father: Derevlianiy, Yuri Tarasovich. Missing with weapons since July 2, 1986."

"What's the matter?" Ivanov asked.

"I know this man," I replied.

"Derevlianiy?"

"Yes, Derevlianiy. Moreover, I've talked to him."

"In Afghanistan?"

"In New York."

"Wait one moment. I must get the chief of the special office."

While Ivanov was getting the *osobist*, I had just enough time to begin reading the next entry: "Private Shapovalenko, Yuri Anatolievich. Drafted 3/8/83. High treason."

Just as I had imagined, the *osobist* turned out to be a man of very few words. There was nothing memorable about his face; it was this, apparently, that made him special. He examined me carefully, and in his eyes I could detect a mixture of curiosity and mistrust. I thought that he must have had some trouble deciding how he felt about me; he listened but did not speak.

"Did you see Derevlianiy before or after the declaration of amnesty?" Ivanov asked.

"After."

"I know that you're tired, but I can hardly let you go to sleep without a story about your meeting," Ivanov said. He tossed half a sugar cube into his mug.

The *osobist* took a notepad and a pen out of his chest pocket.

"Very well," I said. "But in return you must tell me in detail about your life, about the division, and about the war. Deal?"

Ivanov smiled. "Deal."

The *osobist* jotted something on his notepad.

5

New York was already melting under the early morning sun. Could a chicken in a broiler be any hotter? It seemed as if the ghosts of this gigantic city's once-luxuriant vegetation, which at the dawn of the last century had been buried under the streets and buildings, were now sighing with fatigue; the spirits of chestnut, mulberry, and oak trees pushed their way through the asphalt. The city couldn't do without air conditioners, which today were straining to keep up with the heat. The sickeningly sweet smells of tar and automobile exhaust hung in the air.

Craig Copetas and I finally reached Freedom House, a small building (at least by American standards) that was the headquarters of a human rights organization by the same name. At ten o'clock today, July 14, 1988, there was to be a press conference with six former Soviet soldiers, all of whom had fought in Afghanistan, been taken prisoner for one reason or another, and then been freed and brought to the United States.

It was only a quarter to ten. After an anxious glance at the air conditioners that stuck out of the windows of Freedom House, we decided to take a couple more turns around the building.

Copetas was the national correspondent for *Regardie's*, a monthly magazine published in Washington, D.C. It had approached *Ogonyok* with a proposal for a two-week exchange of journalists. *Ogonyok* agreed, thus transforming me—temporarily, at least—into a special correspondent for *Regardie's*. I would be flying to Atlanta in a few days to cover the Democratic National Convention for the American magazine. Copetas was to write several articles for *Ogonyok* about *perestroika* as seen through the eyes of an American. To be quite honest, I wasn't as interested in the Democratic National Convention as I was in the possibility of meeting the former Soviet POWs. Before leaving Moscow I'd called Copetas to ask him to arrange a few meetings for me. Thanks to him I was now in New York.

In my breast pocket I carried business cards that identified me as a part-time reporter for *Regardie's*; they helped me in situations where my *Ogonyok* cards would have been useless.

At exactly ten o'clock we crossed the threshold of Freedom House. I signed my name in the visitors' book, and underneath it I wrote "Correspondent of *Regardie's*, Washington, D.C." It was a peculiar feeling, probably resembling the sensation that someone who's had plastic surgery gets when he looks in the mirror for the first time. It seemed to be me, but . . .

Inside Freedom House the journalists were already bustling about, setting up their lights and television equipment. Soon we heard some footsteps, and six young men entered the room: Mansur Aliadinov, Igor Koval'chuk, Mikhola Movchan, Vladimir Romchuk, Khadzhymurat Suleimanov, and Taras Derevlianiy. While they were taking their places behind a long, microphone-studded table, I took several Freedom House brochures from a rack. In one of them I read that Aliadinov, Romchuk, Suleimanov, and Derevlianiy had recently arrived in America, while Koval'chuk and Movchan had already been living here for several years.

"Was that it?" the *osobist* asked me. "Wasn't there any other information about them?"

"Yes, there was," I replied, lighting a cigarette. "As a matter of fact, the numbers of all the regiments, battalions, companies, and platoons in which they served were listed exactly—not just as P/P so-and-so. Much of what we try so desperately to conceal, the Americans know better than the Soviets. If I try to publish some information that we consider top secret, but that appeared in the American press a long time ago, the censor will still cross it out. An obvious question presents itself: once the American people know something about the

Soviet army, why don't the Soviet people have the right to know it, too?"

Our attitude toward the soldiers and officers who were captured in Afghanistan evolved as our outlook on the nature of the war itself changed. At the beginning of the 1980s we were suspicious; the stereotypes of the Stalin era still predominated. I don't know how to sum up our attitude toward the deserters, or toward those who fought on the side of the rebels against their own people, but the inescapable impulse was to hate them. More than once or twice in Afghanistan I was overcome by hatred. But how could one rationalize such hatred when from a political standpoint the war was unofficially acknowledged as a tragic mistake and from a moral standpoint it was recognized as evil? Toward the mid-1980s, as new moral and ethical ideals came to shape public opinion, hatred was on the verge of becoming an alien emotion. Its targets understood the changing climate; so did those who promoted hatred and those who denounced it as a relic of the older time. The latter point of view gained an official victory in July 1988, when A. Y. Sukharev, the general procurator of the USSR, declared amnesty for all Soviet prisoners of war—regardless of what they had done.

And yet I still haven't found a simple answer to the question of how we should view someone who decided to end the war not on February 15, 1989, but in, say, 1982 by signing his own separate peace treaty. Indeed, it seems impossible to answer the question without saying, "On the one hand . . ., but on the other hand . . ." Maybe there is no simple answer.

"The press conference started," I said. "Romchuk spoke first. He thanked the U.S. government for granting him political asylum and the president of the United States for helping to secure his freedom. There were many kind words about Freedom House and Liudmila Thorn and about the organizations of Russian and Ukrainian immigrants that had taken care of the POWs. Special thanks were given to the mujahedin. Then a frail young man took the floor. It was Movchan."

Movchan spoke in Russian, but every now and then he borrowed words or phrases from English. He had a strong Ukrainian accent.

"It's nice to see that the USSR is finally concerned about its own people," he said. "Naturally, we aren't against the declaration of amnesty. But what guarantees does it offer? So far there are none. *Glasnost* hasn't yet reached the point where all questions can be openly discussed in the press. What will happen to us if we return and there's another change in policy toward deserters? We surely won't have the right to independent legal counsel, and we won't be able to write to the press to stand up for ourselves and our causes.

"A lot has been written about us lately in the USSR, as well as about Ryzhkov.* But we feel that this isn't enough. We hear nothing about our comrades who returned to the USSR from London. Ten or so people returned from Switzerland, not just the two who took part in the Moscow press conference."

Movchan took out a cigarette and lit it.

"There is little *glasnost* regarding Afghanistan. And even though the war has been unofficially acknowledged as a mistake, the press still continues to write about the noble behavior and heroic acts of Soviet soldiers."

He looked at the audience and stubbed out his cigarette.

"I don't want to insult the men who sacrificed their lives in Afghanistan. But I just can't understand what it was all for, or who needed it. . . .

"I'm concerned that the other side of the war is not getting coverage. I'm referring to the atrocities committed by our troops in Afghanistan. Such atrocities did take place; each one of us can testify to them. We're not denying that there was brutality in the treatment of Soviet POWs by the mujahedin. But as far as my particular case is concerned, I had a pretty nice life with the rebels. The Soviet press, however, does not write about the fact that Soviet deserters were bombed. Yes, even that would happen. So if there is talk of truth, it must be complete. Soviet newspapers write about prisoners of war, but only their own. It would be interesting to find out about the conditions that captured rebels live in.

*Nikolai Ryzhkov, a former Soviet POW, had been brought to the United States but voluntarily returned to the USSR before the 1988 declaration of amnesty. Even though he'd been guaranteed freedom upon his return by representatives of the Soviet consulate in New York, Ryzhkov found himself sentenced to twelve years in prison shortly after he arrived home.

"As for the International Committee for the Liberation of Soviet Prisoners of War, we have nothing against it. We are concerned only that Andronov is one of its members, especially considering his past. If this committee is pursuing such high-minded goals, why isn't he worried about the captured mujahedin?"

Igor Koval'chuk, a robust, black-haired fellow with a fierce glare, took the microphone in his hand and said that he was against the idea of bringing the mothers of Soviet POWs to the United States so that they could visit their sons. This, he said, would resemble moral blackmail.

At this moment Andronov shouted that the international committee stood for the liberation of Soviet POWs not only from Afghanistan but from America as well.

"I am Ukrainian," Movchan replied. "Among us there is a Tatar, as well as men of other nationalities. Each one of us has his own nationality. Don't try to make all of us fit into the same pattern."

Koval'chuk interrupted him.

"Mr. Andronov," he said, "you have claimed that I was liberated with the help of the British MI-6 service. That's a lie. The Soviets threw bombs on me rather than free me. They bombed the whole area. It was the rebels who hid me."

As I listened to Koval'chuk I got to thinking. If you joined the mujahedin of your own accord, surely the last thing you wanted was to be "liberated." His logic was a bit lame.

Koval'chuk passed the microphone to Aliadinov.

"It's hard for me to forget the attitude of the USSR toward prisoners of war during the 1940s," Aliadinov said. "And besides, the whole idea of granting amnesty to deserters seems strange. I don't think a single country has ever done that. What kind of lesson will this teach future generations of draftees? It will lead to a weakening of the army. Every army is built upon discipline. Statements of this sort are capable of wiping out discipline at the root. Right now they're pardoning us, but later they'll inevitably decide to correct their mistake. And then we'll get punished anyway. I'm not a deserter myself, but this problem really concerns me."

Suleimanov broke in. "Let me have the mike," he said in a somewhat toneless voice. "Here is my opinion. We sat in captivity for more than five years. We received no aid whatever from the Soviet

Union. They didn't even think about us. Now they're gathering together all the prisoners of war. Once they get them together, they'll definitely come up with a reason to put them on trial."

"Don't worry," said someone in the audience. It was Andronov.

Movchan spoke next. There was more than a trace of passion in his voice, which was trembling now.

"I have lived in America for four years," he said. "I certainly don't consider it an ideal country. It's far from that. But I've come to realize here what it means to be free and to have the ability to fight for your rights and opinions. I don't see this in the Soviet Union. And until they get it there, there will be nothing for us in the USSR. I'm not a man who needs amnesty. I did not betray anyone or anything. I simply came to the conclusion that the war in Afghanistan is an unfair war."

"I have no faith!" Romchuk exclaimed. "I'm willing to explain why. There have already been many changes in the USSR. But until the system itself changes, I will have no faith in the present reorganization. Let's suppose I do come back. But what if a year after my return Gorbachev is out of the picture and his whole *perestroika* no longer exists? What will happen then? Life will return to its old course. I have said all I have to say."

The atmosphere in the room had become tense, heated. The men interrupted one another. Thorn barely had time to translate.

Koval'chuk stood up. His eyes were bloodshot. The hair on his temples was damp with perspiration. He cracked the joints of his fingers nervously and grasped the microphone.

"I have been given amnesty now," Koval'chuk said. "What for? For honestly serving my two years and choosing the country in which I want to live? But what about the lie the system used to send us off to war? We were told that we were going to fight Americans. Americans? All right. If it has to be Americans, we'll fight Americans. And each one of us was thinking, We'll show these guys what it's like to deal with the Soviet army! But now I'm asking you, what about the million guys like me who believed this lie? And what about the murdered Afghan children? I've killed them myself and know what it's like. I was given orders. What could I do when I had orders like that?"

"You killed children?" Andronov asked with feigned amazement.

"Fine!" Koval'chuk shouted. "Don't believe me if you don't want to. Let's say I didn't. But imagine an officer giving an order to someone like me. The punishment for failing to follow orders is the disciplinary battalion."

"You should have shot the officer," Andronov said.

The American journalists followed the discussion with great interest. They were watching Soviets who, at least for the moment, were on opposite sides of the table.

"You there," Koval'chuk said, pointing to Andronov. "You think you have a lot of guts? *You* should have shot the officer. Don't give me that! If you have so much guts, why don't you go and shoot him? I'm grateful to Gorbachev for granting us amnesty. But I'm convinced that I've been deceived. And a million other people were deceived along with me. The Afghans were deceived. And *I* am granted amnesty? *I* am the one who should be granting amnesty—to you and to the Soviet government of that time."

Derevlianiy spoke. He spoke softly and hesitantly. He looked up at the audience only once or twice.

"I completely agree with everything that has been said before me," he said. (At least you learned something in your Komsomol meetings, buddy, I thought to myself. It's permanently ingrained in you.) "Perhaps I could believe in the amnesty, but I've already lived here in America for three months. I like it here very much."

The words struck me as blatant, somehow very childish, fawning on his part. I couldn't help but cringe. This, I thought, was how a homeless puppy tries to win over someone who's picked him up off the street on a cold, rainy day.

Derevlianiy raised his head, tossed back his hair, and continued. "The Americans took me in and gave me work. I'm going to study here. There"—for some reason he nodded toward the far corner of the conference room—"I wouldn't have this opportunity."

Once again I silently asked him: But why?

Derevlianiy's voice suddenly grew stronger.

"I don't want to go back home," he said. "How will people treat me if I come back? 'He ran away and now he's run back,' they'll say. 'He's a traitor.' I saw children murdered in Afghanistan, too. I have no need for amnesty. I'm going to live in America. I'm renouncing my Soviet citizenship!"

He almost shouted these last words.

Aliadinov concluded the press conference with a statement. One of the Soviet diplomats then took the floor to explain some of General Procurator Sukharev's suggestions. As soon as he finished, everyone stood up, stretched their legs, and put their tape recorders back in their pockets.

"Was Derevlianiy the only one who renounced his Soviet citizenship?" Ivanov asked me.

"Yes, he was the only one at the press conference who did," I replied. "As early as February 1988 the *New York Times* mentioned the publication of his 'Address to the Soviet Occupation Troops in Afghanistan.' Derevlianiy was urging soldiers to refuse to serve in Afghanistan. I remember looking at Derevlianiy then and trying to figure out why we were fighting so hard for these guys when they themselves didn't really seem to want to return all that much."

By the time I finished my story, night had stolen into the mountains and stretched its invisible blinds over the windows of the building. The howitzer still growled in the distance like an angry guard dog.

After returning to the hotel, I couldn't fall asleep. I lay there for a long time, finishing off one cigarette after another as I thought about the events, meetings, and conversations of the last few days.

The soldiers who have emerged from captivity and returned to the Soviet Union—especially those who made an interim stop somewhere in the West—have encountered all kinds of reactions back home. Once, while addressing a group of Afghan veterans, I made the point that it was wrong to condemn all prisoners of war indiscriminately. It was necessary, I said, to look at each case separately. There was whistling [the Russian equivalent of booing] from every corner of the room. I could understand why.

On another occasion, while addressing a meeting of Moscow's creative intelligentsia, I reiterated the idea. There were cries of indignation.

Igor Morosov fought in the same area of Afghanistan as Igor Koval'chuk and later wrote a now-famous song about the war ("We are leaving, leaving, leaving . . ."). He told me the story of how, in the early days of the war, his company had been ordered to execute a deserter who'd killed two Soviet soldiers during his escape. They hadn't been able to find him to carry out the order. "That guy is now hanging around in the States somewhere," Morosov said, glancing at his hands. "If he dares to come back here, I'll kill him, regardless of any amnesty." In May 1989, during a concert at the Moscow Variety Theatre, Morosov repeated the same words. His audience responded with an ovation.

The memory of the applause lulled me to sleep.

The howitzers woke me up.

6

After my first hot breakfast in days, I went to the first aid station to have a word with Misha Grigoriev, the chief of Jabal os Siraj's mobile epidemiological laboratory. He'd promised to give me a few water-purification tablets.

Two foil-covered corpses were lying on the ground in front of the first aid station. Bandages had been wrapped around the foil so it wouldn't be ripped away by the mountain wind.

The foil shimmered under the bright morning sun, its metallic gleam masking its grim purpose. The corpses of Sergeant Kiper and Private Zhabraev now resembled huge, silvery Christmas-tree ornaments. Just two hours ago the men had been driving down the Bagram–Jabal os Siraj road with Lieutenant Goriachev. Their MT-LB had almost reached the division's command post when it was caught in the cross fire between two rebel detachments. Zhabraev, the driver, got a bullet through the head. The MT-LB spun around on the ice and turned over. Kiper didn't make it. Goriachev was brought to the hospital in Pul-i-Khumri. He was unconscious, but the doctors hoped he would survive.

"He'll pull through," Grigoriev said. "He's the strong and healthy type."

Goriachev didn't pull through, however. He died twenty-four hours later, never regaining consciousness. In a few days, the death notice would reach his next of kin in the Soviet Union.

Grigoriev's eyes narrowed as he nodded toward the foil-covered bodies and said, "I hope they'll be the last ones in this war."

Once again, however, he was mistaken.

Every time I visited the medical battalion in Bagram I was reminded of July 1986, when I saw a soldier whose skin had been completely charred after his helicopter was shot down. No one could survive such extensive burns, they said, but somehow he clung to life. Every two hours he was given a shot of morphine. He told the nurse, who never left his side, that he didn't regret coming to Afghanistan. He made it through the day, but spent the night in the morgue.

I later spoke to the soldier's wife in Leningrad. "If Petenka hadn't gone to Afghanistan," she said, "he would have found some other way of committing suicide."

Misha Grigoriev's brother, a military doctor in Bagram, didn't know about the incident; it had been before his time. We spoke in the mobile operating room.

"About thirteen thousand patients pass through this medical battalion in a year," he said. "The worst of it was in 1984 and 1985. In 1988 we did somewhere around fifty amputations; in 1985 we did two hundred and sixty-four. Naturally, these numbers don't include the Afghan wounded."

Grigoriev took out some notebooks, flipped through them, and spread his hands in a gesture of helplessness.

"It hit us hard, especially considering that we didn't—and still don't have—a single piece of factory-made medical equipment or a conventional operating room. I had to build everything with my bare hands. Lately we've been transporting injured soldiers to Kabul mainly in armored carriers and KamAZs; some of them sit, others lie down. The Rescuers [planes specially equipped for transporting wounded soldiers] have been reluctant to fly out here. I know that there's an excellent operating room at the KamAZ base. There are only two such operating rooms in our entire armed forces—I saw pictures of them. One of them was sent to the Turkestan Military District for exercises, but they wouldn't send it to war. They were afraid that we'd wreck it. Isn't that absurd? We've suggested an entirely new system for setting up a first aid station and a medical battalion in wartime conditions, but it's been ignored by our command.

"For nearly fifty years we prepared for a global war, but in

Afghanistan we've had to conduct small-scale warfare. We weren't prepared for it at all. If we can't make it in a small-scale war, how can we possibly handle a big war?

"Until 1987 all of the wounded were evacuated by helicopter to the hospital in Kabul. I couldn't have been happier. But the arrival of Stinger missiles put an end to our massive use of choppers. So we're forced to cram the injured into armored carriers—fifteen in each one—and send them down the local roads to Kabul.

"All of our medicine comes to us in glass containers. How am I supposed to take the stuff into the mountains? Everything will be shattered. Even the rebels pack their medicine in plastic; it's both convenient and compact. Meanwhile, we're doing things as they were done in World War II."

Grigoriev opened the door. A stiff breeze blew into the operating room, bringing with it the smell of burning paper. Gray ashes drifted onto the floor.

"We're burning letters," Grigoriev explained. "Nearly everyone has returned to the USSR, but the mail keeps coming. The rest of us are leaving, too, and I don't know how these guys will make it here without us." He nodded toward an Afghan air force pilot who was walking along the tree-lined lane. "They haven't learned anything from us. It's a tragedy! The other day I showed their doctor a triple tooth hook, and he had no idea what the thing was. Recently they had someone here who'd been shot through the stomach; there was a hole where the bullet went in and another where it came out. The Afghan surgeon took out some regular black sewing thread—the kind I use to mend my pants—and went to work stitching the wounds. And that was it!

"Another time they brought us a soldier with a bullet lodged in his abdominal cavity. His stomach was puffed out like a drum. When I operated on him I discovered that they'd patched up the hole in the poor guy's intestine with plaster."

A surgeon's assistant popped into the room, took a pile of bottles from the night table, and left as suddenly as he'd entered. His white coat dissolved into the darkness.

"Still, my conscience is clean before the Afghans," Grigoriev said thoughtfully. "And before me. I *healed* people. To the extent that it was possible, I tried to save them. In just a few weeks I won't be here anymore. I don't know if I should be laughing or crying. I have a feeling that I'm going to the Soviet Union to live out the rest of my days. I have given all of myself here. There will never be anything like this in the Soviet Union. Maybe I don't even need any more of this, I don't know. But who will I be when I return?"

He was silent for a minute. He wound his wristwatch, even though he'd wound it just thirty minutes before.

"I'm very afraid of coming back," he whispered to me. "Very afraid."

I could see the fear in his eyes. The kind of fear that one has of darkness in childhood, of failure in middle age, and of damp earth in old age.

The Grigoriev brother in Jabal os Siraj, however, looked calmly toward the future. He gave me a whole handful of water-purification pills, each the size of a *pyatak* [a five-kopeck coin that's slightly larger than a quarter]. He wanted me to keep what I had: my life. "That's all we really need," he said.

I thought back to Baghlan at six o'clock in the morning on a Sunday in April 1987.

The battle had been joined between Eighth and Ninth streets. Gayur's men were putting up a desperate fight. Our division had kept them tightly surrounded for more than two weeks but had so far been unable to destroy them. The operator of the *dukhi*'s grenade launcher had scored a bull's-eye by hitting one of our men from a distance of three hundred meters. Everything that remained of the soldier could have fit into the cartridge case of a DShK machine gun.

None of the usual expressions—"he died," "he was killed," "he passed away," "he gave up the ghost"—applied in this case. There was nobody left to talk about and nothing left to describe.

7

Colonel Sergei Antonenko had fought in Afghanistan for twenty-one months. For a long time he'd been the commander of the Jabal regiment, but in the fall of 1988 he had become the deputy commander of the division.

Although the division's forces were stretched along the Kabul road almost up to the Salang Tunnel, Antonenko remained chiefly in his former regiment's zone of responsibility. He knew the area like the back of his hand.

Antonenko was a tall, broad-shouldered man. He couldn't have been more than forty years old. He was in superb shape and cut a striking figure in his uniform. His gray eyes stared savagely from beneath his heavy brow, which was draped with a thatch of wheat-colored hair. His angular face was divided into perfect halves by the ridge of an aristocratic nose. There was the barest hint of blush on his dark, clean-shaven cheeks, and a golden stripe of a mustache highlighted his mouth with a short but forceful stroke. A deep dimple cleaved his chin, which took on a metallic gleam in the sun.

"Here's a man the whole army should take after!" someone whispered. I felt warm breath on my frozen ear, but when I turned around there was no one behind me.

Antonenko spat out his cigarette butt with a scowl.

"Lately we have really been buddy-buddy with the *dukhi*," he told me quietly. "You could say that we're best friends, but you can't count on that. The East is a dark and cunning business. They say one thing, think another, and do something else entirely. That's why we're fortifying our route as much as possible. Just a few days ago two battalions arrived—airborne troopers and motorized infantry. Right now we're positioning people at the posts. It's a little crowded, of course, but it makes living and fighting possible. I'm not concerned about North Salang; the *Ismalit* have straddled the road there. Here, at the southern approaches to the tunnel, it's more complicated. It's here that the Ahmad Shah's heavy forces are concentrated, and Basir's group alone numbers more than four hundred bayonets. They believe that we'll be engaging in combat here in the near future. To the extent that I can, however, I'm trying to pacify Basir and the other commanders. If you guarantee that we can safely withdraw our troops through the Salang Tunnel, I told them, we won't fortify the road. I even suggested that we sign a treaty: they would promise to guard the road from other rebel detachments and to let the columns of regular Afghan troops pass through, and we would promise to refrain from combat. But they refused, saying that a Muslim's spoken word is law. At any rate, we'll have to see. Would you like a smoke?"

"What kind do you have?" I asked.

"We've got Yava. How about you?"

"We've got Lejeros, the last of the Kabul stock." As I took out an open pack, Battalion Commander Abramov came up to us.

"*Estas cigarros!*" Abramov exclaimed. "*Il madre mia!* May I take one?"

"Please do," I said. "But why am I all of a sudden hearing Spanish at the approaches to Salang?"

"What do you mean, why?" Abramov asked with a smile. "From Cuba, naturally. I had to serve my time there, too. This is my twentieth month here. Cuba was a bright spot in my life, seventy-three to seventy-five . . . the golden years. Have you gone swimming there too?"

"No, I haven't had the chance," I replied. "But I spent a whole day in an airport there once. I drank five daiquiris and flew somewhere else."

"Havana-mamma!" Abramov cried. He took a long drag on his

One of the book's
heroes, Sergeant
Dzhabarov.

The encirclement of Ortabulaki's camp near South Baghlan.
All photographs © Artyom Borovik.

Jalalabad. Senior Lieutenant Nikolai Zherelin of the Special Forces, ready to go out on an ambush mission.

Captain Zakharov at an ambush.

Lieutenant General Boris Gromov, Commander of the Fortieth Army, at his Kabul residence.

Soviet vice-consul Podchitshaev says good-bye to his dog and villa in Kabul.

Soviet troops withdrawing along the Salang Pass in February 1989.

The commander of the Afghan battalion at Salang. The withdrawal of Soviet troops displeased him.

The Salang Pass. Soldiers attached toy parachutes to the antennas of their vehicles. This was out of superstition, so that their cars would not be swept away in an avalanche.

Division Commander
Colonel Ruzliaev.

Occasionally at Salang soldiers had to push their vehicles by hand.

Mikhail Kozhukov, a *Komsomolskaya* correspondent, and battalion commander
Ushakov at the Soviet-Afghan border, February 1989.

Captain Kozlov (*above*), Jalalabad
Special Forces.

A military pilot (*at right*) at the Bagram
air base before embarking on a mission.
Each star on the plane signifies ten
military missions.

An Afghan man, the father of a downed pilot.

A captive mujahedin from Ortabulaki's camp. South Baghlan, spring of 1987.

Exhausted soldiers, early morning.

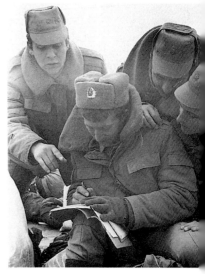

A letter home.

Soviet vehicles burning after a grenade attack. Soviet troop withdrawal, February 1989.

February 15, 1989, the day the war ended. The photograph was taken from the bridge over the Amu Darya River, which marks the border between Afghanistan and the Soviet Union.

The Soviet-Afghan border on the morning of February 15.

The war is over!

The body of the last Soviet soldier killed in Afghanistan. His name was Igor Liakhovich.

cigarette. "All right, buddies, time for me to go. I've got to go around the posts."

Antonenko waved to him as he left. Then he turned to me and said, "Abramov's battalion is stretched out for thirty-seven kilometers along the route; there are seventeen sentry posts, not counting the mobile posts. Something is always happening somewhere."

"So far we haven't seen any regular Afghan troops along this route, and it's a strategic road," I said. "The division will go north in a couple of weeks. Who will control the road?"

"That's the whole problem," Antonenko replied. He brushed some tiny flakes of tobacco from his mustache with the tip of his index finger. "The *dukhi* won't allow the greens anywhere near the road."

"Once we're gone, will the rebels try to take over our posts?"

"How would I know? In principle, they don't really need to. They feel quite comfortable in their *kishlaks*. All the bands here are made up of the local male population. All the leaders also come from these parts."

"Are you referring to Basir?"

"Yes, I'm referring to Basir, and to Malagaus and the others. I recently met with Malagaus. When I greeted him, I tried to touch my right cheek to his right cheek—an Afghan custom to show special respect for someone. But he stopped me. He took me aside, away from his guard, and said, 'Commander, don't do that. You are undermining my authority in the eyes of my men. You and I are living like neighbors—you at your post, I in my native *kishlak*. But we haven't made any deals with you.' And that's exactly how he put it. Arrogant bastards."

Suddenly an armored carrier rushed by, splashing us from head to toe with muddy water.

"Scum!" Antonenko hissed angrily. He brushed the mud off his *bushlat*. "They think they own the place."

"What is Basir like?" I asked as I stepped to the side of the road. An empty KamAZ was heading toward us at full speed, lurching up and down with each bump and hollow in the road.

"He's a wise man, that Basir," Antonenko replied, smiling with the corner of his mouth. "The local folks love him and respect him. And are scared of him, of course. He always wears an American army jacket and dark sunglasses. He knows everything about the Soviet Union. One time he asked me, 'Commander, how are things in Armenia?' "

"Could I meet him?"

"It's out of the question. He talks only to people whom he already has checked out and trusts, namely Abramov and me. When I go to negotiate with him, I'm not even allowed to take a new interpreter with me. A strange face will immediately make him suspicious, and he will simply not come."

"Still, ask him. What if he does agree? Tell Basir that I've had the opportunity to meet not only with the field commanders of the rebels, but with Gailani as well."

"You and Gailani?" Antonenko squinted in surprise. His cigarette drooped from his lip.

8

Gray light oozed through the dirty, overcast sky. People were going through the brightly decorated shops, buying presents for one another, and returning home with packages wrapped in crinkly multicolored paper. The air smelled of an approaching Christmas.

You could hear the laughter of children and the clink of glasses everywhere. The music of the Christmas season (which is sometimes merrier than Christmas itself) had taken over England. Pedestrians moved with a lilt in their step.

Sayed Ahmad Gailani, the leader of the National Islamic Front of Afghanistan, had come to London to visit his family for the holiday.

The organization, which had been founded in 1978, was headquartered in Peshawar, with branches in Quetta, Miram Shah, Chaman, and Parachinar. It had a whole flock of committees—committees on military issues, recruitment of new members, counterespionage, and refugees, for example, as well as committees on culture, communications, and finance.

As early as 1978, the National Islamic Front had declared the following goals: a holy war against infidels and foreign aggressors, the deposition of the current regime, and the establishment of a republican system of government based on Islam and nationalism.

The organization was known for its close ties to Mohammed

Zahir Shah, the former king of Afghanistan, and was especially strong in the Afghan provinces of Kabul, Nangarhar, Paktika, and Paktia. Until recently it had seventy-five detachments and other units in Afghanistan, and its total membership came to twenty-seven hundred well-armed fighting men.

Gailani, who carries the title of *pir* [His Supreme Holiness], was born in 1931 to a family of *khasrat-nakib*. He received a solid education in his youth and learned to speak four languages. His power derives not only from his religious authority and the sizable military force under his command, but also from his family's impressive financial holdings.

For the past nine years, Gailani's armed detachments had proved quite an annoyance to both the Afghan government troops and the Soviet Fortieth Army. It wasn't difficult to understand Gailani's opinion of the USSR and the PDPA—especially the Afghan state security services. Since the late 1970s, many friends and comrades in arms had died at their hands.

I entered his apartment house, a luxurious multistory building across from Hyde Park. A gray-haired doorman greeted me in the hall with a slight bow. A butler led me to the elevator; he smelled of Drakkar, an expensive men's cologne. The doors opened noiselessly. I stepped in, pressed a button, and sped upward.

Neither the doorman nor the butler had uttered a word, yet it somehow seemed as if both had known me for a long time. As I stepped out of the elevator, I saw a dark silhouette framed in a doorway. The silhouette vanished, and I entered a well-lit apartment.

From behind me came a woman's calm voice. "Good afternoon. Please come with me."

It was Fatima, Gailani's daughter. I'd seen her several times on American television, but she was even more beautiful in real life.

Fatima's brows were lightly angled, like a gull's wings, and when she spoke they arched ever so slightly. Her widely spaced eyes—a sign of talent, they say—were the color of a nighttime ocean wave. Her thick black hair, which was bound tightly at the back of her head, fell loose down her slender back. Tiny blue veins showed through the thin skin of her temples, tinting them with just a hint of dark undertones. The refined line of her nose gave the chiseled features of her young face a classical completeness.

As I looked at Fatima, who like the rest of her family was believed to be a descendant of the prophet Muhammad, I thought of one of our generals, who'd told me in confidence that Fatima had the sympathies of Najibullah.

"Why are you staring like that?" she said, smiling at me. "Please, I urge you to come. Father is expecting you."

In a few moments she was introducing me to Gailani.

"Father," she said, "this is our guest."

Gailani, who was sitting in an armchair that faced away from us, half turned his head toward me. Instantly I was burned by the glare of his glittering brown eyes. His gray hair was brushed back, revealing the thin, shallow lines of his high forehead.

The leader of the National Islamic Front rose up from his chair and let me shake his wide, warm hand.

"Please, sit down," he said in English, in a soft baritone. "I will speak in my native language, and Fatima will translate."

"Thank you," I said as I sat down on the couch next to his chair. "As you wish."

"I know that you're from *Ogonyok*," he said. "I once spoke to two Soviet journalists in Pakistan, but what wound up in print was a severe distortion of our conversation."

"I'll try to be as accurate as possible."

"We'll see," Gailani said with a smile. "Frankly, I still can't quite believe in your *glasnost*. Would you care for some tea? Coffee?"

Fatima beckoned a maid, who was dressed in native Afghan clothes.

"Coffee, if I may," I replied.

"Tea for me," Gailani said, turning to the maid. She quickly disappeared through the doorway.

The room in which we sat was spacious and well appointed. Soft light filtered through the ash-gray curtains. I noticed a lot of dictionaries on the bookshelves.

"I was told that your son is also in London now," I said to Gailani. "Would it be possible for me to meet him today?"

"No, unfortunately," Fatima replied. "I tried to find him so that you could meet, but nothing came of it."

"The problem is that my son was seriously injured in Afghanistan," Gailani explained. "At the moment he's with the doctors. It's imperative that he get better, so that he can return. I regret that he isn't with us right now."

"Mr. Gailani," I asked, "have you had the opportunity during the war to visit Afghanistan yourself?"

"No," he replied. "My people are there, and that's enough. One time I was planning a trip to Afghanistan, but some religious leaders whom I trust a great deal advised me not to go. If I went there, they said, it would immediately become widely known and expose the area to shelling, shooting, and other attacks. Why take this unnecessary risk? My son and my nephews are fighting in Afghanistan. That's quite enough."

"Did you come to London from Pakistan?"

"Yes, from Peshawar," Gailani replied, nodding his head gracefully.

"Have you lived in Pakistan since 1978?"

"Yes. I was forced to leave Afghanistan in October of that year, after the communist coup. We were unhappy with the course of events there, however, and with the fact that Taraki had come to power. I feel that Daoud's regime was also forced on the people. I tried to convince Daoud to follow our path. But then there was a communist coup, and right away it became clear that the new regime was hostile to the Afghan people and their traditions. A rebellion against such a regime was inevitable. I had two alternatives: to remain there and share the fate of the relatives of Sibghatullah Mujaddidi [the leader of a moderate faction of the Afghan armed opposition] or to leave the country and continue fighting against the regime. I chose the latter."

The maid reentered the room and silently placed a tray of coffee, tea, and cups on the magazine table. Fatima poured tea for her father. I reached for the coffee pot, but she gently pushed my hand away. "Allow me," she said with a smile.

"So," Gailani said, concluding his thoughts, "we began the struggle even before the invasion of Soviet troops."

The aromas of freshly brewed green tea and strong coffee filled the room.

"If you're studying Afghanistan, you ought to be switching to tea," Gailani remarked.

"But since we're in England now, coffee is permissible," I replied. "How do you feel about the former king of Afghanistan?"

"We were very happy with his rule, especially during the final years, which are now known as the ten years of democracy. It was during this period that a democratic constitution was written and parliamentary elections were held. The country was evolving into a full-fledged democracy. While the king was in power, a legislative process was set up to create a multiparty system in Afghanistan. But then, as I mentioned, Daoud's coup took place. You know, I'm convinced that it was the first step on the path that eventually led to Taraki's coup and the military invasion. It's very sad that Afghanistan suffered this fate. Everyone should have treated democracy very cautiously."

"Whom in particular do you blame for the tragedy that's been killing Afghanistan for the last nine years?" I asked. I signaled to Fatima with my eyes to pour me some more coffee.

Gailani paused to think, taking a large sip of tea. Then, slightly arching his brows, he answered. There was a slight tremor in his voice.

"We are not so naive and rancorous as to blame the Soviet people," he said. "You had no idea about the oncoming decision to send troops into my country. But the people in power made a terrible mistake, which caused a great tragedy. . . . You must understand that we allowed our officers to go to the Soviet Union and study at your military academies, which meant that we trusted your government. But the Soviet Union betrayed our trust. And we're still suffering from that betrayal, reaping its bitter fruit."

Gailani put his cup on the table and stared into it for a long time, his lips pressed lightly together.

"You wanted to spare your troops, and you evaded direct confrontations on the battlefield. But later you killed off peasants in the *kishlaks*. . . . Today I'm not ashamed to thank the Americans for their military and monetary assistance. We were forced to accept it so that we could defend ourselves against a modern army. But everybody should remember that if anyone attempts to establish control over Afghanistan, we will fight him the same way we fought you."

He paused for a moment, then said, "Would you like to smoke? Please do, I don't mind."

"And you, Fatima?" I asked.

"Of course, not at all," she replied.

"The mothers of Soviet soldiers who were captured have waited for years for their sons to return," I said to Gailani. "How much longer will they have to wait?"

"The problem is that most of the captured mujahedin have been shot already," Gailani said, pausing as he fell silent once again. "If you tell me how to bring them back to life, perhaps I could answer your question. We need to wait and see how everything will turn out in Afghanistan. I can assure you that your soldiers' lives will be safe. No one wishes to take his anger out on them today. . . . You must understand that a terrible violation of my country has taken place. A whole generation grew up knowing nothing besides the war. All they know how to do is fight. Think of the beautiful Afghan rugs for which my country is famous. Even as recently as ten years ago, people embroidered them with pyramids and camels. But today there are only tanks, military planes, and bombers. This is what happened to my country. Great numbers of educated people, who were the true bearers of the Afghan culture, have been killed or have been forced to leave the country. Those who left have to be brought back, but to where? To a half-ruined country? It's imperative to rebuild Afghanistan, and we're hoping to receive assistance—yours among others. We have to teach the people how to live in peacetime all over again, to teach them the meaning of democracy. And that will take decades."

Gailani spoke as if to himself, looking past Fatima and me. Suddenly he switched to English.

"I can't understand—and I return to this question again and again—how such a great country could trust the promises and assurances of a few men. How could it allow itself to be led into war without weighing all the pros and cons beforehand? Aren't policy decisions based on real information rather than on promises? Here, take a look at him."

Gailani pointed to a boy of about fifteen who'd quietly entered the room. He wore a flowing shirt that reached almost to his knees and wide, light-colored pants. As the boy came closer, I saw his disfigured face.

Fatima, making room for the boy to sit down, moved over on the couch. "His whole family was destroyed," she said.

"But I doubt that you could explain," Gailani said, rising to his feet, "what made that necessary."

Then the four of us—the boy, Fatima, Gailani, and I—slowly made our way to the front door.

Gailani lifted his eyes as if he were following the flight of a disappearing butterfly. "You have come to see us at a difficult hour," he said. "That is so. But every hour on earth, be it bitter or sweet, is great in its own way. Farewell."

I went outside and walked slowly past the Hyde Park Towers. I felt a weariness in my body, as if I'd just run a great distance. The evening descended over London like a black umbrella. Nothing extraordinary had happened on that chilly pre-Christmas day; I could still hear the laughter of children in the parks and the ringing of glasses in the restaurants.

But I realized I'd aged a whole year.

9

"**I** wish you all the best," I said to Antonenko as I shook his hand heartily.

"We aren't parting for long," he said, hiding a smile behind his mustache. "We'll meet again in Salang."

The driver pressed the accelerator and our armored carrier pushed up the mountain with a roar. If the roads weren't too congested, we would be in Salang in five hours or so.

Our APC slowly but confidently climbed the icy road. The clouds, which had seemed beyond reach just two hours ago, now floated serenely to our left and right. The light of the January sun barely broke through them. The snow was now everywhere: it blanketed the road, swirled in the air, accumulated on the cliffs, fell between your collar and neck, and dimmed the taillights that stretched along the road ahead in an endless dotted line. Millions of tons of it lay silent on the mountains, threatening the retreating army with avalanches.

The soldiers clung in bunches to the tops of the military transports and armored carriers, which had been jam-packed with all kinds of stuff wrapped in blankets and hidden behind mattresses. The men's woolen caps were pulled down to their noses. The higher we went the harder our lungs worked, but they still couldn't draw in enough oxygen. The engines of the trucks roared with all their might, but every hundred meters made our slow ascent even slower. Our lighters and matches turned stubborn in the rarefied air; you needed half a matchbox just to light one cigarette. The four-kilometer altitude made your head spin a little and your legs feel weak.

The sentry posts along the winding road flashed by us one after another. Many sat behind rows of barbed wire that had been strung with empty cans. The cans jangled in the wind, sending echoes deep into the surrounding mountains.

From time to time we stopped at one of the posts for a little food and drink. The vodka warmed our blood, improved our mood, and dampened the feeling of impending danger. In these parts it was easier to travel when you could travel without fear, and a shot or two of vodka seemed to lift a ton of weight from your shoulders. Sometimes we were invited to watch a Bruce Lee or Sylvester Stallone movie on videotape. We'd see the beginning of the film at one post, the middle at another, the end at the next.

Here and there we sped by thin, naked trees that stuck out of the rocky soil like the bony hands of dead men, their frozen fingers spread wide apart. High up in the snows and solitude of the mountains, we could barely make out the mobile posts through the blizzard. They had peculiar names: The Swallow's Nest, Mars, The Moon, The Pearl, and The Dream. The higher and the more remote the post, apparently, the more romantic its name.

Imperceptibly the sun turned into the moon. It was full tonight and looked like a white bullet hole in the black shield of the sky. It was time to look for a place to spend the night.

"See those lights over there?" the driver shouted to me.

Looking through the windshield of the carrier, I nodded.

"That's the Fifty-third Post. You can spend the night there. I'm going to keep pushing on toward the tunnel."

He pressed on the accelerator and the carrier moved forward at a livelier pace.

In five minutes we said good-bye. I hopped off the carrier and walked down a narrow path toward my dimly lit destination.

The post was sunk in the snows of the gorge, surrounded by mountains whose peaks dissolved into the darkness.

The roar of the APC gradually grew fainter, and I felt the silence slowly descending on the earth. Candle bombs hung motionless in the sky, like faraway fireflies.

The post was dirty and untidy, in the war style, and when I opened the creaky door a damp, sweet odor hit my nostrils. A wireless radio crackled in the corner of a dark hallway. The man on duty was sitting near the radio on a stool. He'd been warming his hands over a can of burning diesel fuel, and his palms were black with soot. Specks and streaks of light chased after one another on the hallway walls.

"Who are you here to see?" the man asked, raising his inflamed eyes toward me.

"One of the officers," I replied.

"Battalion Commander Ushakov is right there, behind that door," he said, rubbing his hands above the fire.

Suddenly the door flew open and I saw a big, bony, middle-aged man. His entire body—stooped shoulders, sunken cheeks, creased forehead, bloodshot eyes—spoke of a man suffering from chronic exhaustion.

"U-U-Ushakov," he stuttered.

I introduced myself and told him that I needed a place to spend the night.

"W-W-Welcome." Stepping a little to the side, he let me enter the room.

"So, you're the famous Ushakov?" I asked.

"Famous or not, I am U-U-Ushakov," he replied. "And are you that journalist who disgraced the airborne troopers?"

"In what sense?" I asked, not quite understanding his question.

"In the d-d-direct sense," he said. He tossed some wood into the stove that was sputtering next to him. "You were the one who wrote about an ambush in which the Jalalabad airborne troopers wore *kimri*, not the mountain boots they were supposed to be wearing."

I immediately recalled a letter that I'd received in Moscow a year ago from an outraged major in Rukhi. When I'd opened the envelope, out had come the smell of exhaust fumes, of gunpowder, of war.

"Your letter was the angriest one I got after the Afghanistan book was published," I said. "You were still a major then; congratulations on your promotion. To be honest, I didn't quite follow your criticism. The *kimri*, English sleeping bags, *dukhi* flasks—all of that was true."

"I'm going to say this to you," Ushakov said, hitting the stool with the palm of his hand. "While a normal officer's soldiers are dressed according to the regulations, you showed a band of bums who were decked out in trophy garb. That's despicable!"

"Of course it's despicable," I replied.

"But you were d-d-delighted by it!" Ushakov shouted. He'd gotten so agitated that he was having a hard time lighting his cigarette.

He'd imagined it, I said to myself. Now I'm really in for it—I'll have to listen to his sermonizing all night.

Ushakov took a comb from the table and groomed his red mustache, twirling the ends upward. The sight calmed me down.

"There's already enough crap in the army as it is," he said, blowing out a stream of smoke. "There's no need to propagandize it. Well, never mind—I wasn't really serious. The past is dust."

Ushakov took a long drag on his cigarette, but when he exhaled I saw no smoke.

"Would you like to eat something?" he asked. "The trip must have made you hungry. We'll fix something for you right away."

He stood up, cracking the joints of his stiff legs, and disappeared behind the door.

Ushakov's battalion had come to Salang from Rukhi in September 1988. As part of what later became known as the Rukhi regiment, it had been in many of the war's worst battles and in an even greater number of shelling attacks. Ushakov's men saw Salang, where it had been reasonably calm of late, as something of a lyrical digression—at least compared to Rukhi, which was notorious for being the most godforsaken and dangerous place in all of Afghanistan. Merely flying there and back was regarded by some field officers as an act of heroism. Ushakov and his soldiers had fought there for two years.

Arriving at the southern approaches to the Salang Tunnel, the battalion had taken over five posts along the Kabul-Salang road and put up three mobile posts in the mountains. Ushakov himself had settled in at the Fifty-third Post, which was home to the mortar battery of Ura Klimov, a twenty-four-year-old senior lieutenant. The two battalion commanders had been living together since September 1988. Ushakov's battalion was assigned a twenty mile long zone of responsibility that extended to the Forty-second Post, which was occupied by Colonel Valery Vostrotin's airborne troops.

"I'm s-s-starving, too," Ushakov said as he appeared in the doorway. In his right hand he was holding a frying pan, which was sputtering hot pork grease in every direction. "Toward the end of the war our grub has become a bit scanty. We're consuming the last of our reserves: ground pork, canned potatoes, onions, rice, and condensed milk. The main thing is that the soldiers are fed and clothed. A while ago the *dukhi* gave us a lamb as a present. Our Uzbek cook made a great meal out of it. So sometimes we still get to have a feast.

"Take some more. This is supper. There won't be anything else tonight."

Ushakov closed his eyes and inhaled some of the steam that rose from the pan. Then he smiled and piled a czar's portion in my bowl.

I looked at Ushakov carefully. There was something about him that resembled the country of his birth: enormous, trustful, forgetful of past hurts, happy and sad at the same time. He had nice eyes with a gloomy gleam. At times an invisible wave would pass over his face and it would grow sorrowful, but usually it was illuminated by a vague smile. His voice had become toneless from cigarette smoke. His reddish brown skin was stretched tight over his high cheekbones. Even though Ushakov was only thirty-seven, bald spots showed through the light, thinning hair on both sides of his strong, high forehead. His whole countenance made me think of the mustachioed Russian soldiers in paintings that depict the battles of 1812.

As I talked to him, he struck me as the kind of man who'd known from the minute he was born some of the things that I had to learn much later from books. While he let me know from the very beginning that he wasn't very fond of journalists, I could see, or rather sense, that underneath his hostility was a gentle—and in wartime quite rare—kindness toward strangers.

"The m-m-man who sees the snow as simply white, the sea as simply blue, and the grass as simply green is an impoverished man," Ushakov said as he tossed a couple of sugar cubes into his mug. "The whole meaning of life comes from combining and blending different colors. A journalist should know that, too. There's no other w-w-way to write about this war. Otherwise it's going to be nothing but lies and insincerity. I've read so much about battles that never even happened, while not a word has been written about real battles. We've proclaimed so many cowards to be heroes, while the truly brave have been ignored by the newspapers. A *chizhik* [military bureaucrat] is covered with medals, while the soldier . . ."

He waved his hand in exasperation. A moment later a finger of flame jumped across the stove from one side to another. Ushakov used a piece of bread to wipe the frying pan clean and then put it down on the floor.

"Here, for example, is what happened once at one of the posts," he said. "A soldier went in the bushes to r-r-relieve himself. At that moment a recoilless gun hit the post, killing everyone but the guy who was in the bushes. Later the incident was presented to the higher-ups as if the guy had fought alone while he was completely surrounded."

"What happened then?" I asked.

"They honored him as a Hero of the Soviet Union. Here's another episode. A company commander was driving an inspector from the USSR in an armored personnel carrier. They drove up to a grove of p-p-peach trees. The inspector says, 'Oh, it would be so nice to pick some peaches and take them home with me!' The company commander stopped the carrier and hopped out—right on top of a mine. Both his legs were blown off. The inspector, feeling that it was his fault, did everything in his power to get them to award the commander the Hero of the Soviet Union. Don't get me wrong: I d-d-don't envy him. God forbid. I s-s-simply think that Hero of the Soviet Union is a sacred title. Do you know what I mean?"

I nodded.

Outside the window a diesel generator roared as it pumped electricity into the post. Somewhere in the mountains, a D-30 howitzer fired with a crash; the windowpanes bowed in a bit and then snapped back. A rocket whizzed by above the roof, howling like a second-rate opera star.

"Do you know how to tell, when you're back home in the USSR, if someone really fought in the war or if he was just one of the people who hid out at headquarters?" Ushakov asked suddenly.

He took the kettle off the stove, poured some boiling water into the mugs, and proceeded to answer his own question.

"The one who runs his mouth off to the girls about his great exploits never heard a single bullet whistle by his head. A real veteran will keep quiet about the war. Hey, watchman, come here."

In a few seconds the door opened and a soldier in a grungy *bushlat* appeared in the doorway. He'd been nicknamed Chelentano after the great Italian singer and movie star. No one at the post called him by his real name.

"Soldier, why don't you get us some more water?" Ushakov said, handing him the kettle.

Chelentano disappeared without saying a word. He was an Uzbek and spoke Russian no better than an Afghan.

"In one of my companies, the Uzbeks decided to form their own gang and began terrorizing the Russian minority," Ushakov said. "So I was forced to show them reverse Russian terror. I won't stand for this kind of stuff."

Outside the window, somebody fired a round out of an AK.

"Some sentry probably discharged a magazine into his shadow," Ushakov said. "That's all right. It happens a lot. We only have four weeks left to fight. Our n-n-nerves are giving out."

"Really?" I asked. "I thought it was an alarm."

"N-n-no," Ushakov replied with a smile.

He looked at his watch, scratched the back of his head, and said, "It's one in the m-m-morning already. Maybe we should sleep a bit. Any objections?"

I shook my head no.

"Good . . . sleep it is, then," he said, falling onto his cot with a groan. "I won't undress; they'll have me up twenty times in the night. You get sick and tired of pulling on your uniform. I suggest that you keep yours on, too."

I took off my mountain boots and stretched out on the cot. It murmured something underneath me.

"Don't mind me if I start cursing in my sleep," Ushakov said. "You can wake me up if I start getting really bad."

I smiled and turned off the light.

Making a great noise with his boots, the watchman entered the room and put the kettle on the stove. Its wet bottom hissed peacefully.

Ushakov lifted his head from the pillow and looked at the soldier. "Don't forget to put some coal in the stove in about an hour," he said. "Otherwise our correspondent here will freeze to death. Go on."

Ushakov dropped his head back on the pillow. In five minutes or so I heard his peaceful and rhythmic breathing. The flames from the stove barely illuminated his face, and I could see that he was sleeping with his eyes half-shut and rolled back. The yellowish whites of his eyes shone from under his lids. A wisp of hair, damp with sweat, lay across his smooth forehead.

10

Ushakov had been promoted to lieutenant colonel only recently, even though the paperwork had been submitted two years ago. Some time back, at Rukhi, one of his newly arrived lieutenants had gone AWOL so that he could trade one armored carrier for another in a blockade; the lieutenant, lacking experience, thought that he could manage without sappers. He was blown up by a mine. After the incident, both Ushakov's recommendation for a medal and his promotion had been denied.

The ringing of a field telephone transported me from the past to the present. Before I could lift my heavy eyelids, Ushakov's toneless bass was bellowing into the receiver. "Hello, Mountain Pass? Hello, Mountain Pass? Do you copy? Put me through to Courier. Yes. There have b-b-been no incidents on the road. Everything is normal."

A moment later Ushakov wearily threw the receiver down and muttered, "This is how it goes all night."

"But isn't it still better to be here than in Rukhi?" I asked.

"In some sense it is better, naturally," he replied. "But of course here you never know what to expect. I have a feeling that in our last days we'll have a real showdown at Salang. The *dukhi* will surely attack our tail. I've lost all d-d-desire to sleep.

"In Rukhi we were fired at almost every day. Our superiors were afraid to fly out there. And when they finally did come, nothing good came of it. They would be livid by the time they left. First, we wouldn't give them any cars; they were all being used. Second, we wouldn't give them any vodka or baksheesh. We didn't have direct contact with the *dukhanshiki*, so we instituted a dry law. That's why they weren't happy when they left and why our regiment was in ill repute. Our commander, a d-d-decent man, didn't know how to stick up for himself at the Party meetings. Or maybe he just didn't want to. I always used to whisper to him, 'Come on, Commander, let them have it!' But he'd just sit there and not say anything. So I was always the one to fight with the higher-ups."

"Weren't you afraid of them?" I asked.

"Why should I be?" Ushakov replied. "I believe that a normal, healthy person has nothing to be afraid of anyway. When they discharge me from the army I'll become a coal miner. I'll make more money at it. These hands will come in handy anywhere. Look at our ancestors: they didn't have anything, and what a nice sixth of the earth they got themselves. My friends tell me, 'Watch out, Ushakov, you aren't going to m-m-make it.' I tell them, 'They won't give me anything less than a platoon or send me farther than Kushka [a small, remote town in northern Russia].' "

"But didn't they send you here?" I asked.

"Yes, they did," Ushakov replied with a quiet laugh. "Well, they won't send me farther than Afghanistan. A real worker in the army always stays in the shadows, while the worthless bastard who knows how to click his heels or kiss a general's butt always climbs to the top. It's the same old s-s-story."

Ushakov went to the stove and tossed some coals and kindling into its fiery maw. The damp wood hissed, and in a few minutes the room grew brighter. Wrinkling his glistening forehead, Ushakov returned to his corner, sat down, and propped his elbows on his bony knees.

"No matter what the army is like, I don't think that I'll leave it on my own accord," he said. "Even though there is, of course, lots of nonsense. This one pretty decent guy served as the commander of a rocket battalion that was under the authority of the army, not the division. He was a stern man with strong p-p-principles. And they cost him a lot, these p-p-principles of his. His predecessor's career, on the other hand, had gone very well, because he knew how to do everything: how to heat up the bathhouse, how to get the girls together at the right time, and how to unobtrusively slip the boss— even the lowest-ranking one—a baksheesh. Well, the guy I'm t-t-talking about didn't know how to do any of that. He refused to. Sometimes he'd even get indignant. 'Comrade Commanders, where am I going to get the dough to get you v-v-vodka?' he'd say. 'I don't want to part with my own money—I've got a family back home. And I won't steal. Don't force me to.' Soon he started having troubles: inspections, that sort of thing, till they ate him alive. He came to me after he'd been demoted to armament deputy. My administrative deputy is also in exile. He used to s-s-serve in one of the best regiments, but his honesty did him in. He got a kick in the butt and landed here."

I looked at Ushakov. His eyes were glowing feverishly, as if he were delirious. The light in the room almost seemed to be coming from them. His left brow was knit in a tight arch and was quivering slightly. Ushakov licked his dry, whitish lips and went on.

"A little farther south there's a battalion commander who never sees a single paycheck here—he has it all transferred back to the USSR. He's made a killing. D-D-Do you want to know how? V-V-Very easily. He sells submachine guns to Basir but writes them off as lost in combat. It's all very sad. A s-s-soldier sees something like that and immediately follows suit. And if you start fighting any of this they'll say, 'He's crazy—send him to the psych ward!' I've spent enough time there already. I don't have any d-d-desire to go back."

The first time that Ushakov wound up in an army psychiatric clinic was in April 1971, while he was attending the Kiev Military Command School; he got eighteen days for fighting with a teacher. The second time was in May 1983, while he was serving in Cuba; he got ten days for quarreling with his superiors. The third time was in November 1985, in Kaliningrad; he got forty-seven days, again for arguing with higher-ups.

"In Cuba they didn't like it when I said that the army should be doing some real work rather than just showing off. I've always believed that if there's order within the unit and the soldiers are willing to lay down their lives for their country, then the commander knows what he's doing and there should be no need to bother him with dumb inspections. That's when I lost my temper. Not surprisingly, I wound up in the nuthouse. The doctors began to evaluate my mental condition by asking how a normal man could blurt out something like that to his superiors. Each question was more idiotic than the preceding one. What's the difference, they asked, between a capital city and a town? What's the difference between a horse and a tractor? Between an airplane and a bird? How can a normal p-p-person respond to such questions? If you say that a horse neighs and a tractor roars, that a bird flaps its wings and an airplane doesn't, they'll surely say that you are cracked."

The light in the small window was growing brighter, like the screen of an old television set just after it's turned on. A slight blush appeared on the glass: the sun was lazily commencing its umpteenth ascent to the top of the sky. Ushakov's left cheek, which was turned toward the window, also turned rosy, while the right side of his face remained as black as the dark side of the moon.

"Or else they make you answer a question like: 'If I had a normal sex life, I would . . .' 'How am I supposed to answer that?' I told the medical panel. 'I don't feel deprived in any way when it comes to sex: you couldn't pull me off a woman if you tried!' "

"What did the doctors say to that?" I asked.

"What could they say? They laughed and let me go. You see, the psych ward is an excellent way for the men in charge to take care of an unwanted crisis in a unit."

Ushakov unfolded a pack of cigarettes, which had already been opened from the bottom—a soldier's trick to outwit Afghan infections (this way the filter ends of the cigarettes were never touched by dirty fingers). Lifting his eyes, which had narrowed into a tired squint, he asked, "Shall we have a smoke?"

Suddenly the door creaked and opened a little. I saw a face with neatly cropped hair and small slits for eyes.

"Comrade Lieutenant Colonel, may I come in?"

"Come on in, Slavka," Ushakov replied, directing a heavy stare toward Senior Lieutenant Adliukov.

Adliukov was quite short and still a boy. His black hair, which curled a little at the temples, magnified the pallor of his girlish face.

"Pour yourself some tea, have a smoke, relax," Ushakov mumbled, his voice dull and heavy.

Adliukov had just now, at five o'clock in the morning, returned from Rose, a mountain post that had failed to come on the air at the designated hour. After firing three single shots with his AK and getting none in return, Adliukov and a sapper had climbed the mountain in the middle of the night. For more than an hour they'd trudged through the deep snow, only to find that the post's radio batteries were dead.

Adliukov settled down next to me and started to take off his rubber leggings; lumps of packed snow fell onto the floorboards. Then he poured himself a cup of hot tea, held it between the palms of his hands, and stared for a long time into the steaming liquid.

Adliukov had been orphaned as a small child. He'd been taken in by an aunt, but eventually he came to worry that he was a burden to her. So as soon as he'd finished the eighth grade he enrolled in the Suvorov Military School. From there he went to the Tbilisi Artillery College, and from there to Afghanistan.

Ten minutes later Ushakov returned to where our conversation had left off. "To a commander, the psych ward is often like a magic wand," he said. "A soldier hits an officer, for instance. The soldier has to be put on trial—it's a crisis. But if a regiment has a crisis situation and a man has been convicted, then a commander cannot rise to the next rank. So the incident is reported as a nervous breakdown, and that's it. This is how they reason it out among themselves: Could a normal soldier hit an officer? No, he couldn't. Therefore, this guy must be crazy."

Ushakov gazed at the crooked ceiling, which was crisscrossed by broken pipes, as if his whole life story were written there. He told me why he'd turned down three invitations to apply to the Frunze Academy.

"Let's see, the first time they asked me to go was in 1981," he said. "That was after I was made the battalion's chief of headquarters. Naturally, it's a great honor to wear striped trousers* in your old age; when you die, they'll give you a ride on a caisson and see you off with a salute. But I don't have much of a protective covering on my head, and the bosses are trying to gouge a hole in it. I'll end up with a heart attack at fifty. So I've refused to go any higher than a b-b-battalion.

---

*Part of the special uniform of those in high command.

To keep on climbing to the top, you have to be either a cynic or really well connected. I am neither."

Already it had grown quite light outside. Ushakov glanced at the window. "The white nights are over; the black days have begun," he said with a smile. "Whoever's in charge, don't spare yourself."

Ushakov threw a kitchen towel over his knees, dipped a shaving brush in some hot water and soap, and began to whip up a lather on his cheeks as he hummed a little song. As I watched him I thought: Here they are, the army's two assets—Antonenko and Ushakov. The first is dashing, confident that he is in the right, a true personification of the might of the armed forces. The second is a sickly stutterer with stooped shoulders and silver teeth who's grown old before his time and who doubts not only himself but everyone else.

Ushakov, who was loudly scraping the stubble and lather from his cheeks, intercepted my stare.

"You are studying me?" he asked. "Go ahead. I am a Pomor [one of Russia's numerous nationalities]. Pomors have never been serfs."

Suddenly the assistant to the battalion's doctor entered the room. He was a man of forty with a thin face, sharp nose, and beady, watery eyes.

"Go ahead and sit down, Petro," Ushakov said, pointing with his safety razor toward his cot. "Why are you d-d-dressed up this way? Why are you wearing those spiked boots? And what's the submachine gun for?"

"The spikes are to keep from slipping, and the submachine gun is to have something to shoot back with," the doctor's assistant replied. He seemed to be a little offended.

"Boy you're a clown, Petro," Ushakov said. "The only place you ever go is from the boiler room to the mess hall. Where are you going to slip? And put that submachine gun down. You're just making p-p-people laugh. If something starts, we'll cover you. But seriously, my friends, do watch yourselves. Don't pop outside unless you have to. We have so little time left here that it would be a p-p-pity if something happened on the last day. Once we cross the border I'll leave two ensigns in the unit—the ones that I caught drunk—and the rest of us will head to the best pub in Termez. We won't be celebrating a victory or a defeat, but just our withdrawal. It's been a strange war. We went in when stagnation was at its peak and now leave when truth is raging."

As Ushakov wiped his freshly shaven face, we heard pounding footsteps in the hall outside the door. "Colonel Yakubovsky is here," Ushakov said. "He's the only one who makes this much noise. All right, guys, look alive."

Yakubovsky, a tall man with ruddy cheeks, entered the room. It seemed as if the blizzard had followed him into the post.

"Brrr, it's cold out there," he announced with a smile. Then he turned to Adliukov, who was standing at attention by a cot, and said, "Hey, little swallow, organize some tea for me."

"Comrade Colonel, I am no swallow," Adliukov replied. There was a tremor in his voice. "I am a human being."

Ushakov's eyes were laughing underneath his eyebrows.

"All right, buddy," Yakubovsky chuckled as he patted Adliukov on the head. "Don't get offended. It's just that I got chilled to the bone on the way from Salang. You've got quite a temper, don't you?"

Adliukov's little boots tapped on the floor as he went into the kitchen.

Yakubovsky questioned Ushakov about the situation on the road, rubbed his brown face with his hands, and then, without waiting for his tea, disappeared through the doorway. In a few moments we heard the dull roar of his armored personnel carrier.

"That man is like a tornado!" Ushakov exclaimed as he nodded toward the door. "If it were up to me, once we cross the border I would give each soldier half a mug of vodka, each platoon commander a mugful, each company commander two mugfuls, and each battalion commander three mugfuls. Oh, God . . ."

Adliukov pushed the door open with his hip and entered with the teakettle and more wood for the fire.

"Watchman!" Ushakov shouted, cupping his hands around his mouth like a megaphone. "Watchman!" Hearing no answer, he threw his *bushlat* over his shoulders and ran out into the hall.

"Don't really believe Ushakov about the vodka," Adliukov said. "He's a sworn teetotaler. When he came to the post he personally instituted a dry law. I can even recall him saying, 'We'll fight without vodka and without women.' "

"That's right, without women," Ushakov bellowed as he burst

back into the room. "This concerns not only the married men but the bachelors as well."

"Why the bachelors?" I asked. I didn't quite understand.

"Because there aren't any decent women here," Ushakov snapped. "The reason I prohibited married men from seeing women is based on elementary logic: if your wife is waiting for you back home, then why aren't you waiting for her?"

Then Adliukov spoke. "In short, the relationship between the battery and the battalion that September was a little strained," he said. "Some even dared to inform Comrade Lieutenant Colonel about it. 'Don't try to run another man's house,' they said. 'Let the people keep living a normal life until the fifteenth of February.' "

"That's when I told them that if they kept living that way they wouldn't make it," Ushakov said, brushing the snowflakes off his eyebrows.

While Ushakov's battalion had been stationed in Rukhi, the commander of the regiment had once suggested that all the officers pitch in ten checks apiece to buy gifts for the ladies on Women's Day. Ushakov flatly refused. "Why?" the commander of the regiment asked. "Don't you feel like parting with your checks?" "No, it's just that I don't see a single lady here," Ushakov replied. "There's only . . . here!" He took out a bill worth ten checks and tore it into bits. At that point the commander of the regiment threw up his arms and said, "Your reasoning is pretty antisocial."

Ushakov later explained his reasoning to the ladies of Rukhi. "You've been milking the soldiers and the officers," he told them. "But I won't let you get away with it anymore."

Ushakov, it seemed, didn't like women all that much. And he had his reasons.

One day, back in the USSR, he had returned home from a firing range to find another man in bed with his wife. Without giving the matter a second thought, Ushakov drew his pistol from its holster and forced the man to write a note of explanation as he sat naked at a table. Then Ushakov summoned the chief of the regiment's political office to the scene of the crime and had him stamp the man's confession.

Later, at the divorce trial, a female judge suggested that Ushakov was making unsubstantiated accusations. "Most likely," she said, "this is just slander." Ushakov pulled out the note with the regiment's seal and put it on the table. In granting the divorce, the judge remarked that she had seen many things in her career, but nothing like this.

Ushakov had neither the desire nor the luck to remarry. Last summer, however, he'd met a wonderful woman with a rare name—Taisiya—while vacationing in the south of the Soviet Union. One look at her was enough to make him forget about the war. With something stirring in his petrified heart, Ushakov gathered the last remnants of strength from the bottom of his soul and fell in love with her. He threw himself into the abyss of this new feeling like a boy flying down a mountain on a sled.

"Ta-i-si-ya, Ta-ech-ka, Tai-ka," Ushakov cooed as he glanced at his spent cigarette.

"Apparently someone is really thinking about you, Comrade Lieutenant Colonel," Adliukov said.

Ushakov's smile revealed his steel teeth, which were stained from cigarette smoke. "If someone is thinking of me," he said, "it's the devil in his grave."

Many of the soldiers I met in Afghanistan showed me their letters from home or read them to me like prayers. Often I saw letters from children that started, "Dear Mister Daddy." Many didn't even remember their fathers, knowing only that they were at war.

A major from Jalalabad once told me the story of his fateful trip home in the summer of 1987. His wife and daughter met him at the airport, and they all climbed into a taxi for the ride back into the city. His wife cried the whole way home and kissed his graying temples with her cold lips. As they were driving up to the house, his daughter asked, "Daddy, will you give me two chocolate bars before school?"

"Two is too many, but one—definitely!" he said with a smile.

"Daddy, I want two!" his daughter pleaded. "Uncle Valera gave me two every morning before he left the house."

The major, his joyful intoxication knocked out of him, closed his eyes. He asked the driver to stop the car. Heavy drops of rain were falling on the roof. He handed the driver a twenty-five-ruble bill and asked him to take his wife and daughter to their house. Then he took his bag and walked away. He hadn't seen them since.

"Oh, my life," Ushakov said, slapping his bony thighs with his palms. "It's a comedy with a tragic ending! Do you guys know how to find out whether or not your wife has been faithful when you come home from training camp?"

"I'd like to finish sowing my wild oats first!" Adliukov said, his eyes glistening.

"You'll have plenty of time to do that, provided you manage not to disappear accidentally," Ushakov said. "So anyway, here's how: you drive to your house and go up to the door, making as much noise with your boots as possible. The old women who sit together on the benches in the street freeze in their places and grow quiet from fright. You gather as much air in your lungs as you can and yell to them with all your might, 'So what do you have to say for yourselves, you old whores?' 'You think *we're* whores?' they'll answer. 'What about that such-and-such wife of yours?' That's when you'll find out everything."

Kornienko, the deputy commander of the battalion, and Lieutenant Colonel Liashenko, the deputy commander of the regiment, had quietly entered the room during Ushakov's monologue. They shook with noiseless laughter. Adliukov clapped his hands.

"That's the battalion commander for you," Kornienko said as he brushed tears of laughter from his eyes with the back of his hand.

Suddenly Ushakov grew serious. "I wish you would laugh less," he said, "and work more."

"Why do you change moods like that?" Kornienko, who was still smiling, asked. "One minute you're cracking jokes and the next you're mad."

"I'm mad because I gave you my ensign and you've let him become undisciplined," Ushakov replied. "He's gotten completely out of hand, the bastard."

"He hasn't gotten completely out of hand," Kornienko said. He smiled again. "It's just that the guy's wife left him."

"Tell the ensign that he's lucky," Ushakov said. "It's much better without women. Much calmer. I should know. I feel it right here."

With this Ushakov gave himself several hard slaps on the back.

"No, Ushakov, you've just tightened up like a fist," Liashenko said softly. "Once you go back you'll open up again. Here, at war, we're together day and night. We fight together, sleep together.

There we spend the days together and the nights apart. You won't be able to act there as you do here. Don't even think that you will."

"B-B-But they're not to be trusted at all!" Ushakov shouted as he angrily hit the night table with his hand. "As soon as you're gone to the training they try to get in bed with your neighbor."

"We put our wives under tighter restrictions, Serezha, than we put ourselves," Liashenko said. "In reality, we get away with the kinds of things we won't even allow them to think about."

Ushakov caught hold of Liashenko's sleeve and hissed with burning hatred. "Listen here. In the ten years that I was m-m-married I never cheated on her once, even though as soon as she would go away somewhere all the women from the neighborhood would immediately come running. But I showed them all out. Only after we were divorced did I let certain ones stay. So here I've set up a 'dry law'—for both alcohol and women."

Liashenko put his arms around Ushakov. "Don't try to convince me that a man can run like a lone wolf his whole life," he said.

Ushakov's face was pale.

"A man just can't," Liashenko continued. "There has to be somebody there to help you when you get old. As long as you're in the army an ensign will take care of you. But what about later? Why can't you understand, you silly man, that each year it will get more and more difficult?"

11

At nine o'clock in the morning the wind herded the clouds together, the sky turned turbid, and the snowstorm began raging with renewed strength.

I went out on the road and headed toward the Fiftieth Post. The armored carriers and military vehicles stretched northward in an endless dotted line. They moved very slowly. The wind whipped the armor with snow. The soldiers, having nothing else to do, smoked one cigarette after another, bringing them to their bluish lips with frozen fingers. About five hundred meters down the road I caught up with a lieutenant who was walking quite briskly. His face was completely covered by a woolen cap, except for two handmade eyeholes, over which he'd pulled a canvas hood. The two ends of the hood's drawstring, which was tied in a knot underneath his chin, were slapping him on the cheeks. We walked together for quite some time, exchanging brief phrases every now and then.

We drew near the Fiftieth Post. A collapsing snowdrift had forced an armored carrier off the road, and the lieutenant wanted to speed up the soldiers who'd been trying to dig it out since morning. While the two men trapped inside had received only light bruises, several hours had passed since the accident and they were getting quite cold.

The wind was picking up speed and threatened to push us off the side of the road.

"Look at this bastard blow!" the lieutenant said, cursing the blizzard. "Whose idea was it to withdraw the troops in February? So much equipment has been wrecked already."

He pushed up his knit cap, exposing his wide forehead and deeply set black eyes. Then he ran a hand over his eyebrows, which were covered with hoarfrost.

"Whenever Russia is at war it's always a fierce winter," the lieutenant said. "I'm not sure who has worse luck—us or the *dukhi*. They're having a rough time, too. All the mountain paths have been buried in snow; communication between the detachments has been broken. Are you coming from Ushakov's post?"

"Yes," I replied.

"Then where is Ushakov himself?"

"He went to the *chaihan* [an Afghan tea shop]. A watchman reported to him that three airborne troopers were looting a *dukhan*. He ran off to investigate it, taking Company Commander Zaulichniy with him. Apparently the airborne troopers had taken a liking to the Hong Kong perfumes and audiocassettes."

"The airborne troopers know what they're doing," the lieutenant said with a smile.

After walking another seven hundred meters or so we met a captain and several soldiers who were taking apart a makeshift monument on the side of the road. The driver of an armored carrier had been killed here a year ago, and his comrades in arms had memorialized him by erecting a metal pyramid with a five-pointed star on the top.

"It's been three months since we received orders from General Gromov to remove all the Soviet symbology, to take down all the memorials to the dead on the roads," the lieutenant explained. "That way, when the army leaves, the *dukhi* won't be able to mock or befoul their memory."

Two soldiers were beating the frozen ground with shovels in an effort to pull out the rusty scraps of metal. A KamAZ was growling nervously next to them. The truck was decorated with cheerful posters and banners.

The captain, who was trying to keep warm by hopping from one foot to the other, picked up a piece of plywood nailed to a blackened wood cross and, breaking it with a blow of his boot, tossed it into the nearby fire. The flames clawed at the dry wood, which crackled sharply in the heat. Part of the sign had been broken off, but this much I could make out: MUNISM IS OUR BANNER!

I squatted, stretched my hands toward the fire, and used a smoldering piece of wood to light a cigarette. The lieutenant put his foot on a blazing log, which hissed under the pressure and sent wisps of smoke rising from under the thick sole of his boot.

"Oh, this is great," he murmured. "I really thought that my toes would freeze and fall off. Hard to believe, but it's warmer in the USSR."

"When did you get back?" I asked.

"A week ago," he replied.

"Vacation?"

"No, I was accompanying a shipment number two hundred."*

"Where to?"

"Near Tashkent."

"Did you have time to go home?"

"Yes, they gave me fourteen days, but first I got stuck in Bagram—the planes couldn't land because of the weather. We finally got to Kabul right before New Year's. The refrigerators in the morgue there are the same as in a meat locker. For several days we sat in a shabby room of the infectious disease clinic, which was near the morgue, and that's where we spent New Year's Eve. They put the corpse in a zinc case, soldered it shut, and then put the zinc case in a wooden coffin. They left a window in the zinc case, though, because the body wasn't disfigured."

The lieutenant fell silent for a few minutes as he followed the chaotic dance of the flames with his eyes. He shifted his left boot closer to the fire; his other boot was enveloped by rank gray smoke. Then he continued.

"They say that the kind of New Year's you have will determine the kind of year you'll have. I spent mine in the Kabul morgue. Before I could even come back here from Tashkent, I received a death notification from the Soviet Union. My brother had been killed in a fight."

The lieutenant looked into the wind with despair, squinting to

*The code name for a zinc coffin holding the corpse of a soldier.

protect his eyes from the stinging snow. "I've survived the war, but he couldn't survive there," he said with feigned indifference. "So that's the way it is."

"Did you have to go far from Tashkent?" I asked.

"No," he replied. "I got there and gave the recruitment office the soldier's death certificate, the certificate of monetary compensation, and his closed military card. The military commissioner went off to notify the parents, taking an ambulance with him. The father, you see, had a bad heart. The mother wailed at the funeral; the father tore at his few remaining strands of hair. 'How could they let this happen?' he cried. 'How could they let this happen?' He looked at me as if I were the one who had killed his son. The relatives surrounded us, speaking very rapidly in their own language. I asked the military commissioner what they wanted. 'They're asking, "Why did you bring this black load?"' he replied. Then he took me to the airport as soon as possible; there have been cases in which the officers accompanying a soldier's corpse have been stoned to death. The atmosphere was very heated. They'd just shown *Little Vera*, and the crowd had broken all the windows at the movie theater. And now comes this casket . . ."

Several Afghans with submachine guns came up to the fire and began trading antibiotic tablets for cigarettes.

"Cool *dukhi*," the lieutenant said, smiling at them.

"Is there any chance that these very *dukhi* will open fire all of a sudden?" I asked.

"None at all," he replied. "There's mass fraternization all along the road, in the form of trade. No one has any desire to fight."

The monument still wouldn't budge. One of the soldiers suggested blowing it up, but the captain flatly dismissed the idea. He ordered the driver to turn the KamAZ around and use its bumper as a battering ram.

The pyramid stubbornly resisted, as if the dead soldier were grasping at it from underneath the ground. The sight of five living men struggling against one dead man gave me a sensation of vague but bitter distress.

The bumper came within a few centimeters of the star.

"What are you waiting for?" the captain shouted into his bullhorn. "Push forward. Hook it on the axle!"

The metal monument screeched desperately as the KamAZ slowly drove over it. When the KamAZ backed up, however, I could still see the pyramid. It was leaning a little bit but hadn't fallen. The mangled star lay nearby.

"Let's go, one more time!" the captain yelled into the bullhorn, trying to compete with the roar of the engine. "Come on!"

"Let's go, one more time!" the mountain echoed after him. "Come on!"

Suddenly one of the soldiers took a running start and jumped on the pyramid with both feet. The monument let out a metallic moan but withstood the attack.

"There's no need for that," the lieutenant said. "Not with your feet."

The captain gave us a hostile look.

The KamAZ turned around and tried again. In a minute it was all over: the monument was toppled, defeated.

The soldier had lost again.

The lieutenant and I moved on. We had twelve hundred meters to go before we reached the place where an avalanche had hit this morning and blown an armored carrier off the road and over a cliff. The road was congested with the rear of the Bagram division. The vehicles were bumper to bumper, engines idling. The ice and the asphalt seemed to be trembling under my feet. Above the road the exhaust fumes swirled in the snowstorm, making it all but impossible to breathe.

The lieutenant pulled his woolen cap over his nose. I took a dirty handkerchief from the pocket of my *bushlat*, folded it into fourths, and pressed it to my mouth, using it like a gas mask. As the wind shifted we crossed from one side of the road to the other in an effort to avoid the choking fumes. The sun was struggling to fight its way through the blizzard, the exhaust fumes, and the murky sky.

"Yesterday a soldier disappeared without a trace!" the lieutenant shouted as we approached the avalanche.

"Where?"

"On the other side of Salang. Near the lake."

"Near the lake," came the echo.

"They say he took a dog with him!" the lieutenant yelled.

I tried to picture the missing man and imagine what had happened to him.

But, as we trudged along, my thoughts shifted to New York, to Freedom House, to my meeting with the former Soviet prisoners of war after the press conference. I shared the story with the lieutenant.

12

"Fine," said Mikhola Movchan. He took the jean jacket off his shoulders (which were as thin as a woman's clothes hanger), draped it over the back of a chair, and lit up a black cigarette. The drops of sweat in his sparse blond hair glistened under the lights. "You want to hear my life story? Then listen . . .

"I was born in the village of Lazorianka, near Zhitomir. It's a small village. Do you know it? It's okay if you've never heard of it—that's not what matters. Still, that's where I spent my childhood. I went to the city for the first time when I turned eight. I didn't like school. I still don't. It's boring. What I remember most is the village—the road, the trees, our house. I remember my favorite chestnut tree; I always hid in it. As I talk to you I can see the road from my village into town. I can see myself walking down that road for the last time. I used to read books when I was in school. It wasn't easy to get them in our village, but my aunt worked in the school library. I remember that the library's copy of *Spartacus* was missing half its pages.

"I had no idea what I should do with my life. I was born in 1963. I was never active as a Pioneer [a Soviet youth organization], and especially not as a member of Komsomol. Childhood friends? I probably won't be able to remember any of them now; it's been six years since I left home and joined the army. Six very long years.

"In Ashkhabad they told us that we would be sent to Afghanistan, but I wasn't frightened. I believed the press, which carried picturesque accounts of how we were *not* fighting there. This was in 1982. Once, at a hospital in Ashkhabad, I accidentally saw some men who'd been wounded in Afghanistan and realized that there *was* a war there, that there *was* shooting there. At first I didn't tell my parents anything, but I later wound up writing to them. I remember trying to comfort them by telling them that I was going to be eating watermelon and would send them some.

" 'Son,' my father had told me, 'serve and obey.' My father is a tractor operator. My mother works as a milkmaid. I ended up disobeying."

There was no ashtray at the table where we were sitting, so Movchan made one out of an empty cigarette pack and flicked his ashes into it. As he talked he rubbed his cheekbones with his slender index fingers.

"Where did Movchan serve?" the lieutenant asked.

The question startled me. I was talking merely to break the monotony of our walk, to keep my mind off the cold. I hadn't thought my companion was even listening. We walked on, and I continued with the story.

Movchan lit a cigarette and placed his hands on the table, interlacing his fingers. He continued with his story:

"In Afghanistan I served at Ghazni—the fall and winter of eighty-two, the winter and spring of eighty-three. In the beginning of the summer I left. Before I defected I served in a motorized infantry unit. Life in the unit was fairly calm, unless we were involved in operations, when everything was different. I have nothing bad to say about our army, but the things that went on outside the regiment were terrible. We didn't see any friendly Afghans anywhere—only enemies. Even the Afghan army was unfriendly. Only one village in the whole area had a more or less tolerant attitude toward our presence. When the propagandists would go out to solicit support for Soviet rule, so to speak, they would take along a company of men and tanks. They used to say that the situation was better in 1981. I really couldn't say.

"I served as a sergeant, but not in combat subunits. A regiment generally would send one battalion and one reconnaissance company to fight. But I was never in any of them. I served for six months and then took off. I deserted early in the morning, just before dawn. I was lucky.

"I kept feeling as if I were watching a movie about myself. This feeling grew stronger when I found myself among the rebels. It's strange, but I didn't notice any animosity in their eyes. They saw that I'd deserted, and when a Soviet helicopter began searching for me by going through each *kishlak*, they helped me hide.

"The urge to defect came toward the end of my tour of duty. At first I had some doubts about whether we were in the right; then I was overcome with a feeling of despair. Everyone around us was an enemy. I remember an intense feeling of anger toward the rebels because so many of our guys were getting killed.

"I wanted revenge.

"Then I began to doubt the goals and methods of international aid. I had a difficult time deciding what I really believed. I just knew what I had to say during the political instruction meeting: that we were fighting 'American aggression' and 'Pakis.' Why had we mined all the approaches to the regiment? I asked myself. Why were we aiming our machine guns at every Afghan? Why were we killing the people we came here to help?

"Whenever a peasant was blown up by a mine, no one took him to the medical unit. Everyone just stood around, enjoying the sight of his death. 'This is an enemy,' the officer said. 'Let him suffer.'

"It's grim. I didn't listen to my father. I deserted at dawn.

"That's my life. And now it's America. Another life. A movie. Yes, a movie.

"On the morning that I'd decided to desert, I stared at a field for a long time. Everything was still—very still. I just stood there and looked. The muscles of my legs tensed up involuntarily. I froze. Then I glanced at the rising sun and ran. When I looked back, the regiment was far, far away, on the other side of the field. Some of the Afghans who were working in the field helped me hide. I saw the helicopters approach. They saw me running and understood everything.

"After two days had passed we left the *kishlak* and went into the mountains. After walking for a long time we finally reached the rebels' camp. The rebels looked at me with curiosity but not hostility.

They were armed only with ancient augers that went back to the time of the British invasion. In 1983 they had no other weapons. Can you imagine using flint augers against tanks, helicopters, and bombers? This is the truth. As it turned out, I was in Sayaf's group. They treated me well. At first I didn't understand a word, but later on a man who spoke decent Russian arrived; he'd studied in the USSR, served as an officer in the Afghan army, and then deserted."

"Sayaf is still fighting in Afghanistan," the lieutenant said thoughtfully. "Our battalion has had to cross swords with him more than once. He's a wild fighter, that's for sure."

Movchan rubbed the surface of the table with the palm of his hand, took out another cigarette, and clicked his imported lighter.

"Sayaf asked me why I had deserted," Movchan said, taking a deep puff. "I replied that I didn't like the war and that I didn't want to kill Afghans. Sayaf told me that his people didn't want to fight either, but that they had to defend their country's independence. Otherwise, he said, the struggle of a million Afghan forebears would have been reduced to nothing. As he put it, 'The lives of our ancestors must not be made meaningless.'

"I stayed in Sayaf's detachment for a year. I moved around the country with the rebels. That's when I saw and understood what the Afghan resistance is all about. Whenever we came into a village we were greeted with joy by everyone, young and old. The kids brought us food. The women brought us clothes. It was during this year that my attitude toward the war was formed and became a conviction. I realized that all of our—er, I mean all of the Soviet—propaganda about the war in Afghanistan is a complete lie from beginning to end.

"I started to learn the Afghan language and eventually came to speak it pretty well. I was willing to do anything to atone for my sins before these people, even though I hadn't come to their country of my own free will. I couldn't see any difference between myself and a Nazi in my native Ukrainian land. It's the same thing: rolled-up sleeves, submachine guns, cries, villages. . . .

"I came to the United States in 1984. I was one of the first Soviet soldiers to arrive. I have no desire to discuss exactly how I got here. It might make it more difficult for other prisoners of war to follow in my footsteps.

"I ended up here because I was lied to from the very beginning—when I was sent to Afghanistan. I don't want the world to put me on trial, the way World War II criminals are still being put on trial now.

"I know that in the USSR they're now starting to speak badly of the guys who fought in Afghanistan. They started to talk when it became safe to talk and to criticize the war. They should have spoken out sooner.

"I tried writing to my family, but they later let me know that they were having problems. I stopped writing. I don't want them to suffer because of me. It's not their fault. They wanted me to serve and obey. But I didn't heed their advice. This is my life, and if it's shattered it's not my parents' fault."

Movchan couldn't hide the tremor in his voice. He loudly inhaled the smoky air.

"When I was running across the field to desert from my unit, I wasn't fleeing to America," Movchan said. "I had no plans to come here. I wasn't even thinking about it.

"I didn't flee from the Ukraine. I fled from the war. I wasn't particularly thrilled to come to the United States, but I had no other choice.

"Right now, I feel that there's no way back."

"Well, he shouldn't have said that," the lieutenant said, hearing the end of the story.

"Movchan will never return," I replied. "If he didn't feel guilty, he'd come back. Actually, each person should live where he chooses. Otherwise you have slavery."

"He'll come back," the lieutenant said. "He'll remember the chestnut tree and the village road. His memory will show him the way. You'll see. He just has to stand up tall one more time and start running—the way he ran then, across the field. . . . Back it up!"

A soldier jumped off an armored carrier and threw down a cable. The driver of the second carrier backed up a little. The soldier threw the cable down a precipice, where the vehicle that had been blown off the road by the snowslide lay helpless, its wheels in the air. The men had dug it out from under five meters of snow.

Down below, a soldier caught the cable and attached it to the crampon of the disabled armored carrier.

The lieutenant told them to attach a second cable to an MT-LB as a backup.

They fussed with the second cable for about ten minutes. It was so short that the MT-LB, spewing its bluish exhaust fumes over everybody, had to drive up to the very edge of the cliff.

"Now it'll reach!" shouted the soldier who was standing below. Then he waved his hand.

The lieutenant dislodged a rock from the cliff and, banging its sharpest side into the ice, placed it under the left tread of the MT-LB.

The engines of the two armored carriers and the MT-LB roared, and soon one of the carriers was pushing the other forward with dull thuds.

The lieutenant shouted something. His words resounded everywhere, competing with the roaring of the vehicles and the echo of his voice. He probably couldn't even hear himself.

The soldier below was also shouting something. I could see his mouth opening and closing but could hear none of his words.

The stranded carrier jerked and began crawling up the cliff's almost vertical face, leaving behind a swath of tightly packed snow about two meters wide.

The MT-LB was spinning its treads with all its might. As they slid across the snow, chunks of ice shot out from underneath. A soldier threw his *bushlat* under one of the treads; within seconds it emerged from the other side as torn rags.

He shouted something and began to laugh hysterically.

I couldn't hear his laughter.

An Uzbek sergeant began pushing the second armored carrier with his hands, but the lieutenant shoved him aside with a sharp blow of his fist.

The guys who'd been dug out from under the snow were now warming themselves in a nearby carrier. One of them stuck his head out of the hatch and looked nervously in every direction.

In about fifteen minutes the carrier that had fallen from the cliff was back on the road. It took another fifteen minutes or so to turn it over on its wheels.

The lieutenant, who was furiously exhaling pinkish clouds of steam, came up to me and showed me his hands. The skin on his palms was torn and bleeding. "Look!" he said.

"Where are you heading now?" I asked.

"I'm taking those two to Pul-i-Khumri," he replied. "Want to come?"

"Yes. And from there—to Naibabad."

We climbed in the armored carrier that only half an hour ago had been lying below the precipice. The carrier's starter screeched but refused to turn the engine over.

The MT-LB drove up and pushed us several times from behind.

"It's going!" the driver shouted.

The lieutenant closed the hatch, switched on the blue light, and started looking for his dry food ration.

Suddenly the world had shrunk to the size of an armored carrier.

"It's about a three-hour drive," he said, offering me some tinned compote. "We'll have time to talk to our heart's delight.

"So the case of Movchan is clear," he continued. "But what about the others? Did you try to convince them to return home?"

"No."

"Why not?"

"It's their own business."

"Did they know how you felt about them?"

"Quite frankly, I still don't know that myself."

"The *afghantsi* hate them."

"I know."

"So what about the others?"

"The others?"

13

The roar of the armored carrier dissolved into the hum of an air conditioner. I wasn't wearing a military uniform; instead I had on a faded T-shirt and a pair of sky-blue jeans.

Igor Koval'chuk sat across from me at a small round table. His bovine face was calm. His expression seemed to change with the shadows, now resembling that of an ancient Roman tyrant, now a Basque peasant. Like Movchan, he sucked incessantly on cigarettes. His bloodshot eyes shifted back and forth. I thought I could hear the blood pumping heavily and rhythmically in his temples.

"I'm from Kharkov," he said, forcing his pudgy lips into a smile, which he immediately wiped off with the back of his hand. "I was born in 1960."

"We're the same age," I said.

"Great," he replied. "Like all young people, I was involved in many different things. What I loved most of all were poetry, the sport of rifle shooting, history, music, and, of course, girls. Anyway, I had no problems with the first three hobbies in our freedom-loving society. But I got into a lot of trouble because of music and girls— they would lecture me, reprimand me, have talks with me.

"Girls were by far the most complicated issue; they caused me problems both at home and in school. The teachers told my parents that they must keep their son from depravity. I was told that I should be ashamed of myself for not spending the nights at home, for sleeping with girls. I'd blow up and yell, 'I'm seventeen now, and I'm not allowed to go to bed with a girl because I'm too young. But when I'm old and have gray hair, everybody is going to say, "Can you believe this guy? So old—and still chasing girls." ' My whole class would laugh, but the teacher would get mad and threaten to call my mother.

"And so in 1978 I graduated from the tenth grade of School Number Ninety, in the city of Kharkov. I became an airplane electrician, and went to work at an aircraft plant. My days, which were occupied with work, flew by; my evenings were filled with poetry and rifle shooting. I got to know new people, experienced success, failures, and love, and put my words to rhyme. I saw our humdrum, incubated people, bred by the Party. Two years passed and then the powerful hand of the system drove a wedge into my life, ripping apart my monotonous existence by sending me to the army.

"At the recruitment office there were one hundred and sixty of us, athletic guys who knew how to shoot. I ranked one hundred twentieth in Special Detachment Eighty.

"After saying good-bye to my parents, my sister, and my friends, I left my native and beloved city in the spring of 1980, taking with me my memories, my poetry, and my ability to shoot.

"The train took us south. We spent the time playing cards and drinking vodka. We spent twelve days like this and then found ourselves in Turkmenistan. We were in Kizyl-Arvat, a dirty provincial town, where an airborne regiment that had been decorated with the Order of the Red Banner was stationed. This is where my friends and I were sent in the spring of 1980.

"The hard days of basic training started. For each ten recruits there were two sergeants who taught us everything—attacking, defending, working with the bayonet and the butt of the gun, and, of course, shooting. My marksmanship was excellent, but otherwise the basic training didn't come easy to me.

"In two and a half months we took our oath of allegiance. We were all lined up and told that we were very lucky, that we had the great honor to be trusted by the Party to fulfill our international duty in Afghanistan. We had to help the Afghan people retain the conquests of the April Revolution, they said, and defend them from the bloodthirsty actions of imperialism, which, by invading the territory of our ally, threatened our southern border.

"Within two days we were mobilized. One hundred and sixty soldiers were scattered throughout Afghanistan.

"I and twelve of my friends arrived at a subdivision of reconnaissance airborne troopers, known by the call sign Daisy, which was twenty-five kilometers south of the city of Mazar-i-Sharif."

"We'll be in Mazar-i in an hour and a half," the lieutenant said with a chuckle. "Would you like some tea?"

"All right."

He tossed me a cold flask.

"Is this Pakistani?" I asked.

"Yep," he replied.

The lieutenant flattened the empty can of compote with the heel of his boot, opened up the hatch, and tossed it to the side of the road.

For no apparent reason, Koval'chuk unbuttoned and then buttoned the collar of his shirt. He smoothed his hair, pinched the bridge of his nose, and closed his eyes. He was silent for a minute. Then he spoke.

"We reached the Seventh Company after dinner. Captain Rudenko looked at us solemnly. 'Well, my boys, now you are meat—genuine meat—for jackals,' he said. 'Heed my words: you must either become wolves or die—one or the other. If you can't smell blood, you can't live and you can't run. You'll get devoured.' Then he called a sergeant and ordered him to give us our weapons. The captain's words sank into my brain like a wolf's fangs. Why is he so mean? I thought. We didn't do anything to him. Why did he pounce on us like that?

"But after only one month I was even worse.

"As soon as I'd received the title of reconnaissance landing trooper and secured the trust of the older guys by telling some dirty jokes, I began to feel as if I were being sucked into a giant, bloody whirlpool, where I was losing my ability to think and where all I did was wield my gun. Soon I lost my friend Oleg. Then it was Vitia.

Vitia's frozen blue eyes have left a scar in my heart. His last words: 'You know, Garik, we somehow could have lived a different life.'

"I'd lose control, screaming through my tears and spraying the area with submachine-gun fire.

"After six months of service, however, I became like everyone else. My hands wouldn't shake anymore when I'd close the eyelids of a fallen friend. I smoked dope. The sweet-and-sour smell of blood no longer turned my stomach inside out with nausea. I no longer closed my eyes when I was firing at point-blank range.

"By January 1981 I understood Captain Rudenko's words. I'd turned into a hardened wolf who was being eaten alive by lice and who was soon to disappear. I was given the rank of private; three months later I was given the rank of junior sergeant and assigned to be the gunner of an armored carrier.

"I didn't know what I wanted. I was the same person, yet somehow I was different. During the whole time of my military service, my submachine gun hadn't hit a single American. I'd wake up and think: Why won't the government tell us the whole truth? *You see, boys, this is the story, we need you to conquer the Afghans. Everything is clear and simple.* But no, they deceived us, their own soldiers. They played with us as if we were toys, while we were dropping like flies.

"In the evenings I'd howl with anguish, and in the mornings I'd laugh.

"Several episodes were turning points for me.

"One of them happened in the three hundred and ninety-fifth Regiment in Mazar-i-Sharif, the Sixth Mountain Rifle Company. Three inseparable friends were serving there: a guy named Panchenko and two guys—one from Kiev and another from Altai—whose last names I don't remember. One night, after drinking a lot of home-brewed beer, they decided that they wanted some hash and some lamb, so they set out for a neighboring *kishlak*. They ran into an old man on the way there. Well, they were drunk to the gills, and they struck the old guy on the head so hard that a piece of the rifle's stock fell off. For some reason, however, they didn't notice it. They dragged the old man into the bushes at the side of the road and kept walking.

"Soon they reached the *kishlak* and entered a house. There was a woman inside. They started raping her, and she started screaming. When her sister darted out of the house, there was nothing left for the fellows to do but to stab both of them. Then they entered the house next door. There were children inside, and the soldiers opened fire on them with their AKs. They shot all of them but one, who managed to escape. (Later, at his court-martial, Panchenko said that he didn't notice the boy because he was drunk—that's why they didn't finish him off.) Then the soldiers went into a *dukhan*, took a whole sack of hashish and a lamb, and returned to their unit. That's when Panchenko noticed that a piece of his rifle—the part that has the number of the gun on it—was missing.

"The soldiers staggered back down the road. They finished off the old man so that he wouldn't talk, found the missing piece of the rifle in the bushes, and returned to the unit.

"In the morning, all the soldiers in the company were ordered to line up. Then the boy who'd survived came out, followed by the commander of the company, the political deputy, and an *osobist*. After he walked up and down the whole line, the boy pointed his finger at Slavka. Panchenko and Slavka look like twin brothers. Slavka couldn't bear it. 'There's Panchenko!' he shouted. '*He* was the one doing the killing. *He* should pay for it!' Then Panchenko stepped forward. 'He!' the boy screeched. 'He shot at me!'

"The court-martial took place in Pul-i-Khumri. It lasted six months—a real circus. Then the condemned men were taken to Termez. Before leaving they said that they would write to Brezhnev and ask him to pardon them. Their only regret, apparently, was that they hadn't finished off the kid.

"While they were on trial in Pul-i-Khumri, the guys from the regiment would regularly slip them hashish and opium. They'd somehow gotten a syringe and would shoot up every day. By the fifth month they were really gone. They couldn't even walk on their own—they had to be led by the hand.

"At the trial, Panchenko said, 'When I was knocking off twenty people at a time on your orders, you said, "Well done! Here's an army man with excellent results in combat. Put his name up on the board of honor!" But when I got hungry—all right, I did get plastered, I was drunk then—and went to get a lamb because there was no food, I killed the same people that I always killed. This time, however, it wasn't on your orders. So now you've decided to try me?'

"The court stated that Panchenko was spewing anti-Soviet propaganda.

" 'Here's a case where three fools got caught,' the commander of the company told us. 'Do whatever you want, but don't get caught.' "

"I don't believe that the company commander would say such a thing," the lieutenant said as he spat out of the hatch. "I don't believe it, and that's the end of it!"

"I found plenty of inconsistencies in Koval'chuk's story," I said. "But what interests me isn't so much the degree of his truthfulness as his way of thinking. He, Movchan, and the other former prisoners of war were trying, of course, to rationalize their desertions. They really couldn't have cared less about me. They knew that it was unlikely we'd ever meet again."

"Who can say what they're about?" the lieutenant asked thoughtfully, putting his feet up on the seat. "Does Koval'chuk think he's any more noble than Panchenko?"

"I don't think so," I replied.

I got the flask from the heater and took a big gulp of strong tea.

Koval'chuk poured some Coke into a plastic glass and drank it down, throwing his head back as if he were drinking vodka.

"There have been so many times when I was forced to do the same things," Koval'chuk said. "The only difference is that Panchenko got caught and others didn't."

Koval'chuk twisted a cigarette in his strong, calloused fingers. (From the looks of things he bit his fingernails a lot.) He sniffed the cigarette and then lit it.

"We once accumulated three broken-down armored carriers," he said. "When the officers decided to send them back to Gorky, we had to squirm around on the ground for three days so that we could unscrew the bottoms of the carriers and hide all the contraband inside. The contraband would later be taken out back in the USSR. No one at the border ever bothered to take apart the frames to see what might be in there. If the border official didn't want to sign the inspection papers for some reason, he'd be bought off.

"Two of our soldiers accompanied the carriers to Gorky. To make sure that they'd keep their mouths shut, the officers were allowed to hang out at home for a couple of weeks. The soldiers kept half the stuff for themselves. Do you think the officers could possibly remember exactly what they were bringing? It's scary to think how many weapons and drugs were smuggled into the USSR.

"Hashish gives you a great high, but you immediately develop a ferocious appetite. That's when you trudge over to the *kishlak* to get a lamb. You can really fly when you get drunk and stoned at the same time. But here's the problem with hashish: if something is troubling you, it'll really start killing you. Hashish would drive me nuts. I'd start thinking again and again about the war and whose number was going to be up next in this fucking company.

"It's best to go into an operation stoned—you turn into an animal. If you drink vodka or dry alcohol that's diluted in water, you can still feel your whole body. But taking a drug is like anesthetizing your soul; you stop feeling altogether. Later, when you come back, you just collapse, like a watch spring that needs to be rewound. And all your muscles ache. As long as you're in combat, however, you just get high and run around like a maniac. Hashish stifles emotions, smoothes over nervous fits. And there are lots of those, especially in the beginning.

"You watch your buddy knock a door down in a *kishlak*. Out comes a dark, bony hand with a sickle. It slashes his belly open and his guts fall onto the ground. Your buddy is just standing there, looking—he can't believe that it isn't a dream. Whenever you see something like that, you don't care who or what's in the house. You just throw a grenade at it, then another one. Bang! The roof is blown off. When you're stoned, you don't notice that you're tired. You run up and down the mountains and the *kishlaks* like a billy goat, without ever stopping."

Koval'chuk took a blue handkerchief out of his pocket and wiped his glistening forehead. Beads of sweat rolled from his temples down his cheeks. The right corner of his mouth was trembling slightly.

"I lost myself there," he said in a cheerless voice. "Lost myself . . .

"Then there was this other incident. Actually, wait—let me read you a poem."

Koval'chuk leaned against the back of his chair and looked up, as if something were inscribed on the ceiling—something I couldn't see. Then he began to recite in a soft, low voice:

> *The road.*
> *A soul is crushed by the wheels.*
> *Nerve endings.*
> *I take a can of vodka.*
>
> *Nightmare.*
> *Shreds of a destiny.*
> *I remember a little girl dressed in white:*
> *Ramadan.*
> *She is so young.*
> *She swam across the road like a swan.*
> *A jerk, a jolt,*
> *A bloody tear fell on the windshield*
> *And into my heart.*
>
> *And only the pulse*
> *Of the bloodshot eyes.*
> *I imagined my sister in the other one's place.*
> *And again comes the scream.*
> *The brakes screeched.*
> *They pulled at my veins;*
> *They hummed for me the song of hell.*

Koval'chuk sat in silence for a few moments, slowly lowering his gaze. He broke into a faint smile as his eyes met mine, waiting several seconds before resuming his story.

"So anyway, there was this incident," he said. "That's what the poem happens to be about. We'd just returned to our unit from a week-long operation in the streets of Aybak. We were just trying to get some sleep, but all of a sudden we had to deal with a group of actors who'd turned up out of the blue. The chief of headquarters had called us up and said, 'Hey, you guys, these actors came here to do a show for the Afghan communists. They need a ride to Dzharkunduk. Plus, it'll be fun for you to take a ride with some girls.' All right, we said, we'll do it. We got into the cars and drove out onto the road.

The armored carrier roared as its treads touched the asphalt and expelled a cloud of black smoke as it picked up speed.

"A young female singer, an ensign, and I sat in the gun-control section of the carrier. The ensign was pestering the young woman with dumb jokes, showing her his gun, and telling her stories of his wild adventures. As for me, I looked up at her only when I could tear my eyes away from the gun sight. Because she sat behind the control panel of a laser, however, our eyes would meet from time to time. 'You have beautiful eyes,' she said to me at one point. 'I'd love to have eyes like that. Let's trade.'

" 'Look, young lady, leave me alone,' I replied. 'If I take my eyes off the gun sight we'll both go to our resting place. You know what I mean?' In the meantime, the ensign kept telling her what a great fighter he was. Suddenly she said to him, 'Why don't you get lost?'

"On hearing this, the driver turned around and shouted, 'Nice going, lady!' Then he turned to the ensign and said with a grin, 'She really showed you!'

"It took only a split second for the driver to lose control of the carrier. It skidded toward the side of the road, where two kids were standing—a girl of twelve or so and a little boy who couldn't have been older than seven. The boy managed to avoid the treads; the girl didn't have enough time. Her black eyes were wide open, staring at me through the gun sight and imprinting a black-and-white photograph on my heart.

" 'Kolia!' I screamed, 'Go to the right!' But it was too late. The left side of the carrier rocked a little as the girl got wrapped around the tread. I could see bloody pieces of flesh through the windshield. I could still hear her scream. The ensign rushed to the radio and shouted, 'Daisy! Daisy!'

" 'You just get back here,' the captain yelled. 'I'll show all of you fuckers.' All the numbers on the carrier were covered with mud—no one could have remembered which one it was.

"When we reached our destination, the singer, seeing the blood on the carrier, said, 'Oh no, what's this?' The ensign began to explain. The singer stood there, nodding her head and saying, 'Yes, I see. . . . What can you do . . . ? War is war.' Then she turned around and went off to sing her idiotic songs.

"I sat on the carrier with Kolia, smoking hashish and cursing myself, the singer, and the ensign."

Koval'chuk crossed his hands on his chest and blew a jet of smoke in my face.

"In the course of two years, I carried out all the orders that I was given," he said. "Then I told myself: I can't live like this anymore—I can't live this lie! God, I thought, this lie will haunt me for the rest of my life. I can try, of course, to drown it in vodka, but I'll never be able to find myself. I won't even be able to write about the past. At that time, back in 1980, the political deputy had told us that after we returned from Afghanistan we would have no right to talk or write about the war.

"I decided to desert when there were only ten days remaining until my demobilization. All the documents were in my hands. I wrote one last letter home, gathered all the ammunition and weapons I had, and left.

"The guerrillas in a nearby *kishlak* gave me shelter. I remember sitting there, drinking tea, when suddenly I felt in my bones that Soviet soldiers were surrounding the *kishlak*. They grabbed me, returned me to the guardhouse in Kunduz, and began a four-month investigation.

"On July 31, 1982, I made another attempt to escape. I went to the bathroom, tore a board off the wall, crawled through the hole, and took off. This time I won. I spent four long years in a rebel detachment. Now I'm here. That's it."

Koval'chuk sat there in silence, hanging his head as if he were suddenly tired. I waited several seconds and, catching his heavy stare, looked him straight in the eye.

"And now, as succinctly as you can, try to explain your reasons for leaving," I said. "In two or three sentences."

Koval'chuk, who looked at me without blinking, seemed to be gazing at something far away. I saw my reflection in his black eyes.

Soon I felt my eyes smarting, but through sheer will power I managed to keep them fixed on Koval'chuk. I held on for another fifteen seconds or so.

Only after I'd blinked did he answer.

"I realized that I wouldn't be able to look the mothers of the soldiers who were killed in Afghanistan in the eye," Koval'chuk said slowly. "That's why I left. And this time for good."

"Interesting fellow," the lieutenant said thoughtfully. "Only I'm having trouble understanding why he wouldn't be able to look the mothers in the eye. I don't see the logic."

I didn't either.

"Was this the last of your New York meetings?" he asked me.

"No," I replied. "After saying good-bye to Movchan and Koval'-chuk, I caught up with Mikhail Shemiakin in the lobby of Freedom House. He was standing there in his leather boots, enveloped in solitude and yellow cigarette smoke. 'Misha,' I said, 'let's meet and talk tonight.' He turned the more severely scarred side of his face to me and said, 'Sure. Why not? My apartment, at eight in the evening. Will that suit you?' Reviewing my plans for the next five hours, I replied: 'Of course. But let's not invite anyone else. All right?' Shemiakin nodded his head in agreement.

At exactly ten minutes to eight I was approaching his house. I went up in the elevator and rang his doorbell. Andronov, the special correspondent of *Literaturnaya Gazeta*, opened the door for me. This was odd: we did agree not to invite anyone else. Shemiakin was still wearing a military uniform and boots. We sat at the dining table, on which there were tall wine glasses, Swiss cheese, and ham. I asked Shemiakin, "Misha, when did you decide to devote your attention to the issue of the Soviet prisoners of war?" "Recently," answered Andronov, "relatively recently." Moving closer toward the artist, I inquired, trying to catch his eye, "Misha, is there a real possibility of helping the boys to obtain freedom?" "Of course," smiled Andronov. After a minute-long pause, he asked, "With whom do you work in Moscow on the POW issue?"

"Work is not really the right word for it. I am simply gathering material to write about it," I replied.

The conversation could not get off the ground. Shemiakin was silent. Andronov kept grinning. I was drinking water. "In that case," Andronov smiled once more, "why don't you write about Shemiakin, the great Russian artist."

"Unfortunately, I am practically unfamiliar with his work," I tried to explain.

Shemiakin held up his index finger and said, "Yes, write about me as an artist, and not as the chairman of the international committee for the liberation of Russian prisoners of war."

Soon afterward we said our good-byes. After thanking the artist for a most informative talk, I headed to the airport.

14

An early twilight darkened the sky above Pul-i-Khumri. For a long time the wind chased the clouds, like a dog chasing after pigeons. After it had driven them away, and decided that this was enough for one day, the wind settled down, and now only from time to time howled in its sleep somewhere far in the mountains. What kind of dreams did the wind see?

For a while not a single star could be seen up above, but then, finally, one star lit up, spreading a soft emerald light all around it. There was no snow here: we had left it behind in Salang. Thick mud mired the road.

"If you love a filthy base, Pul-i-Khumri is the place," quoted the lieutenant grimly, jumping off the armored carrier and looking around with murky eyes.

He spat into his palm and brushed the grayish drops off his *bushlat*.

"Are we here?" I found myself asking, even though I knew the answer.

The driver-mechanic took out a rag and began cleaning mud off the carrier's number.

"Go over there." The lieutenant pointed to the outlines of a remote building. "That's where the regiment headquarters are located."

A miniature woman appeared from behind the stone wall. She slipped out of the gate, bent down, picked something up, and walked back.

"Wow," said the lieutenant, "I thought all the women had already been sent back." A smile froze on his face. For a few moments he just stood there in silence, dreamily following her with his eyes. Suddenly he spoke in verse:

> "*A beautiful name*
> *For heroism and for romance .*
> *A help and a burden*
> *From every corner of Russia*
> *They came here to fight*
> *They came here for fun.*
> *Signalers, doctors, and sergeant-majors*
> *Men have fallen apart because of you . . .*"

After a pause, the lieutenant asked, "Have you ever heard this little verse?"

I nodded.

The woman's body had almost completely disappeared in the darkness. She walked down the moonlit path in the wet mud, which resembled a stripe of wrinkled-up tin foil.

"Well, God willing, we'll see you later. Bye!" Holding down his hat, the lieutenant ran to the place where a second armored carrier was hidden by darkness.

He disappeared, and I suddenly realized that I hadn't even asked his name.

After showing my ID card at the checkpoint, I walked down the moonlit path. I soon caught up with the tiny woman who'd inspired the lieutenant to recite poetry.

"Excuse me," I said. "Where is the regimental headquarters?"

The woman turned around. Her face was pale in the moonlight.

"Over there," she said, pointing to the west. "But there's no one there now except for the officer on duty."

She was beautiful—in the kind of garish, provocative way that's impossible not to notice.

"Where are you from?" she inquired.

"From Salang."

"I'm going to the mess hall. Are you hungry?"

"Extremely. Are you a waitress?"

She nodded, smiling a little.

The mess hall was empty, bathed in cold light by the fluorescent lamps. The woman went into the kitchen, and for a while I heard the clattering of dishes and banging of doors. She reappeared in about ten minutes with an aluminum kettle and a plate of noodles in her small, dark hands.

"Here, it's hot," she said, sitting down in the chair next to mine.

"Have you been here long?" I asked.

"It seems like my whole life," she replied.

"Are you sick of it?"

"Yes and no."

"I can see why you said yes, but why no?"

"I'm a little bit frightened to go back to the USSR," she said, leaning on her fist. "Actually, I left to get away from some problems— family problems, financial problems, you know. . . ."

"How could your husband possibly let you go?" I asked, pouring some more hot tea into my mug.

"Well, I got tired of our poverty and our debts," she said. "One day I just couldn't take it anymore. I told him, 'Why don't you go north, Kolia, and make some money?' "

"What did he say?"

"He flatly refused." Her gray eyes grew distracted, like a child's. "Then I said to him, knowing full well that he wouldn't agree to it, 'If you don't want to, then I'll go myself and bring us back some money.' "

The woman tapped the table nervously with her cherry-colored nails and then added, "He didn't say anything. He just turned to the wall. He didn't even ask where I was going. So that's how it goes."

She took a pack of Belomor Kanal cigarettes from her pocket and spent a long time trying to open it. She finally extracted a cigarette and lit it.

"But I didn't manage to make any money," the woman said. She let out a thin stream of smoke, which hit the surface of the table and slowly spread over it, enveloping the two mugs and empty plate like the morning fog. "Last year there was an explosion at the army warehouses—all the things we'd accumulated were burned. That's why they call this the burned-down regiment."

I detected the sweet scent of powder and lily of the valley perfume. The woman, chilled by a sudden draft, clasped her arms to her chest.

"All kinds of things have happened here," she said. "Last month this Afghan major got into the habit of coming to our unit. Just the other day he tells me, in broken Russian, '*Khanum* [woman], I you marry.' 'Allah forbid,' I tell him, 'I'm already married.' But he just keeps saying that he'll marry me and that's the end of it! Then I realized that he wants to get married so he can go to the USSR. He's scared to be left one on one with the *dukhi*. I don't know if I should laugh or cry."

I spent the night in a temporary structure near the mess hall. The rats, who were having a wild feast underneath the floorboards, wouldn't let me fall asleep. After tossing and turning on my cot for a while, I lit up a cigarette.

On the other side of the thin wall, the officers were watching videos into the wee hours of the night; I could hear their thunderous laughter. But soon all the noise died down, and Senior Lieutenant Varenik entered the room, which was divided in half by parachute cloth. He sat down on a chair and cursed for a long time; the infantry, it seemed, was being sent back before the pilots. Varenik kicked the hot plate with his smart new boots and quickly caught a pot that fell from it. Then he took out a suitcase from underneath his bed and started to stuff the enormous white parachute into it.

"What's that for?" I asked.

"I'm going to make a tent out of it in my backyard," he snapped.

Around four o'clock in the morning we heard the booming of a recoilless gun. The plastic on the window looked as if it were breathing, keeping time with each shot, and the tank wheels that hung on the walls—a homemade defense against rocket missiles—jangled a little.

I lay down again but soon felt drops of rusty water falling from the air conditioner onto my face. I changed my position so that I was lying in the opposite direction.

Just before dawn, after tossing and turning all night long, I finally fell into oblivion—a nervous, shallow sleep.

I dreamed of an airstrip that stretched beyond the horizon, of fighter planes taking off and landing. Even in my sleep their roar made my temples ache.

I've spent so many hours at so many airfields in Afghanistan—under the ferocious suns of Bagram, Jalalabad, Shindand, Kunduz, Kandahar, and Herat—that I couldn't count them now. The thirty-nine minutes and forty-two seconds I spent aboard a MiG-23 in June 1986 cut into my memory like a sharp knife. At the time, the combat flight seemed strange, intoxicating, exhilarating—imagine riding on a supersonic roller coaster in hell. As time passed, however, the exhilaration wore off. It was replaced by a cold, gray emptiness that gradually gave way to a vague sensation of anguish and guilt. We'd flown in fours to the northeast, to the Pakistani border, hiding from the Paki radar stations in the shadows of the mountains. Lieutenant Colonel Karlov and I were in a double bombing formation. Even though our MiG-23 didn't do any bombing, I still don't feel any better about it. That day, after I'd come back to the airfield in Bagram, I lay down on a cot in a pilot's lounge and listened for a long time to an Afghan cricket. He played like a virtuoso, with complete abandon. It was his music that woke in me the first doubts and anguish. The incongruity of a cricket and a MiG split my consciousness.

I was last at the airfield in Bagram just the week before, at the very beginning of January. I lived in a building right next to it, and I could never sleep because the attack planes accelerated right above the roof. I met Anton, a dashing and intrepid air force pilot who had a loose walk and kept his hands in the pockets of his luxurious and fragrant leather coat. Once I sat with him in the control tower, a spacious room that was barely illuminated by the panels of its electronic instruments. The walls were covered with photographs of our aircraft, as well as potential enemy planes—Afghan, Pakistani, Iranian, Chinese, and Indian fighter-bombers—and their identifying markings.

"Each of our pilots has a strong sense of professional pride," Anton said as he lightly tapped the map that was spread out on the table. "Therefore, he tries to go for a direct hit, to bomb the target exactly as ordered—even if it's a *kishlak* that might have peaceful civilians as well as a band of rebels. The way I see it, once you're up in the air it's important to make an accurate strike. I've forbidden myself to feel anything during the bombing attacks; I either leave all my personal feelings and doubts at the airfield or keep them to myself. Otherwise, you inevitably have to ask yourself, 'Why are we here?' "

I looked up at the wall and read: "G-17. Crew—one person. Maximum altitude—18,000 meters. Maximum speed: 1,400–2,100. Maximum overload—seven to eight units. Armaments: Volcano gun, bombs, NURs." Then I thought, Was this man merely frightened by a journalist? Or was the story I had heard about him a lie?

The story, more or less, went as follows: Several months ago, he and his leading plane flew north to bomb a *kishlak* in which a band of rebels was hiding out. A few seconds after the attack, the leading pilot yelled into his radio, "I think we missed!" Both bombers performed an antirocket maneuver, hid in the clouds, and turned around. Instead of heading back to the *kishlak*, however, they returned home to Bagram.

Only as they were approaching the base did the leading pilot hear a response: "So we missed—good for us!"

When I was in Bagram back in June 1986, I remember sitting down next to a boyish-looking pilot. A little volume of Antoine de Saint-Exupéry's short novels, which had been published by *Ogonyok*, was sticking out of the pocket of his beige summer pants. His gloomy eyes were as light blue as the sky, and his prematurely wrinkled forehead was knit in a perplexed grimace. I opened my mouth to ask him a question but stopped myself as the chief of the political office placed his heavy hand on my shoulder. "Leave the guy alone," he told me. "Don't interview him. This is our pacifist. You see, he really loves to analyze things too much."

The Bagram aviation division worked days and nights. It dropped nearly two hundred tons of bombs every twenty-four hours, sometimes even more. For instance, during the 1988 operation code-named Magistral, which ousted armed rebels from the strategic road to

Khost and delivered food and matériel to the blockaded town, the daily expenditure of explosives hit four hundred tons.

Bagram's pilots didn't have it easy. They were exposed to danger not only in the air but also on the ground. Beginning in the latter half of August 1988, the rocket attacks became more and more frequent. They were especially bad on November 13 and December 26.

The Afghan pilots settled down on the other side of the airfield. They weren't having an easy time of it, either—especially considering that in two weeks the entire Soviet airborne force was going to take off and head back to the USSR.

"National reconciliation?" they asked, spreading their dry brown hands in exasperation. "What's that? Why are we making peace with the enemy? An enemy should be fought!"

Amin, a twenty-seven-year-old major, slowly got up from the table. Everyone grew quiet. "I'm the chief of the OTP [firearms and tactical training regiment]," he said. "Six years ago I finished the summer college in Frunze. In five years I've accumulated fifty-five hundred hours of flight time. You can believe me. I am a Khalq soldier. Tell me, why did we first call the enemy 'bandits,' then 'basmatch' [counterrevolutionary robbers in Central Asia during the civil war], then 'terrorists,' then 'extremists,' and now 'the opposition'? It's impossible to fight with the opposition. Meanwhile, the enemy hasn't changed!"

Two question marks flashed in his eyes as he got up from his chair and began pacing nervously up and down the room.

"And what about the regular politics?" he asked. "Why do we have so many corrupt men as our commanders? A man suddenly appeared in Bagram and was given a MiG. So he flew over to Pakistan. Why was he sent to us? I always knew that he was a traitor. He always missed when he had to hit a *kishlak*, even though everyone knew that a rebel band was hiding there. But they told us that he was a revolutionary, and we were persuaded. Why did it happen?"

He came up to a map on the wall and leaned against it with his narrow, bony back.

"You're leaving!" he yelled out. "We'll still keep fighting. But if we have a hard time again, will you come help your Afghan friend?"

Amin was silent for a little while. Then he came up close to me and asked, "Will you come?"

The question sent a chill down my spine.

15

From Pul-i-Khumri I took a chopper to Naibabad, the site of the Fortieth Army's reserve command post. It was after dark by the time we lifted off the pad, and the weather was lousy. The helicopter shook and swung from one side to another, like a truck on a country road. My teeth were doing a desperate tap dance against one another.

Next to me sat a procurator [legal official] from the former garrison in Kunduz. He had a neat little black mustache, quick, attentive eyes, and a slightly crooked nose. He took a portable flashlight from one pocket and a wrinkled-up, unopened envelope from the other. "These sons of bitches!" he cursed, pointing a ray of weak yellow light at the letter. "They don't trust the procurators. It happened again!" I could hear the suppressed anger in his voice. "Just look at this!"

He handed me the envelope, which had been stamped: "Received with evidence of tampering. Operator 548, YFPC [Office of the State Postal Courier]."

"And here's the one that came before it—from my wife." He stuck his hand underneath the parachute straps that crisscrossed his chest and produced a faded envelope. This one bore a different stamp: "Received in soiled condition. Operator # . . ."

The procurator spoke up again. "One time, I couldn't take it anymore," he said. "I called the postal courier and laid into him.

'What kind of treatment is this? I'm a procurator, for God's sake, and a colonel, too!' "

"What did the courier tell you?" I asked, returning the envelope.

"He told me that he wasn't the one who read the letters. He said that the special service in Alma-Ata does it. Incidentally, are you armed?"

"Only with these," I replied, showing him my two fists. "What about you?"

"You bet!" the colonel said. He gave me a sly smile and slapped his holster with his hand. Inside was a Stechkin pistol.

"And there, too," he said, nodding toward the seat. A new submachine gun that had been equipped with a grenade launcher was shaking up and down. A little later I noticed that the colonel's vest was packed solid with AK magazines and grenades.

"You're the most well-armed man in Afghanistan," I said. "I'm scared to sit next to you."

"Don't laugh," the colonel replied. "You never know!"

"We have a long flight ahead of us," I said. "Why don't you tell me about some of the interesting cases you've worked on?"

"I'm afraid that you'll be disappointed," he said, dismissing my question with a wave of his hand. "They won't let us catch the really big fish. They only let us get close to the small fish. Everything is done so that a procurator can't get close to the real crime—to the racketeers. A few years ago, for example, we received a directive to concentrate all our forces on the exposure of—I hope you'll pardon me—illegal bathhouses in the units and subdivisions and to severely punish the individuals who'd built them. They use the small fish, you see, to distract us. And if you do happen to get a big fish on the hook, they start calling from as far as Moscow, telling you to close the case."

"I once met a procurator in Kabul," I said. "I think he spent a whole day questioning a soldier who'd decided to earn himself a medal."

"Had the soldier shot himself?" the colonel asked.

"Yes," I replied. "He shot himself through his bulletproof vest. What about the deserters and the soldiers who are missing in action? Do you ever investigate any of them?"

"Sure," the colonel said with more than a trace of excitement. "Of course we investigate them."

I pulled back the curtain and looked out the window. It seemed as if the earth and the sky had traded places. The entire area below us was studded with thousands of little stars that flickered weakly in the night. Above our heads it was pitch-black.

"That's probably Rabatak," the colonel said.

"Not Aybuk?"

"Perhaps. When we get there I'll give you a cassette tape with a recording of an interrogation of one of the deserters."

"Does the Sukharev amnesty apply to him?"

"Until we've received a decree from the Supreme Soviet, it concerns us very little, to be quite frank." The colonel smiled and winked at me. "Politics is all very well. But the soldiers must be kept in check."

"What's happening with Tseluevsky right now?"

"Is he the one who came back from the United States last fall?"

"Yes."

"His case was closed. He wound up in a psychiatric clinic."

The procurator rummaged around in his bag and produced a battered thermos. "Would you like some tea? Tell me a story and I'll pour you some good Indian tea."

Rita Sergeevna Peresleni, a small, withered woman who'd grown old before her time, smoothed down a worn tablecloth on the round table. She walked with an unsteady, faltering gait toward the kitchen at the far end of her communal apartment.

This Moscow flat had the permanent smell of trouble and loneliness. The floorboards creaked plaintively underneath our feet. The dirty windows rattled forlornly, keeping time with the trucks that passed by on the street.

Yuri Sergeevich Kuznetsov, Rita Sergeevna's brother, closed the door behind him, sat back down in the armchair, and lit up a pungent cigarette. Then he turned to me and said, almost whispering: "You know, she's still pining for him. She misses him so badly that she's just wasting away. When I look at my sister, this old man's heart bursts with grief. I'd give my right arm just to see her smile. Just once."

His eyes were watering, but instead of wiping them dry he took off his thick glasses and cleaned them with the tail of his untucked shirt. Then he put his glasses back on and pushed them firmly up the bridge of his nose.

"He attended School Number Eighty-three," Yuri Sergeevich said. "You know, not far from here there's a trolley stop called 'School.' After graduating from an eight-year school he went on to technical school. Then he worked at the Salut factory. He was drafted on May 11, 1983. Neither of us has seen him since."

I heard Rita Sergeevna's footsteps. She paused, put the teakettle down on the floor, and opened the door. Then she bent down again, picked up the kettle, and quietly entered the room.

"As we were saying good-bye at the train station, Aliosha's grandmother was sobbing," Yuri Sergeevich said as he helped his sister set teacups on the table.

"She saw the other two grandsons off very calmly," Rita Sergeevna said as she got some biscuits from the cupboard. "But when it came to my Aliosha, she wailed and wailed, as if she knew there was going to be trouble."

"Aleksei spent his six months at the Ashkhabad training camp," Yuri Sergeevich said with a wheezing sigh. "Then he was off to Kabul. Then to some unit somewhere in the mountains. Then—"

Rita Sergeevna interrupted. "Then, on January 26, 1984, the Krasnaya Presnya military enlistment office informed me that my son, Aleksei Vladimirovich Peresleni, was missing in action in Afghanistan."

She covered her face with a patched-up apron and sat there for several minutes without moving or making a sound.

Yuri Sergeevich brought an index finger to his lips. "Shhh . . ."

It was getting dark outside. The rainy August day was waning. It was dying and yielding to a warm stuffy evening that promised no relief from the heat.

"She's exhausted," Yuri Sergeevich said after a pause. "She works at the Uzbekistan restaurant from morning to night, making *chebureki* [fried dough]. It's hot there, and the drunks are always shouting."

Suddenly Rita Sergeevna tore her apron away from her eyes and looked at me attentively. "Tell me, are you from the KGB?" she asked in a slightly hoarse voice.

"Not quite," I replied with a smile. "I'm from *Ogonyok*."

"The magazine?"

"Yes, quite right."

Yuri Sergeevich got up from his armchair and sat down at the table. Breaking off a piece of a biscuit, he dipped it in his tea. "So," he asked, "when do you leave for America?"

"Tomorrow," I replied. "I'd very much like to meet with your son, but unfortunately I don't have his address."

"I wonder what Aliosha is like now," Yuri Sergeevich said as he blew on his tea.

"He's larger, more grown-up," Rita Sergeevna said proudly. "Here's a snapshot of him. He sent it to me recently. He's lost some of his good looks, though. He isn't a boy anymore. Liubashka, my daughter, could barely recognize her brother."

She went to the dresser and took a cardboard box from one of its creaky drawers. Carefully holding it in her hands, she brought it to the table.

"This is my Aleksei," she said as she handed me a color photograph and a few letters. "In San Francisco, with his car and his own garage in the background."

"Aliosha has gotten rich," Yuri Sergeevich said, shaking his head. I couldn't tell whether it was a sign of pride or disapproval.

"You may read the letter if you wish," Rita Sergeevna said with a smile. "His address and telephone number, by the way, are in it."

I took the folded sheet of ruled notebook paper from her slightly trembling hand, which was covered with liver spots.

The paper was worn out in the creases and filled with the awkward handwriting of a schoolboy. I began to read:

Hello, my dear Mama and Liubashka! I have received your letter. I was very, very happy. Finally, the first letter in three years. I'm very glad to hear that you're alive and well. I didn't recognize Liubashka in the photograph. She's changed so much. She's turned into a beauty. You've lost weight, Mama. But otherwise you look as good as you looked on May 11, 1983. I'm glad to hear that both grandmothers are alive and well. I'm working as a chef. I've learned a lot already, and I really love my job. I have a feeling that I was born to be a chef. I prepare

French, Italian, Chinese, and American cuisine. That's quite a range, isn't it? I'm sorry that I'm not with you; I wouldn't have let Liuba go to work at sixteen. I have a little bit of experience behind me, and I would advise her to go to college. She's intelligent, and education will open up many opportunities for her. Well, actually, she's not little anymore. She's got a head on her shoulders; she's not dumb. Let her do whatever she sees fit. Yes, I do feel bad about our little village. I've thought about the days that we spent there many, many times. But whatever happened was meant to happen. I'm glad that everything is okay with Grandmother. What's happening with her? I didn't expect that Mishka would get married so quickly. I wonder if I know his wife. Tell him to write me. One more thing—how is Igor Orekhovsky? Does he help you out? How is he doing? Well, that's it for now. It seems like there's nothing else to say. Besides, I don't particularly care for writing big, dramatic stories.

I live in San Francisco. Everything is going well. I have a huge apartment, a garage, a car. You ask what my dreams are, Mama? You probably know them as well as I do. You see, Mama, America is not my motherland. And that says it all. Maybe the time will come when we will all meet again.

Well, write to me—don't forget me. And please send at least one photograph of all the relatives and people who are close to me. And my father's photo, too.

Well, I love all of you and keep you in my thoughts.

I'm sending you a photo.

—Aliosha

P.S. I'm waiting for Irena's address!

At the end of the letter were his address and telephone number. I wrote them down.

"Who's Irena?" I asked as I returned the envelope and the letter.

"His girl, his bride-to-be," Rita Sergeevna replied. She was struggling to hold back tears. "They used to see each other."

"He asked for her address," I said.

"I don't have it," she said, spreading her hands in a gesture of helplessness. "But you can give Aliosha her telephone number."

Putting on her glasses, she opened a worn address book to the letter *I* and handed it to me.

"While you were reading Aliosha's letter, I scribbled him a reply," Yuri Sergeevich said with an imploring smile. "Won't you take it with you?"

I nodded and tossed the letter in my bag, along with the paper where I'd jotted the girl's telephone number.

A bluish pigeon with pink circles around his stern-looking eyes was hobbling along the window ledge.

"You should really try to be gentle with Aliosha," Yuri Sergeevich said. "He's a nervous fellow."

"What's wrong with him?"

"He had a hard childhood. Rita's family lived in poverty. Her husband drank. He beat her a lot—even when she was pregnant. Aliosha saw all this as he was growing up; first he cried, then he became very withdrawn. And when Aliosha turned ten, his father was burned to death."

"How?"

"Bare high-voltage wires. It happens."

I turned to Rita Sergeevna. "Does he write to you often?" I asked.

"Not very often," she replied. "But he does call us sometimes. The last time he did I hung up on him."

"Shhh," her brother hissed from the other side of the table. He beckoned me with his hand and I moved closer to him. "You see," he explained to me in a whisper, "Rita and I think that the man who calls us from America, who speaks in Aliosha's voice, isn't Aliosha."

"Then who could this man be?" I asked in a whisper, following his example.

He lowered his head until his chin almost touched the table. I could feel his warm breath as he said, "I guess he must be from American intelligence."

"But what makes you think that it isn't your nephew?"

"First of all, he spoke with a very slight accent. Rita caught on to it immediately. Second, in one of the letters Aleksei wishes his mother a happy Easter. But our Aleksei has never even been to church! This, of course, is where the Americans really botched it. It wasn't very professional of them at all. Anyone could see that."

By now Rita Sergeevna had calmed down. As she stared obstinately out the window, faint specks of light passed over her face.

"The letters aren't from him, either," she said in a hushed voice. "They were all dictated to him. If anyone knows my Aliosha, it's me. And those aren't his letters."

"To be honest, I don't follow your reasoning," I said.

Yuri Sergeevich broke in to explain. "The reasoning is very simple," he said. "After his father's death, Aliosha was the only man left in the house. He helped his mother with everything. He might have forgotten about his friends from time to time but never about Rita. Now he writes that he has a car, a garage, a house. But if this were our Aliosha, he'd deny himself everything to help his mother. He knows very well that she lives in poverty!"

I was having trouble understanding them again. "How could he possibly help you from San Francisco?" I asked.

"He would send us money."

"Just like that? In an envelope?"

"Yes," Yuri Sergeevich said, "in an envelope!" After dwelling on this for a little while, he once again beckoned me closer with his finger. "There's a sure way of checking whether this is Aliosha or his double, an agent," he said. "When Aliosha was a child, he planted a tree near our house in the village. When you meet him, ask him what kind of tree it was. And let us know afterward—that way we'll be able to check."

"Fine," I said. "Tell me, when did you receive Aliosha's first letter?"

"A long time ago," said Rita Sergeevna, who was still staring out the window.

Yuri Sergeevich was drumming on the table with his fingers.

"May I take a look?" I asked.

"We don't have it," Yuri Sergeevich replied.

"Where is it?"

"The KGB has it," Rita Sergeevna said. "I took it to the KGB myself the same day that I received it."

"Why?"

Yuri Sergeevich looked me straight in the eye and said, "Oh, young man, if you were the same age as I and had gone through everything I've had to go through, you wouldn't ask these kinds of questions."

Rita Sergeevna added some water to her cup from the kettle. "Would you like me to warm yours up again?" she asked me.

"Thank you, but it's time for me to be going," I said gratefully. "Tell me—Peresleni, is that a Russian name?"

"Why do you ask?" Yuri Sergeevich said. There was a touch of fear in his eyes.

"Just out of curiosity. But don't answer if you'd rather not."

"No, why not?" He got up from the table, pressed his fingers against it, and explained as he looked at his sister. "I believe that its roots are Italian. But first of all, that was a long time ago. And second, Peresleni was Rita's husband's name. As you know, he's been gone for more than fifteen years."

"Maybe you could bring Aliosha something from the house as a souvenir," Rita Sergeevna said to me. She hugged the cardboard box again, pressing it to her chest.

"Sure. But what should it be?"

"It could be a comb," she said as she began to search hastily through the papers, keepsakes, and other things in the box. "No, I'm going to keep the comb—it still smells like Aliosha's hair. Here's his union card, if you like."

"Okay," I said, taking the green card from her. "If we meet, it will be nice for Aliosha to hold it in his hands."

"Here's a photograph," Rita Sergeevna said. "Aliosha is only fifteen here . . ."

"So you took the union card, the uncle's letter, and the girlfriend's telephone number with you to San Francisco?" the procurator asked, demonstrating his aptitude for listening and remembering.

"Yes," I replied. "Along with a copy of the Sukharev amnesty."

"Did you call the girlfriend?"

"Of course. But unfortunately Irena wasn't home; she was vacationing somewhere in the south."

"Well, don't make me wait," the procurator said with a smile. "What happened in San Francisco?"

"You know, I should be the one asking you all the questions, not the other way around," I said. "I'm the reporter. If I leave here with an empty notepad, it'll be your fault."

"Reporters, procurators, interrogators, and intelligence agents all share a common character trait."

"What's that?"

"They'll sell their souls to get interesting information."

The sun was rising very quickly above San Francisco, like a yellow balloon. By nine o'clock the city was brimming with a flood of Sunday sunshine.

In the western outskirts of the city the ocean was roaring, diligently licking clean the beige beaches. A salty breeze rushed through the neat streets, rustling leaves and caressing faces with the warm palms of its hands.

After the long, suffocating weekdays in New York City, San Francisco was like a holiday. Gleaming in the golden light of the seasoned summer sun, it resembled a ripe, juicy melon, ready to burst with youthful energy.

I caught a taxi at the airport and was in the center of the city in less than half an hour. My cabbie, dropping his speed to fifteen miles an hour, was lazily gliding down the avenue in his old Dodge. As he came to a stop across from the house numbered 1221, the car rocked a little, as if there were a wave underneath us. As I paid the driver and got out, I felt little hammers banging furiously on my temples. A window on the second floor of the compact house attracted my gaze like a magnet. In its frame I saw a pale face and two alert, cautious eyes.

The little hammers began to bang even harder. I wiped the warm sweat from the back of my neck and slowly climbed the stairs to the second floor and rang the doorbell. The door opened noiselessly. I saw the same face I'd seen in the window and the same blue eyes, which could outstare anyone.

"Hello," I said in English, not knowing if this was Peresleni. "Are you Aleksei?"

"Yes," he replied. He touched his uneven blond mustache with the back of his hand.

I introduced myself and held out my hand. His handshake was weak and hesitant.

Mikhola Movchan suddenly appeared from the other room. "Hi," he said with a smile.

"Hi, there!" I replied, greeting him in Russian. "What brings you to the West Coast?"

"I'm doing some traveling," he said, shrugging his shoulders.

Judging from his carefree gesture, you'd think he spent his mornings in San Francisco and his evenings in New York.

"Why do you speak Russian with Mikhola and English with me?" Peresleni asked. I detected a mixture of caution and resentment in his voice.

"Because he and I have already met," I replied. "As for you, Aleksei, I know you only from photographs. I was afraid to make a mistake."

"Come into the living room," Peresleni said. He opened an enormous coffee-colored door and invited me to follow him.

The living room was spacious and bright, with a fireplace, a couch, and a coffee table. A sturdy fellow of twenty-five or so, dressed in faded jeans and a nylon jacket, was smoking a cigarette near a big window. He greeted me, inserted a cassette into the tape player, and leaned against the wall. A few seconds later Alexander Rosenbaum was singing:

> Ligovka, Ligovka, Ligovka!*
> You are my family home.
> Ligovka, Ligovka, Ligovka!
> We'll sing together yet.

"Let him sing," said the sturdy fellow. "It helps cut through the tension."

"Did my arrival create that much tension?" I asked.

Movchan sat down on the sofa and gave me a friendly smile. The sturdy fellow (who, as it turned out, was working as a mason in San Francisco) knit his bushy eyebrows.

A bookcase near the fireplace was filled with books in Russian. Nearly all of them seemed to deal with some period of Russian

*An area in Leningrad.

history. My gaze focused on a beige booklet titled *Nicholas II— Number-One Enemy of Freemasons*.

A small dining room sat between the living room and kitchen. A straw basket at the center of the oval dining table was filled with oranges and pineapples. A can of Coca-Cola stood on the edge of the table.

"How long will you be in San Francisco?" Movchan asked.

"Not long," I replied. "I'm thinking of leaving on one of the flights tonight."

"Are you thinking of leaving, or leaving?" he asked, drilling me with his heavy stare.

"I'm leaving," I said.

Movchan and the sturdy dark-haired fellow relaxed noticeably.

As soon as the song had ended, Movchan slapped his thighs and abruptly got up from the couch. "Well, we've got to go," he said. "I need to take care of some things, you know."

"Sure," I said.

Movchan held out his hand to me and said, "Well, good-bye!" Smiling once more, he put his arms around the sturdy fellow and escorted him out of the living room. A minute later we heard the front door slam.

Peresleni came back into the room, changed the cassette in the tape player, and turned down the volume. "What is it that you're so interested in?" he asked.

"Your life," I replied.

He looked around the apartment with an ironic and satisfied demeanor. "As you can see, we're getting by," he said with a chuckle, his cheeks blushing.

"Yes, your apartment isn't half bad," I said. "But where's the garage with your car?"

"You see, right now I don't have one," he answered evasively. "But how do you know about that?"

"Rita Sergeevna showed me your photograph with the car and the garage in the background," I said. "You also mentioned it in your letter, if you recall."

"How is Mama?" he asked suddenly. He was staring out the window and nervously biting a fingernail.

"Yuri Sergeevich said that she hasn't been doing very well lately," I told him. "I visited them right before I left Moscow."

"My poor mama," Peresleni said with a deep sigh. He walked over to the window. Placing the palms of his hands on the glass, he leaned his cheek on it. He stood like that for a minute. Then he turned to me abruptly and said, "Sit down on the couch. We don't have a lot of time. Lenka will be home soon, and she won't let us have a decent talk."

I remembered about Irena. "Is she your wife?" I asked.

Peresleni waved his hand in exasperation. "Girlfriend, wife—what difference does it make? We're just living together. We'll see what happens."

"Are you the one who's doing all this reading?"

"It's Lenka's book collection." He opened the can of soda and filled our glasses. "But I flip through them, too. They're all very interesting. I couldn't get anything like that in the Soviet Union. You could say that I'm educating myself. Well, go ahead—ask some questions!"

"How did America receive you, and how did you accept it?"

"When I arrived here, I was really out of it," Peresleni said, rubbing his forehead with his fingers. "Just imagine—captivity, the trip, my nerves. First they brought us to New York City. It was odd to be a stranger among strangers, you know. It was interesting, mysterious. I walked around the city, peeping in the windows of its stores and looking in the faces of its people. This austere city, shimmering with the cold neon of advertisements, really overwhelmed me. It was as if a shroud of numbness descended upon my mind."

Peresleni plucked a speck of tobacco from the bridge of his nose with his little finger, drank some more soda, and lit a cigarette.

"As I walked around New York, I didn't know whether I should feel blessed or cursed," he said. "Anyway, when they brought us to New York they asked, 'Would you boys like to visit a store—the kind of store that you've never been to before?' 'Sure,' we said, 'take us there.' So they bring us to a gigantic supermarket. Everything is flooded with light, and the shelves are sagging underneath all the food. They take our pictures and record our comments on tape. Then they ask us, 'Well, boys, what's your impression of America?' 'Your women are unbelievably beautiful,' I replied, 'but Russian women are even better!' They gave us a kind of sour smile. You see, I hadn't seen a normal woman for so many years that I was dazed not by the amount of food in the supermarket, but by the women I saw there. The war and captivity had taken away all the normal, healthy feelings that any young man has. In Afghanistan, when I woke up in the morning, I wasn't thinking of a woman's body, but of death—of how long I had left to live. Two hours, a day, a year?"

Peresleni walked softly across the room and put a new cassette in the tape player. Alla Pugachova, another popular contemporary singer, soon replaced Rosenbaum. "You can see a million, a million, a million scarlet roses from your window," Alla sang in San Francisco.

"America," Peresleni said slowly and thoughtfully. He cracked his knuckles. "What about America? America gives you opportunities. America shelters you. America teaches you how to live."

Peresleni sat down on the couch again and suddenly burst into tears. He cried like a child, sobbing violently, full of despair. He wasn't embarrassed by his tears and didn't try to hide them from me. He let them stream down his cheeks and fall onto the floor.

"When you're left all alone, you're like a bird amid the ocean," he said. He was looking at his sneakers and catching the falling teardrops with his hand. "You search for a shore. That's what I did— try to find a place to land. It's not that easy. Thank God, at least, that I landed on this shore. Thank God. You can see that I'm becoming acclimated here bit by bit. Lenka and I have made this slapdash nest together. I get paid enough money."

Peresleni was silent for a few moments. Then he pushed the hair out of his face and continued. "It really is enough money," he said. "But you can never pluck out of your heart what's been planted in it since the beginning—your motherland. No matter where you find yourself, it's in you."

He wiped his red eyes on his sleeve. A strand of saliva hung from his lip.

"America, what is it to me?" he asked in a dreary, uneven voice, struggling with a convulsion in his chest and throat. "Bullshit! Pardon my language, but America is bullshit. Would you like me to speak in English? I know how to!"

He suggested this in a childlike way, as if he were inviting me to play with him.

"No, don't," I replied.

"Fucking America!" he exclaimed in English. By now his voice had become a little hoarse. "I know I don't like this shit! I no like American people. Fucking shit!

"After they took us to that store"—here Peresleni switched back to Russian—"they asked us, 'Boys, where do you want to go?' 'California!' I immediately blurted out. 'Why California?' they asked. 'Because I don't know any other state in this America of yours!' I replied. Well, to make a long story short, they sent me to California. When I arrived a man met me here, and I lived in his house for a few months. He helped me to find a job. And so I started loading trucks. I loaded furniture, delivered it, and was paid good money. I was really happy with all of it. But then . . ."

Peresleni shut his eyes and pressed the tips of his little fingers to his temples, as if he were struggling with a headache. Out on the street, a car screeched to a stop. Peresleni slowly lowered his hands onto his knees and took up where he'd left off.

"But then I got involved with some dope fiends and started taking drugs. I felt too lazy to work as a deliveryman, so I quit my job."

I glanced at the skin inside his elbow but saw nothing except the bluish thread of a vein. "How did you get involved with them?" I asked.

"It doesn't matter," he replied. "They're still trash, filth, crap, carrion. They should be squashed like lice."

"What happened next?"

"Then I found a job as a tailor, and at the same time I enrolled in some computer-technician courses. I was good at all of these things. I was good at electronics. I could still fix a computer right now if I had to, honestly. Would you like to have a drink? I feel kind of awful."

"I have no objection."

"Then let's run down to the store. It'll only take five minutes."

Peresleni searched the store's shelves for a long time, until his gaze finally fell on a squat, one-liter bottle of vodka. His lips and eyebrows moved as he read the name on the label. "It's Finnish," he said with satisfaction. "At least that's near Russia. And now for the pickles!"

He looked through a platoon of glass jars on a lower shelf. He chose one and boldly tossed it in the air a few times, saying, "This could almost be from the Rizhskiy market!"

I paid the cashier and in less than ten minutes we were ascending the stairs to Peresleni's second-floor apartment.

Once inside, he took a few hot dogs out of the refrigerator and dropped them on a red-hot frying pan greased with corn oil. After browning the hot dogs on one side, he flipped them into the air with the practiced flick of a chef's wrist. After doing a somersault about a meter above the pan, the hot dogs gracefully landed on their un-cooked sides—all in a neat row.

We sat down at the coffee table. "In a certain sense, a person's character is his fate," he said. "Try, when you have some spare time, to gain an understanding of your character, and then you'll be able to predict your destiny. Try it."

"I'd think it would be a lot easier to consult a fortune-teller," I said.

Peresleni suddenly turned his serious stare toward the opposite wall, slightly above my head. "Well, let's drink to Russia's destiny," he said. "Let's hope it'll have some luck in the next century. Cheers!"

Peresleni emptied his glass in one gulp. "Nice!" he exclaimed in an unexpected falsetto. He crossed his strong, slightly pudgy, hands on his chest and thought for a little while. Then he resumed speaking in his normal voice.

"Fate is a murky thing. When I was seventeen or eighteen, I was in love with Yuri Vladimirovich Andropov. I wanted to go to the KGB school so that I could serve as his personal bodyguard. I really loved that man. Do you remember his speech from the Lenin Mausoleum at Brezhnev's funeral? He was the only member of the Politburo who wasn't wearing a hat. The wind played with his gray hair. Andropov spoke sincerely, honestly. Nobody had made this kind of address from the mausoleum for a long, long time. He was a strong man; he made the country work during the workday. I was very proud when Andropov became the general secretary."

Peresleni leaned against the back of the couch, stuck his hands in the pockets of his jeans, and smiled dreamily. Suddenly, however, his smile turned into a frown.

"But fate decided otherwise," he said. "It didn't ask me if I wanted to go to Afghanistan. I was a sergeant. Two Kazakhs served in my subdivision. They hated me just because I was from Moscow. They'd beat me until I was black and blue, until I'd lose consciousness and the ability to feel pain. 'The Russian who served here before you was also from Moscow,' they'd keep saying. 'We tried to "reeducate" him because he—like you—was a fool, the swine. The Russian swine who was here before you ran off to the *dushmani*. We'll "reeducate" you, and you'll leave, too.' Their anger was frightening and their rage fierce. It seemed as if they were using me to avenge all the suffering that had befallen their people. 'What are you beating me for, you bastards?' I'd shout. They'd merely laugh and beat me even harder. They used their boots, their fists; they hit me in the groin, in the stomach, on the head. Ohhh, it hurts just to remember it!"

Peresleni closed his eyes. His nostrils trembled a little. He wiped his face with the palms of his hands, as if it were wet.

"They hated me even before meeting me. Maybe that hate was their chief reason for being. Because if it hadn't been for them, I wouldn't have deserted my unit and you and I wouldn't be drinking vodka together. The thought of deserting sprouted in my subconscious during and after the beatings. The Kazakhs themselves beat it into my brain, which they emptied of everything except that one saving dream. All beaten up, I would lie down on the floor, crawl under the cot to stay out of their way, and dream about leaving. I dreamed about it indulgently, rapturously. The dream was my revenge against the Kazakhs and my fate. I wanted to live so that one day I could get even. I had no other purpose. I invested all of my imagination and inspiration, everything that I had, in my feverish dreams. I even smiled when I was dreaming; tears of happiness streamed down my face. Oh, how harsh is my fate!"

We got up and, without speaking, looked each other in the eye. I could hear my breath and his. Peresleni's mouth was as crooked as a snake.

"A third toast!" he said. *

We drank for the fifteen thousand people who, like he and I, had been killed in Afghanistan.

---

*People in the Soviet Union traditionally drink the "third toast" without clinking their glasses, out of respect for those killed in battle.

"Well, to make it short, I left," Peresleni said as he slid the tip of a finger along the edge of the table. "Or rather, ran into a vineyard after one of the beatings, intentionally leaving my rifle behind. So the *dukhi* got me unarmed and defenseless. They, too, gave me a good beating because I'd surrendered without an AK. After just a few days, I was praying to God and to the command of the Fortieth Army: 'Please, my friends, free me from captivity. I fought for you, and I'll be glad to fight for another five years!' But no one set me free. My God didn't hear me, and the Afghans wanted to force me to worship Allah. And theirs is a cruel God."

With the flick of a switch the light came on in the dining room and I once again saw Peresleni's tears.

"I didn't run from my unit because I wanted to join the rebels. Believe it or not, I wanted to get to Italy on foot. I believed that I had relatives there. I thought that I'd find them. When I was little, I used to ask my mother why our last name wasn't Petrov, Ivanov, or Tutekin. She'd answer that one of my great-grandfathers must have been Italian. With each passing year the image of an Italian great-grandfather became more and more real in my mind. I wanted to hide from those two Kazakhs in his castle, somewhere in Naples. But instead of Italy I wound up in captivity."

Peresleni smiled with his eyes only and silently moved his lips.

"There, in Afghanistan, I met other Russian captives. Some of them were still children. How could anyone dress them up in military uniforms and army boots and send them off to Afghanistan just like that? How could silly little kids be sent off to war at all? That's criminal! Let the thirty-year-olds and forty-year-olds fight the wars. Maybe that's stupid, too, but at least it's preferable to misleading mere children. We were all deceived and turned into mincemeat. At least I managed to get out, but the other ones—the fifteen thousand we drank to—didn't. Now I must pay another price for the life that I was given—the price of loneliness. Do you know what loneliness is? Loneliness is an androgynous being who sometimes assumes the guise of a man in a gray hat. I've grown accustomed to him. He isn't a bad fellow. He keeps his mouth shut, doesn't cause any harm, and that's it. And in these times simply not causing any harm counts for so much."

We heard the front door open and a woman's quick footsteps in the living room.

"Lenka is here," Peresleni explained. He went on:

"In Afghanistan I saw people fighting one another for the future of the country," he said. "Today, many countries are fighting for the future of the world. I chose to go to the seminary and fight my own demons. Each person should follow God to the degree that he is able to. While I was there I realized how far Christianity is from Christ and how far communism is from the communist dream. Today, Russia stands at the threshold of a new faith, or philosophy—call it what you like. The world has already gone through the religion of God the Father. It has experienced the religion of God the Son. The time has come for the religion of God the Holy Spirit. I believe that it will come from Russia."

Peresleni flitted from one subject to another, like a bird caught inside a room. He spoke quickly, swallowing his words and licking his dry lips from time to time. His eyes had a feverish glow.

Suddenly a bolt of lightning shot down from the sky outside; it was as if someone had photographed us using a flash. In a few moments a howitzer boomed somewhere to the west of San Francisco.

"Whenever I hear thunder," Peresleni said as he closed the window, "I immediately see Afghanistan in front of me."

"Do you have to go to work tomorrow?" I asked.

"Yes," he replied. "I'll be up at six o'clock in the morning, as usual. It takes me forty minutes to get there. I walk. I have to be at work at seven."

"Where do you work?"

"In a restaurant called Four Seasons. I work as a chef. I really love to cook. My owners are pretty nice people."

My owners. For some reason the phrase made me cringe. Never in my life—all twenty-seven years of it—had I ever uttered those words (my owner was a system, not a person).

"I like working for them, but I'd like to be the boss myself," Peresleni said. "I'm very close to being the boss, believe me. I have what it takes. I'll make it—you'll see! Come back in five years and I'll be a powerful millionaire. Right now I need to save some money. Then I can open my own little restaurant, and then a whole chain of restaurants!"

"I wish you the best, from the bottom of my heart," I said.

"It's so great that my mom taught me to cook when I was little. She's so wonderful! So I'll make all the money I need. I'll definitely make a lot of money. I have a pretty good salary already."

"Aleksei, I have to go."

"Wait, we'll take you there. Lenka drives faster than the speed of light."

I took the letter from my pocket and put it on the table. "This is from your uncle," I said.

He deftly opened the envelope and started reading. His eyes moved from side to side. I took a few large gulps of coffee; it was already cool and no longer burned my mouth. Peresleni refolded the letter, sliding a fingernail along its edge.

"It seems that my uncle has suddenly become overly fond of politics," he said slowly and grimly. "He reads the newspapers now and quotes them, too. Be honest with me, was this dictated to him?"

"Yuri Sergeevich wrote the letter that you've just read while I was there. And nobody told him to do it."

Making sure that the door to the kitchen was tightly closed, I handed him a piece of paper on which I'd written Irena's telephone number. "In your letter to your mother you asked for Irena's address, but Rita Sergeevna did not have it," I said. "She gave me this telephone number. I called Irena, but she wasn't home. She was vacationing somewhere."

"You were given this number by the KGB," Peresleni said coldly. "I should know. What are you? A captain? Or did they make you major already?"

"Wow!" The procurator said above the noise and slapped his face with the palm of his hand. We were nearing the command post. "They must have really scared the guy, those devils! Is that really what he asked you, whether you were a captain or a major?"

"That's what he asked me," I said with a smile.

"Did you tell him that his own mother believes the CIA is helping him compose the letters he's sending her?"

"No. Both mother and son are practically insane with their fear of spies. Why add more wood to the fire?"

"Too bad," the procurator said. "You should have told him."

"If one man believes another man to be a camel," I replied, "it is very difficult for the latter to prove he is not."

• • •

Peresleni gave me a sullen stare.

"It really makes no difference to me whether you are a KGB agent or a journalist," he said. "In either case it's just nice to speak to someone who came from *there*."

"If you don't want to take the phone number," I said, "please give it back to me."

Peresleni didn't answer, but he hid the piece of paper deep in his pocket.

Suddenly I remembered that I was supposed to give Peresleni his old union card. I rummaged in the breast pocket of my jacket again and handed it to him. "This is for you to keep as a souvenir," I said. "Rita Sergeevna asked me to give it to you."

Peresleni looked at his photograph and burst into laughter. "What a fool I am in this picture," he said. "A fool! I had no idea about the things that would happen to me only a year later. Poor, silly boy."

On our way to the airport we stopped at the Russian Orthodox church in San Francisco. It stood alone in the enormous and noisy city, washed by a soft evening drizzle and enveloped in fog and darkness. Inside, it was warm and there was the sweet scent of candles.

Peresleni approached the altar. Out of the corner of my eye I could see that his lips were moving: "And by the holy cross . . . the blessed one . . . holy one . . . servant of God . . . my hope of hopes . . ."

What was Peresleni asking God for on that warm August evening, amid the sprinkling of rain and the sputtering of candles? Did the Lord hear his prayer? And, if so, what was the Lord's judgment?

About two weeks later a man who called himself Aleksei telephoned the consulate general of the USSR in San Francisco. He wanted to arrange a meeting. He said that he was in an area of Seattle that was closed to Soviet citizens. The call was made on a Friday night, just as everyone on the consulate's staff was preparing to go home. The man was told to contact the consulate on Monday morning.

He never called back.

Irena was married recently. She still lives in Moscow, and they say that she is happy. But every now and then, once or twice a year, when a strange melancholy visits her heart, she goes to the telephone and, after making sure that no one is nearby, calls Rita Sergeevna. They exchange news, talk for a long time, reminisce about the past, and say good-bye until Irena's next call. After she hangs up, Rita Sergeevna takes a cardboard box out of the dresser and, crying softly, looks through the things Aleksei left behind: his comb, his Komsomol card, his handkerchief.

As for Irena, she hastily hides in her purse the address book that contains the telephone number of the woman who was destined never to become her mother-in-law. Then she goes off to take care of her housework.

16

As Soviet troops withdrew along the central route through the South Salang area, final preparations were being made for military action against Ahmad Shah Massoud. But here, in Naibabad, lost amid the boundless desert sands some seventy kilometers from the Soviet border, it seemed that the war was already over. The only reminders of the war were the countless columns of military and transport vehicles that stretched despondently from south to north in the direction of Khairaton.

Not far from the town, at the site of the 201st Motorized Infantry Division, Major General Sokolov, the chief of the Fortieth Army headquarters, had established a backup command post. According to plan, Lieutenant General Boris Gromov, the commander of the army, would relocate here about ten days before the last Soviet subdivision was to cross the border. Just in case, a separate building had been set up to accommodate the leader of the Operations Group of the Ministry of Defense, which was still located in Kabul. The soldiers nicknamed it "Varennikov's building."

The division's last lights were dying, and the night's stiff, chilly winds had already dusted the ice-covered puddles with frost.

The procurator said good-bye to me near the division's headquarters. As he disappeared into the darkness, I could hear the crunching sound his boots made on the ice.

Behind the wall and the barbed wire, the last choppers landed for the night.

Colonel Ruzliaev, the commander of the division, was in his office drinking a late-night cup of tea.

Ruzliaev was a stocky man with wide shoulders; his forty-one-year-old body seemed to have been made to last for centuries. The translucent blue eyes on his sunburned and wind-beaten face looked around angrily. His movements were quick, exact, and full of energy. His sly smile was hidden behind a violet cloud of cigarette smoke.

Following his graduation from the Armored Tank Academy, Ruzliaev had been sent to the Siberian Military District, where he became the chief of headquarters of a tank regiment. Later he served as the commander of a motorized rifle regiment on an APC, and in 1983 he was made the chief of headquarters of the entire division.

Ruzliaev arrived in Afghanistan in 1987 and took over for Colonel Shehovtsov. He'd been in charge of the division ever since, first in Kunduz and now in Naibabad.

"I met Shehovtsov in April of 1987," I told Ruzliaev. "He was conducting an operation to eliminate Gayur's gang."

"At Baghlan?" he asked, narrowing his eyes.

"Yes," I replied. "Even though Gayur was surrounded in every direction by Afghan and Soviet subdivisions—there were blockades every twenty-five or thirty meters—he somehow managed to get away. Is he still fighting?"

"He sure is, the fucker!" Ruzliaev cursed. "At that time, in the spring of 1987, Shehovtsov had completely surrounded him. It seemed impossible for him to escape. But Gayur outsmarted everybody. Some people are convinced that he slipped out of the blockade in women's clothes; others believe that he bribed some Afghan soldiers to take him out in an armored carrier—no one was checking them. In other words, it was some act of treachery that got him out. Baghlan is still a sore point with us. I moved the regiment out of Baghlan—it's back in the Soviet Union now—and Gayur and Shams are active there again."

The smile vanished from Ruzliaev's face. He grew noticeably sterner.

The last few days had done a number on Ruzliaev's nerves. At Gray Lake, near the Eighth Post, a Private Starikov had disappeared.

At Pul-i-Khumri, a large part of a regiment's documents had burned in a fire. The airborne troopers who were moving north along the road apparently had been causing a lot of trouble.

"I've had it up to here with those Rambos," Ruzliaev said with a sigh. He nodded toward the darkened window, through which we could hear the muffled roar of military vehicles. "They have a lot of money and not enough to do! Just the other day I met one of their ensigns—he was drunk as a skunk and had afghani bills sticking out of his pockets. Not just tens, but thousands! So there's never a dull moment. And to make matters worse, we now have the Karp and Ignatienko situation on our hands."

On January 11, at precisely ten-twenty in the morning, Ruzliaev had been informed that the rebels had seized a UAZ and, along with it, two Soviet soldiers. He rushed to investigate and learned that two men and a car were missing from the communications regiment. Sergeant Andres Karp and Ensign Pavel Ignatienko apparently had stolen some condensed milk, butter, and canned meat from the provision depot and had gone to Tashkurghan in one of the regiment's UAZs to sell it; somewhere along the way, they'd been captured by rebels from Rezok's band.

Ruzliaev quickly decided to surround the rebel detachment from all sides with the men of the reconnaissance battalion and company. Then he established an artillery formation and subjected the rebels' command post to several severe attacks. The exploding shells shook everything around them and left black puddles on the ground. The air filled with the smell of burning, and gray smoke drifted like fog above the desert sands.

Rezok soon sent Ruzliaev a letter in which he asked him to stop the artillery attacks and promised to return Karp and Ignatienko in return for one hundred million afghanis and fifty captured mujahedin. A little later he sent Ruzliaev a list of the people whose release he demanded.

Within a few days Ruzliaev had managed to collect five hundred thousand afghanis. He made arrangements with the local officials to release twenty-one mujahedin from prison.

One morning he received the following note: "We are being held at the *kishlak* of Kur. Both the driver and I have been wounded in the leg. Basic first aid has been administered. If you can, please don't fire. Ignatienko."

Ruzliaev sent this message in return: "Karp and Ignatienko! Write us about your condition and health. Send me notes with answers to the questions posed through the Afghan elders at sixteen hundred hours sharp every day. Ruzliaev."

Then came Ignatienko's reply: "Our health is in satisfactory condition. We can hold out for a while longer. We'll hang in there for as long as necessary. Our relationship with the *dukhi* is stabilizing. They gave us medicine. Ignatienko. P.S. They won't let us write anything else."

The following day, the elders delivered a new message from Rezok: "Commander of the Soviet Division Ruzliaev! I have two of your men, whose names are Pasha and Andrei. They are in very poor condition. Until you release the mujahedin, I will not give them back to you. I will not allow any further correspondence. When you are ready to release the mujahedin, I will let you know where the trade will take place. Rezok."

On the morning of January 17, after placing the five hundred thousand afghanis in a small chest and loading the mujahedin in an armored carrier, Ruzliaev and Major General Sokolov, the commander of the headquarters, went to Tashkurghan, where the exchange of prisoners was supposed to take place on a bridge over the Samangan River. Several subdivisions of the Afghan MGB under Colonel Khamid's command had blocked off all the streets along the river.

The sun was high above Tashkurghan. The air was clear and cold.

A decision had been made to exchange one of the Soviet soldiers for nine Afghan guerrillas.

On arriving at the designated point of exchange, Sokolov and Ruzliaev carefully examined the opposite bank of the river, which was bristling with machine guns and grenade launchers. Rezok stood next to Karp and Ignatienko. A woman in European clothes was videotaping the scene.

The Soviet vehicles turned off their engines. Their black guns shone dully in the sun as they stared at the other side of the river.

Rezok's men led Karp up to the bridge. Ruzliaev's soldiers,

accompanied by nine guerrillas, moved toward the bridge from the other end. The two groups walked slowly toward each other. The bridge rocked a little. Except for the sound of footsteps and the murmur of the river, everything was quiet.

Karp, drawing alongside the men that he was being traded for, paused for a second and looked them in the eye. Then he looked at Ruzliaev and, ignoring the pain in his leg, broke into a run, hobbling toward his comrades.

Ignatienko's exchange was more complicated. For no apparent reason, Rezok suddenly refused to trade him. Ruzliaev cursed quietly. Sokolov continued to stare intently at the opposite bank. Rezok walked in circles around Ignatienko, gesturing with his hands and saying something.

Fifty minutes had passed since Karp had trotted across the bridge.

Then, without any warning, Rezok put his arms around Ignatienko and gave him a slight shove in the back. After twenty more minutes the exchange was over.

Ruzliaev sent the small chest with the money and four submachine guns to the other side of the river. He turned around one more time and looked at Rezok. Rezok looked at him. They stood like that for a minute. Then the two men turned around and headed away from the gray Samangan River. Ruzliaev went north, Rezok went south.

They never saw each other again.

"I dealt with Karp and Ignatienko from January eleventh to January seventeenth," Ruzliaev told me. His sharp gaze pierced the curtain of cigarette smoke. "Rezok turned out to be a decent guy—he didn't incite them to treason or send them to Pakistan."

Ruzliaev walked across the room and turned off the television set. "You free some bastard from the *dukhi*," he said as he filled our cups with ruby-colored tea, "and then you start thinking, Should I really have done it? I once made the same kind of trade for one of our guys, but he ended up dumping all kinds of garbage on me. 'I ran away from your Soviet government,' he says to me. 'It has never been any good to me.' "

Ruzliaev touched his Adam's apple as if he wanted to make sure that it was still there. He coughed several times, came up to the table, and lowered himself with some effort onto the chair. "When I think of the kind of treatment our guys get on the other side of the border," he said, "sometimes I feel lousy inside." I suddenly remembered the words of a major from Pul-i-Khumri.

The major, who was about thirty-five years old, had a round face and chubby cheeks. He bitterly despised the press—in fact, he hated journalists even more than he hated the *dukhi*. Staring at me with his black eyes, which were ready to open fire at any moment, he muttered through clenched teeth: "I'm surprised that you haven't made a war hero out of Hudalov. I guess you haven't gotten around to it yet." Then he spat, burning a hole in the snow.

Kazbek Hudalov, a graduate of the Ordzhenikidze Command School, was a notorious traitor. After deserting to the rebels, he'd formed a detachment of ten or twelve Tajik deserters and aggressively attacked Afghan government troops as well as subdivisions of the Fortieth Army, shelling their posts. His men sometimes dressed in Soviet military uniforms—a trick that often misled even the most experienced soldiers. In the fall of 1988, Hudalov's detachment had been active around the Bagram crossing, firing at Afghan posts, but in the winter his tracks disappeared somewhere in the Panjshir mountains.

Ruzliaev smoked his cigarettes right down to the filter—a sign of thrift and neatness. Even now, the glowing tip of his cigarette practically touched his fingers, which were yellow from nicotine. Crossing his eyes to make sure that only a centimeter was left on the butt of his cigarette, he put it out with his left hand while he opened a new pack with his right.

For lack of anything better to do, I spent the first half of the day in Khairaton in the company of the most untalkative captain I'd ever met. During the three-hour trip there and back he didn't utter a single word (except for cursing once at a traffic officer for refusing to stamp his driver's pass). In Khairaton we went to get some coal for the communications regiment, but the warehouse was closed and we came back empty-handed.

Upon our return to Naibabad, I went to see Sokolov to ask him for a chopper to Kabul.

"If the wind doesn't die down the choppers won't go anywhere," he said, looking skeptically out the window of his office.

The Soviet journalists in Kabul didn't know Sokolov very well, even though he was the son of a famous Soviet military leader. (His father, Marshal S. L. Sokolov, had been relieved of his duties as the minister of defense in the spring of 1987 after a West German, Matthias Rust, landed his plane in Red Square.) Some officers said that Sokolov was talented, businesslike, easy to talk to, and very demanding. He'd been sent to Afghanistan toward the end of the war (replacing General Grekov). He'd immediately come down with a classic set of infectious diseases, including hepatitis. By the time he got out of the hospital he'd lost a lot of strength. Soon after that, Gromov had sent him to Naibabad.

"The war has come to its logical end," Ruzliaev said. "Lately it's become popular to denounce and revile it. But the army gets reviled along with it, and that's dangerous. Everything shouldn't be blamed on the military. If things continue in this way, should a dangerous situation suddenly arise the army will refuse to fight. . . . Well, it's time to go to sleep. My first presentation is at four-twenty in the morning."

17

I spent the night in a trailer on Lipsky Street, a paved path that the soldiers had named after the chief of the division's political office, who lived nearby. The trailer was covered with camouflage netting, which rustled at night like a forest.

In the morning a warm wind blew in from the south, bringing clouds with it and destroying my chances of getting to Kabul. A cyclone that had originated somewhere above the Persian Gulf was now moving in a northeast direction. It was responsible for everything. It had apparently decided to travel through all the wars on the planet—the Middle East, Afghanistan. . . . Where would it go next? The dry southern wind was infused with the smells of war; it made your hair brittle, caused your skin to peel, weakened your nerves, and numbed your mind.

Sokolov was tall and thin. He spoke softly but confidently in a pleasant bass. He had the smile of an honest, sincere, and intelligent man, and he smiled often.

He was dressed in a dappled shirt whose crisp white collar made his thin face seem even darker. He was just a little over forty.

Back in Kabul, I'd once asked a veteran Soviet journalist about Sokolov; the old-timer knew everything about everybody. "He's an incredibly intelligent man," he replied. "He belongs to a third generation of intelligentsia." The old-timer was right. If the Fortieth

Army held a contest to identify the most cultured man in its ranks, Sokolov would undoubtedly win first prize.

"How long did it take you to adjust to Afghanistan when you first came here?" I asked Sokolov.

"I can tell you from experience that you spend the first year just getting familiar with what's going on," he said with a smile. "The second year you start gaining confidence, and in the third year you can go out and do a little hunting once in a while. Do you smoke? Help yourself."

He offered me a pack of cigarettes.

"From everything I've seen, the Fortieth Army smokes more than any other army in the entire world," I said. "Everyone smokes, from privates to commanders. General Varennikov, I believe, is the only exception."

"War is war," Sokolov said. "What can you do?"

"The negative sides of the war are getting plenty of attention, but what about its positive aspects?" I asked. "How has the war helped the army?"

"In general, our army isn't very well adapted to combat activity abroad," Sokolov said. "What are the pluses of the war? It's difficult to say. The conditions in Afghanistan are unique, and the experience gained here would be hard to apply in a 'classic' war. Here, I think, we realized that our small subdivisions—from battalions on down— must be better trained. Their commanders must be given more independence; not all decisions should be made at the top. Actually, Afghanistan did teach them to be independent in this way. Our officers received real combat experience here. And here is the other lesson: any operation, even an insignificant one, must be planned out to the smallest detail."

"What about the APC #2?"

"We increased its gun's angle of elevation; now an APC #2 can shoot at practically any mountain peak. We've also made the APC #2 more stable on slopes. Finally, we've made it more comfortable. In short, we managed to convince the manufacturer that such modifications were necessary. The same could be said for the APC #80, too."

Our discussion floated from one topic to another: cigarettes,

General Headquarters, military equipment, Afghanistan, children, the fate of the army. . . .

"I'd dreamed about being in the service since I was a child," Sokolov said, looking up. "I wanted to follow in my father's footsteps. But he was against it: the army wasn't very popular toward the end of the 1950s, which was when they began the reduction of the armed forces. . . . But I pursued it just to spite everybody. I went from being a lieutenant to being a general. Now my son is also dreaming about the army, and once again it's not very popular. The newspapers are making fun of military glory, patriotism, even personal courage. . . . It's hard to read all this stuff. Our soldiers are experiencing a difficult time. There are a lot of problems. A lot more of the junior officers are married than in my youth; they need apartments, and there aren't any. We get a lot of undesirables in the army, too: physically and mentally sick people and, more and more often, drug addicts and criminals, some potential and some actual. Where do you think the term *paika* [slang for ration] came from? The answer is clear: the criminals brought it with them. I'm convinced of it. The changes in our society inevitably have a direct effect on the army. There can be no doubt about it."

We were watching "Vremya" [a nightly news broadcast] on television. Igor Kirillov, the anchorman, was reading yet another statement from the Soviet government regarding the situation in Afghanistan. Sokolov listened carefully. When Kirillov had finished reading and froze in a meaningful pause, Sokolov turned the volume down.

"I'm getting the impression that history isn't moving along in a spiral, which is the popular conception, but is going around in a circle," he said. "Everything repeats itself, only with doubled or even tripled force. Would you like me to lend you a book to read?"

"Yes, of course," I said enthusiastically, since I hadn't read a single word in the last month.

"Read it," he said. "You'll see what I'm referring to. But I have the book at home. Shall we walk down there? It's not far—only a five-minute walk."

Sokolov's trailer was near the army's ZKP [alternate command post]. It was furnished modestly—bed, couch, desk, VCR, books—

without even the merest hint of luxury. Sokolov sat down on the couch, opened his attaché case, and took out a worn-out photocopy of *On the First Stages of the Russian-Japanese War*, by Major General E. E. Martinov, who served at the Russian General Headquarters at the beginning of the twentieth century. It opened with the following quotation: "Oh, Russia! Forget your former glory! The double-headed eagle is defeated, and yellow-skinned children play with your tattered flags." In lieu of an introduction, Martinov supplied an article that he'd written in the middle of January 1904, a few days before the beginning of the war. The article had turned out to be prophetic: Martinov predicted Russia's defeat.

Sokolov brushed some dust from the jacket of his samizdat [contraband copy], opened the book with great care, and began reading selected paragraphs to me, adding his own comments from time to time. Sometimes it was hard to tell which words were Martinov's and which were Sokolov's.

" 'At such a serious moment in our history, the world's press is busy comparing the strengths of the two countries,' Martinov begins his article." Sokolov, who was sliding his index finger along each line, looked up for a second as if to make sure that I was listening. " 'However, one factor has been completely overlooked, which is extremely important in its effect on the army—society's attitude.

" 'The Japanese people in their entirety—from their first scientist to their last worker—are imbued with patriotic fervor. The might and well-being of his motherland is the cherished ideal of each Japanese man, which renders his personal interests secondary.

" 'Naturally, when such an attitude prevails in society, the army, which is perceived as a reflection of the state's ideas and as the main tool for the achievement of the nation's goals, enjoys great popularity. In their study of history, even as early as grade school, young boys are taught to admire acts of heroism in combat. At university lectures, students hear preachings of a healthy national egotism rather than some cosmopolitan utopias. When a young Japanese man is drafted, it is a joy for him and his family, not a disappointment. When he is employed in the service, he experiences the same respect that the military uniform receives in his country.' "

Once again Sokolov looked up from his book and glanced at me. "But what do we see in Russia?" he asked with a slight smile. " 'At the same time, in educated Russia, at university lectures, in literature and in the press, an entirely different view is systematically presented; this is the view that nationalism is an obsolete concept, that patriotism is unworthy of a modern "man of culture" (who must love all mankind equally), that war is a vestige of barbaric times, and that the army is the main impediment to progress.

" 'These ideas, which start in university circles, in the literary world, and at the publishing offices, and which are so devastating to the entire state system, eventually penetrate the rest of Russian society, so that every nincompoop who joins in this view thus acquires the license to consider himself to be a member of the "progressive intelligentsia."

" 'A logical consequence of such a world view is the complete rejection of military valor and a contempt for military service as stupid and harmful.

" 'Such an attitude toward the army within the intellectual spheres of our society has not yet managed to corrupt the Russian soldier (although the poison of *Tolstovstvo* [a school of thought originated by Leo Tolstoy] has begun to penetrate the masses). But it does have a rather bad effect on the army officers.'

"Would you like some water?" Sokolov asked me. "I have a couple bottles of Borshomi."

He opened one of them, brushing off the sawdust that stuck to it, and filled our glasses with sparkling water. After a couple of swallows, he once again lowered his eyes to the book. He raised an index finger and read on.

" 'Watching this sad phenomenon, one inevitably comes to the conclusion that, to undergo a radical healing, Russia needs to experience some rough times again, such as the events of 1812, so that our cosmopolitans would have a chance to test the practical applicability of these utopias on their own backs.' "

Sokolov pressed his knees together and opened the book to its last pages. He refilled our glasses and read from Martinov's afterword.

" 'Thus, at a time when even the most democratic countries try to instill a promilitary sentiment in their people in the interests of national security, our progressive intelligentsia is preoccupied with the reverse goal and is not in the least embarrassed to declare this even during an unsuccessful war.' "

Sokolov mumbled to indicate that he was skipping a few sentences. Then he went on.

" 'In the last few years, our government itself has headed the antiwar movement. Naturally, the ostentatious statements of the government's communiqué could not abolish all the wars in the universe, but they did give all the numerous enemies in the country's social structure the right to loosen the very foundations of the army, using the government's authority as their cover. . . .

" 'It's worth mentioning that, after adopting these ideas during the Gaag conferences [the international conventions of war adopted at the 1899 and 1907 conferences in Gaag], which served to utterly undermine the prowar feelings of the people and the army, our censors would not even allow objections against them. Moreover, when I wanted to publish the translation of a brochure by the German professor Shteingel, which proved the impossibility of disarmament, I was prohibited from doing so!

" 'It was under these conditions that we were suddenly attacked by Japan, and there suddenly appeared the demand for the courageous soldier, for the selfless officer, for the kind of military valor that had just been publicly vilified, for the art of warfare whose existence had been denied altogether.' "

Sokolov's eyes slid down the page. He whispered something and then turned the page.

"Here it is!" he exclaimed. "Are you tired of it yet?"

"Not at all," I said. "Please continue."

" 'The uneducated masses were interested in the war only insofar as it affected their families and economic interests. The actual news from the far-off theater of war reached the broad masses only in the form of rumors.

" 'And as far as the "progressive intelligentsia" was concerned, it viewed the war as a convenient opportunity for the achievement of its goal: the destruction of the current regime and the creation of a free state in its place. Since it seemed much harder to accomplish this with a victorious war than an unsuccessful war, our radicals not only wished for defeat but tried to provoke it.'

"Are you tired yet?"

I shook my head no.

"Then listen to this," he said. "Here Martinov has a rather

interesting paragraph on the state of literature during that era, and on its writers: 'While during the whole war Japanese poetry, prose, and song tried to lift the spirits of the army, fashionable Russian writers also gave us two works that were hailed by the critics as being particularly timely: Andreev's *Red Laughter*, which tried to instill in our already cowardly society an even greater fear of war, and Kuprin's *Duel*, which is a malicious lampoon of Russian officers. In addition, throughout the war, the radical press was full of attacks against the army and the officers. Things went so far that a certain G. Novikov stated in *Nasha Zhyzn* ["Our Life"] that students soiled their honor by seeing regiments off to war. In the same newspaper we read that a priest in Samara refused to give communion to a mortally wounded man who'd been brought from Manchuria because he'd killed people at war.' "

Sokolov looked at me intently. After a short pause he shut the book and said, "How horrible that poor soldier must have felt, giving his life for his country and, instead of gratitude, hearing only words of denunciation on his deathbed."

Sokolov was silent. I tried to figure out whether the last sentence belonged to him or to Martinov. Then he threw his spotted *bushlat* over his shoulders and huddled up—either against the cold or against what he'd just read.

"Anyway, history doesn't move along in a spiral, but in a circle," he said. "What Martinov wrote eighty years ago applies today. I'm referring not only to his thoughts with respect to the role of public opinion, but also to his recommendations for the organization of the General Headquarters. Take this book and you can restructure the General Headquarters. I can't really decide if there's more humor or tragedy in the situation. Unfortunately, it's time for me to go to the command post. You should go find out about the weather; they just finished reconnaissance work in the Pul-i-Khumri area. If the choppers can't fly today, I'll give you a car. You can drive down to Mazar-i-Sharif and then take a plane to Kabul. Okay?"

18

The small military airfield at Mazar-i-Sharif was sunk in a thick, heavy darkness. The moon, shrouding its face in a veil of clouds, coldly and arrogantly watched the goings-on.

Transport planes, which landed and took off every thirty minutes or so, became invisible as they switched off their lights.

A bright beam suddenly appeared about thirty meters above the ground and began descending with a deafening roar, like a motorcycle coming down a hill.

It turned out to be an Mi-8 helicopter, which had come to Mazar-i-Sharif to pick up two wounded soldiers. The men were lying silently on a stretcher near a beat-up An-12, staring into the sky. Their faces were paler than the moon. A lieutenant colonel who was also flying to Kabul covered one of them with his *bushlat*.

"I'll get another one in Kabul," he said, addressing no one in particular. "This is an outrage. All the headquarters staff have been given sweaters, but there aren't enough for the soldiers."

The light from the helicopter was reflected in the officer's khaki-colored eyes.

The wounded men were loaded onto the helicopter, along with several bags of mail.

"Poor guys," he said. "Tomorrow afternoon they'll arrive in Tashkent and realize that no one—not their girlfriends or their country—wants them. While we fight here our names are being dragged through the mud. It's disgusting."

He took a heavy windbreaker out of his backpack and threw it over his shoulders.

"I wasn't the one who started this war, was I?" he suddenly exclaimed. "What did I need it for? The government said go, so we went. And now they're blaming us for it. I'm on the political staff— how do I explain all this to the soldiers? These wounded men could have gone back to the USSR last fall; that's when their terms of service ran out. But the command asked everyone who was about to go home to stay another six months. Otherwise the army here would have consisted entirely of new kids who hadn't even had a taste of the war. So they stayed. Now they'll come home and be harassed— 'murderers, assassins!' We have a brotherhood here, maybe the only good thing to have come out of this war. In nine years the traditions of the Fortieth Army have grown strong. But look at what they're doing to it now. They're disbanding it! There won't be a Fortieth Army anymore."

A circle of people formed around us. They stared silently at the ground, smoking their cigarettes. One of them offered me a smoke. I held out my hand and felt the chill of the universe.

The lieutenant colonel continued his monologue:

"They tell us that everything in the USSR is done for the individual, for his own good. But since I've been here I've realized how much the life of a Soviet person is worth. Do you know what it's worth?"

He showed me the nail of his little finger.

"That's how much it's worth! For what did we bury fifteen thousand of our boys here? If the military had been allowed to conduct the war as it saw fit, we would have eliminated all this so-called armed opposition a long time ago."

"You'd have to destroy all of Afghanistan to do that," I remarked.

"Nonsense!" he exclaimed. "They should have listened to the military and positioned garrisons along the Pakistani border. If we'd closed all the roads and caravan routes, we would have squashed the *dukhi* without any military action. Naturally, however, we would have had to increase the limited number of troops so that the politicians could claim credit for an invasion. Gibberish!"

With the tip of his boot he picked at a rock on the ground, finally kicking it aside.

"Oh well, what's the point of talking about it now?" he said, waving his hand in exasperation. "You can't rewrite history. Let's get into the plane. The crew is already in the cockpit."

We took off ten minutes later. The plane took a long time to gain altitude and rise above the airfield. We banked slowly and headed south.

There was a curfew in Kabul from approximately ten o'clock in the evening to four o'clock in the morning. The Afghans had set up checkpoints along the roads every five or six kilometers. They were supposed to check documents, but sometimes they stopped cars just to bum cigarettes. An Afghan soldier, his unblinking black eyes staring at you like gun barrels and his submachine gun trained on the driver, would walk up to a car and ask, in a voice that could send chills down your spine, "*Sigar nis*? [Got any cigarettes?]" But the question generally came across as "Hey, buddy, want to keep living?" The driver would hand a pack of cigarettes through the window, his hand trembling with each heartbeat: "bum-bum . . . bum-bum . . ." The sound seemed to come from his chest; in fact, it was the pounding of the howitzers somewhere outside the city.

During the day, the mountains around Kabul resembled a black-and-white photograph of a storm at sea. At night, however, they seemed more like a giant tidal wave that could wash over the city at any moment.

From the window of my hotel room I could see a very tall cliff that resembled a knotty index finger raised in warning to all those who were watching. The cliff snagged the bellies of the low gray clouds; its tip was covered with shreds of dirty cotton wool.

With each passing hour, fewer and fewer Soviet troops remained in Kabul.

In a week the high command was to lift the restricted zone around Kabul's airport, sending the soldiers manning the defensive ring around the capital back to their posts. The mixed aviation regiment was also getting ready to leave the city. Only the crews of three transport planes—scheduled to move the Fortieth Army command from Kabul to Naibabad on February 3—would stay behind, along with ten or so soldiers to guarantee their takeoff.

Army General Varennikov, who was in charge of the Operations Group of the Ministry of Defense in Afghanistan, was supposed to remain in Kabul as late as the night of February 14. He was to be the last of the Soviet garrison, which once numbered in the thousands, to leave Kabul.

A small group of Soviet military advisers still remained in Kabul. During the nine years of the war, the contingent of military advisers had been cut by 178. The Party and Komsomol advisers had left back in the fall of 1988.

The Soviet press corps had also shrunk a great deal. There was a growing rift between the journalists who were planning to leave before February 15, 1989, and those who were supposed to stay behind after the troop withdrawal; the relationship between the two factions began to resemble that between recovering and terminally ill patients in a hospital.

The wives of the Soviet journalists stationed in Kabul had left the year before. The members of the press corps now led comfortless lives. One especially lonely reporter found three or four cats to share his villa, which brought a barrage of wisecracks from a veteran journalist who was known as the least sentimental guy in the whole Soviet colony. Imagine my surprise one morning when, after spending the night at his house, I heard the cynical journalist whispering: "*Duchik! Duchik!* Come here, my baby, I made you some food. *Duchik*, you bastard, come have some milky-milky that Daddy got for you. . . . *Duchik!*" A minute later a fat black cat appeared and, seeing the famous journalist on his knees with a saucer of warm milk in his hands, lazily licked himself.

Kabul's diplomatic corps was also waning by the day. Some of the embassies were now just empty buildings; others were staffed only by an ambassador and an adviser, the latter often serving simultaneously as a diplomat, driver, courier, groundskeeper, guard, cook, and drinking partner.

At the Polish consulate I couldn't find anyone but the ambassador himself.

"Are you thinking of leaving Afghanistan?" I asked him.

"Who knows where a person can feel safer these days—here or in Poland?" he replied, smiling grimly.

"Have you been in Afghanistan for a long time?"

"Yes, for quite some time." He glanced at the window, which was blocked by sandbags.

"Why do you think the Afghan revolution turned out to be so tragic?" I asked, realizing that our conversation was going to be quite brief.

"Young man," he said, squinting his eyes like an old man, "revolutions aren't the only things that die. So do some much more significant things—like love, for instance."

The streets of Kabul seemed to be filled with Soviet military *bushlats*; people were buying last-minute souvenirs to bring back to their families in Russia. In areas where you could hear the roar of armored carriers, the prices were lower (as if the shopkeepers were being held at gunpoint) than in areas that weren't "controlled." I remember a major who, after buying massive amounts of stuff, loaded all his packages onto a UAZ as he sang a little ditty that went: "Kabul, thank goodness I was there. / You gave me clothes and shoes to wear."

Once I went into one of the shops with my Afghan translator to buy a cigarette lighter. "Peace and health to the customer!" the shop's elderly owner said, greeting us in broken Russian. When I asked about the lighter, he quoted an exorbitant price.

"That's too expensive," I said.

"It's up to you," the old man said, shaking his beard back and forth.

"If I don't buy this thing from you, to whom are you going to sell it?" I asked, trying to convince him to let it go for less. "In just a couple of weeks there won't be any Soviets left here."

"Ahmad Shah will be here," he said with a sly smile. "Ahmad Shah has much dollar from Pakistan, from America. He buy!"

"It'll be a while before Ahmad Shah gets here, believe me," I said. "And we're leaving."

"Leaving, leaving," he said, repeating my words and staring intently at me with his clever, half-closed eyes. He waved his hand and said something in his own language.

After we'd left, I asked my Afghan companion to translate the old man's last remark. "He said that the Russian soldiers are heading north to go home," my translator explained. "And later on they will go even farther north, leaving their Muslim republics behind."

The words sent a chill down my spine. I turned around to see the shopkeeper still smiling amicably at me. He waved one more time.

Not far from the shop I saw a long line of people waiting for bread. Even longer lines of cars and trucks were coiled in spirals around the gas stations. Kabul was connected to the USSR (its only source of flour and gasoline) by a single slender thread: the Salang road. Ahmad Shah Massoud had now blocked the road, cutting off the incoming shipments of food and fuel. General Varennikov had responded by organizing an airlift of essential goods from Tashkent. This, however, wasn't enough to keep the city from being strangled in Massoud's grip. Many people believed that the impending military strike against him at South Salang—the rumors had already spread through the streets—would lessen the tension and give the city a chance to catch its breath. And while Massoud was something of a national hero, the people were annoyed that his tactics had caused privation among the city's civilian population as well as among the government troops. Most of the ordinary citizens, as long as they weren't hungry, didn't really care who controlled Kabul; their political sympathies and antipathies were determined by their stomachs.

I remember meeting a towheaded young soldier near the Jangalak plant, where the Soviet command was distributing free flour. His hair and eyebrows had turned white from the flour dust. "This is some kind of international duty," he said as he brushed the powder off his eyelashes with a sleeve of his *bushlat*. "You shoot them with one hand and put food in their mouths with the other."

19

By January, "optimize" had become the most popular word among the Soviets in Kabul. Y. M. Vorontsov, the Soviet Union's first assistant minister of foreign affairs and ambassador to Afghanistan, had brought the term with him from Moscow. It meant to reduce the number of Soviet personnel to an optimal level. The question "How's it going?" was typically answered, "They haven't optimized me yet. What about you?" My hotel roommate began his daily letters to his wife with precisely these words.

With each passing day the Soviet embassy came more and more to resemble a fortress; it had a double protective wall with barbed wire, heavy steel gates, a bomb shelter—even its own armored personnel carrier hidden underneath a tarpaulin. The Soviet diplomats' contacts with the outside world diminished drastically. One of the embassy's junior staff members complained to me that he had to rely on the BBC and the various Voices (Voice of America, for example) for 90 percent of his information about what was going on in Afghanistan.

I'd suspected for some time that the Soviet military commanders were much better informed about the situation in Afghanistan than the Soviet diplomats. Now I was convinced of it.

In one of the embassy's offices I saw a famous photograph of Che Guevara—the same picture, as I later learned from a British documentary, that Ahmad Shah Massoud carried with him everywhere. As I looked at the portrait of Che, who was gazing dreamily upward, I wondered where Ernesto himself, were he alive, would have preferred to see his portrait—in the military headquarters somewhere in the Panjshir mountains or in the office of a Soviet diplomatic adviser in Kabul.

For three weeks running, a tattered poster on a stand near the embassy's movie theater informed observers that "Today, at 7:30, the new French film, The Unlucky, will be shown." The film never ran, however, and its title hardly improved the mood of either the embassy staff or the members of the Soviet trade delegation.

At the bottom of the embassy's empty swimming pool the wind played with fallen eucalyptus leaves. The tennis court would have completely forgotten its purpose had it not been for the chief of the KGB office, who came every Friday (his only day off). His weekly forty-minute sets seemed quite fantastic to me, especially when the camouflaged helicopters that provided covering fire for the airborne troopers would fly by above his gray-haired head.

Every day, from early in the morning until late at night, the Soviet embassy was deluged by "Sov. citizents"—Soviet women who, after marrying Afghan men and living in Afghanistan, had decided to return to the Soviet Union with their husbands and families, now that the situation was extremely tense and Russophobia had placed their lives in danger.

They had different reasons for coming to Afghanistan.

Svetlana D. came to Kabul by her Afghan husband's invitation soon after their wedding. She was very surprised, however, when her husband suggested that she stay at a hotel. Believing that he was looking for a suitable house, at first she didn't object. But soon she started to worry, and for good reason. As it turned out, her husband already had an Afghan wife—not just one, in fact, but a little harem. Eventually she had no choice but to move in, too. As the years passed she even got used to wearing a veil and to her role in the household.

Natalia N. came to Afghanistan soon after the arrival of Soviet troops. She and her Afghan husband lived in a kishlak so remote that it couldn't even be found on a map. One night, some time after the government had issued a decree that prohibited people from hanging portraits of the Ayatollah Khomeini in their homes, government agents—apparently acting on a tip—burst into their little hovel, ripped a portrait of a bearded man off the wall, and threw the husband in jail. They didn't bother to listen to what Natalia had to say. Only after he'd been released did the couple manage to convince the local authorities that the portrait was of Karl Marx and not Khomeini.

Day after day, many such women and their husbands stormed the Soviet embassy in Kabul, desperately trying to obtain exit visas. They were joined by many ordinary Afghan men and women who had no family ties to the USSR but were afraid for various reasons to stay in Afghanistan after the withdrawal of Soviet troops.

20

The headquarters of the Fortieth Army, which had been located in the former palace of King Zahir Shah (and later Mohammed Daoud), had been moved to the site of our division in Kabul on January 10. Varennikov's operations group had moved here as well.

Army commander Boris Gromov's office was now located in a one-story building. His work day typically began at five-thirty in the morning and lasted until eight-thirty at night. Once in a while he would take a short walk and then return to his desk.

Gromov was stout and sturdily built. Short, boyish bangs hid his strong, prominent forehead and made his tired face look younger. The glare of his light-colored eyes was firm and stubborn. There was something mysterious and Napoleonesque about him. Some people thought that he looked like Vladimir Vysotsky, the popular Russian singer; others claimed that in both appearance and mannerism he resembled Marshal Zhukov.

At any rate, everyone agreed that Gromov was only half a step away from becoming a living legend. The army loved him for his simple manner and his fearlessness. Several years ago his wife had been killed in an automobile accident, leaving him with two sons.

While Gromov was still in Kabul, he'd been made the commander of troops in the Kiev Military District.

"What are your achievements as the commander of the Fortieth Army?" I once asked him.

"There definitely have been achievements, but they've been collective achievements, not mine alone. I came here in the summer of 1987. In the last year and a half, we've managed to reduce the loss of life by approximately one and a half times and the loss of machinery by two times. This is due not only to the decrease in military activity but also to the improved training of our soldiers."

"And what about the losses suffered by the detachments of the armed opposition?"

"I don't have the exact statistics. From 1980 on they lost more and more people each year. In the last four years, however, their losses stabilized and did not increase. They learned how to fight, too."

Through the window we could see the sun slowly falling behind the horizon. The sunset was accompanied by distant artillery fire.

Gromov closed the curtains and turned on the light. He took out a gold-colored pack of cigarettes, opened it, and lit one up.

"These are Astor cigarettes," he said. "Would you like one?"

"Thank you, Comrade Commander," I replied. "I wouldn't mind."

I would have guessed that Gromov, if he smoked cigarettes at all, would prefer something very strong and without a filter. Astor cigarettes were more the kind that women liked—weak, with a gold ring around the long, thin filter.

"What was the most difficult time for you in Afghanistan?" I asked.

"When we started the withdrawal of the troops," he said without hesitation. "First we sent two columns to Kabul. We were expecting the opposition to attack their tails, but everything went smoothly. The hardest part was the removal of the troops from Kandahar. It's a very problematic area. There's a continuous green zone all along the road. There aren't that many Afghan troops, and the level of their training left room for improvement."

"Is it easier now?"

"It's too early to say. The number-one problem is Salang. In the last two days there were thirty-seven avalanches along just a seven-kilometer stretch of the road. In the South Salang area, Ahmad Shah Massoud has amassed a strong force—more than four thousand armed men in all. There's never been such a massive accumulation of troops there. He's hoping to shut off the road to Kabul after we leave, which would be tantamount to blockading the capital. Even though Massoud has promised not to touch our columns, we can't trust his word. It's conceivable that he will soon initiate military activity. You see, the complexity of the situation is rooted in the fact that our time here is limited. We must leave the country by eight-thirty on the morning of February fifteenth. If we stay even an extra few hours, it will cause an international scandal. But our vehicles are moving slowly. There's ice on the road, not to mention avalanches, constant stops, traffic jams, and accidents. And now there's Massoud, with his four thousand troops. So there's still plenty to worry about."

"Which subdivision is going to leave Afghanistan last?"

"The reconnaissance battalion of the former Kunduz division. But I will be the last to cross the bridge across the Amu Darya . . . on foot."

"Do you already know what you're going to say at the final moment of the war?"

"Yes: 'There isn't a single soldier behind me.' "

"Is that all?"

"Not quite. No reporter's microphone would survive what I'll say afterward—it would explode!"

"What does the future hold for you?"

"Kiev. The Kiev Military District. I've never been there. I know Kabul, in fact, a lot better than Kiev. This is already my third time in Afghanistan. There's a superstition among our men here that it's a bad omen to talk about your 'last time' in Afghanistan. Instead of using the word 'last,' they say, you should say 'definitive.' But I disregarded this. Before I flew home after my first round, I said, 'Good-bye, my friends, let's embrace for the last time!'

"A few years passed and I was back. The second time that I left, I told myself, That's it, Gromov, this is your last visit here. But fate had other plans for me. So now, as you and I sit here together, I'm thinking to myself, This is my *definitive* time in Afghanistan."

"Are you afraid that they'll send you here again?" I asked.

Gromov let out a stream of smoke through his clenched teeth and inhaled it through his nose. He leaned against the back of his armchair and said, "No, this is it—the end of it!"

While I wasn't quite sure whether Gromov was talking about the war or about our conversation, I went ahead and asked him my final question: "Do you have frequent contact with Army General Varennikov?"

"Of course," he replied. "If it hadn't been for him our troops would have caused five times more trouble than they have."

V. I. Varennikov was born in 1923 in Krasnodar. In 1942, after finishing a course for platoon commanders at the Cherkhask infantry school, he was sent to the battlefront, where he was in charge of a platoon. In August 1943 he became the artillery commander of a regiment, and in 1945 he became the assistant commander of a regiment. He served on the Stalingrad, Southwestern, Third Ukrainian, and First White Russian fronts, where he took part in the battle of Stalingrad; in the liberation of the Donbass Basin in the Ukraine and Poland; in the battle for Warsaw; and in the occupation of Berlin. He was wounded three times and accompanied the victory flag from Germany to Moscow. After the war he served as the commander of a regiment in a northern district.

Over the years Varennikov changed units, cities, and districts. In July 1967, after studying at the General Headquarters Academy, he was appointed the commander of the corps; two years later, he was made commander of the army. In the summer of 1971 the forty-eight-year-old general was sent to East Germany as the first deputy commander in chief of Soviet troops in Germany. In 1973 he became the commander of troops in the Cis-Carpathian Military District, and in 1979 he began working at the General Headquarters, where he headed the General Operations Office and later became the first deputy chief of the General Headquarters. In the spring of 1985 he arrived in Afghanistan, where he directed the Operations Group of the Ministry of Defense of the USSR while retaining his position as the first deputy chief of the General Headquarters. Since then the various commanders of the Fortieth Army—from Dubynin to Gromov—have been under Varennikov's command. Soviet journalists, however, weren't allowed to mention Varennikov's name right up until the end of the war.

One of our problems in Afghanistan, it seemed to me, was that the Soviet Union never had a central office in charge of the various delegations of its superministries: the KGB, MID [Ministry of Foreign

Affairs], MVD [Ministry of Internal Affairs], and Ministry of Defense. The chiefs of these groups acted autonomously, often sending contradictory information to Moscow and often receiving conflicting orders in return. The four offices should have been consolidated under the leadership of the Soviet ambassador. But there were so many different Soviet ambassadors that none of them had enough time to become thoroughly familiar with the state of affairs in Kabul. There was Tabeyev, then Mozhayev, then Yegorychev, then Vorontsov—all within a two-year period. Of these four men, only Vorontsov was a professional diplomat with extensive experience in Central Asia. While the rest had enjoyed successful careers within the Party apparatus, they had no background in Central Asian affairs. Many people believe that it would have been wiser to put all the power in the hands of Varennikov, who'd served almost continuously in Kabul since 1985.

"During my time in Afghanistan there have been repeated changes of leadership in the various offices," Varennikov told me. "And each newly appointed official would begin his term with more or less the same suggestion: 'Why don't we and the Afghans carefully plan out and execute a large-scale military operation against the bands of rebels so that the people here can have a normal life for once and for all?' Unfortunately, the whole problem has been that the rebel bands don't constitute the overwhelming majority of the opposition. The opposition is concentrated in the native populations, which have been fighting to defend their tribal interests.

"I could name many areas whose inhabitants oppose the central government and at the same time refuse to allow rebel detachments on their territory. They're used to living independently and don't want to take orders from anyone. Naturally, they're against anyone who would attack them with weapons or otherwise try to establish rule over them. During the first years of the war, in our effort to support the Afghan government, we thought that we had to implant the nucleus of a political organization in each district. But the *kishlak* dwellers resisted us at every turn. That's why military force was employed wherever there was opposition. Military units were used to maintain the 'people's' power, and certain comrades were eager to report that 'yet another district has been liberated from the *dushmani*.' It sounds absurd, doesn't it? Naturally!"

We talked late into the night, but Varennikov never turned on the light; he was resting his eyes. I could see the vague outlines of his face, the white spots of his temples, and the thin stripe of his dark mustache.

From time to time the telephone rang, and Varennikov would pick up the receiver and listen intently to yet another report from the field. A few times he placed calls to check the progress of the airlift of flour into Kabul.

"Don't you think the Soviet officials in Afghanistan, who had a duty to keep Moscow accurately apprised of the situation here, often sent only information that was likely to be well received, so they wouldn't upset their bosses and provoke their wrath?" I asked him. "I'm referring not only to 1979 but also to the period that followed."

"I'm not in a position to judge the level of training of the staff at that time," Varennikov replied with a smile. "This must be done by people who are competent to do so. But as far as supplying only favorable information to Moscow, this undoubtedly happened. What's more, the diplomats weren't the only ones doing it. Unfortunately, this was the disease of the stagnation period: to inform the central offices only of what would be well received, rather than what was actually taking place.

"The discrepancies caused Moscow to make decisions that weren't always sound, which harmed the Soviet Union a great deal. Our dogmatism, inertia, and sluggishness also led to many problems. That, for example, is why the proposal to create several autonomous districts within the framework of a unified Afghanistan wasn't accepted. Even though such a system would have significantly reduced the tension between the central government and a number of the provincial leaders, Moscow feared that the creation of autonomous districts would tear Afghanistan apart.

"It's also evident that had we agreed earlier to an open dialogue with the leaders of the armed opposition—both inside and outside of Afghanistan—we could have achieved much more tangible results."

The telephone purred once again. Varennikov picked up the receiver and listened for a little while. "Thank you," he said, nodding to the invisible person at the other end of the line. "I appreciate the information." He put down the receiver and turned to me again.

"I'm told that another Il-76 landed at the airport with more flour," he said. "We're in a dead-end situation because of Ahmad Shah Massoud. He won't leave us any alternatives. I'm afraid that we'll soon have to cross swords with him at South Salang. His detachments have come right up to the road. In principle, we're willing to let Massoud take over all of the sentry posts along the road, so long as he agrees not to let anyone but Najibullah's forces pass through and also agrees to protect the road from other opposition groups.

"While we want Massoud to sign such an agreement with representatives of the government troops, he refuses. As soon as we leave he plans to take over the road—the country's most vital artery—and block the movement of government vehicles, which would place Kabul in an even more critical condition than it is now. We can't allow it. We'll have to fight. We've tried to avoid this by every possible means. . . . Who wants to fight in the last weeks of the war? The Soviet command in Kabul doesn't. But we have obligations to our ally, and, I have to say again, Massoud leaves us no other choice."

Varennikov was telling the truth—the Fortieth Army had no desire to fight in the waning days of the war. First, there was the risk of not being able to leave on the morning of February 15. Second, the possibility of additional Afghan and Soviet casualties produced distress in the hearts and minds of our officers.

The mood was quiet and gloomy. The joy that had accompanied the news that the nine-year war was about to end had been replaced by the heavy feeling of hopelessness.

On the eve of the war's final battle, the men at one post had sung a song that went "A soldier served in the military service. / Military service, the time of hardships." At another post they sang, "My road is sad, and my fate is bitter." At yet another a boyish tenor infused his audience with a chilly sadness as he sang:

> Don't call me, Father, don't disturb me;
> Don't call me, oh, don't call my name.
> We're walking down an untrodden road,
> We're drifting in fire and blood.
> I don't know if there'll be another battle;
> All I know is that the war isn't over.

> *We're just grains of sand in the universe,*
> *And we won't see each other again.*

But Kabul was pressuring Moscow, and the army command had little choice but to follow orders.

21

Winter started to retreat during the third week of January. The sun gained strength by the hour, mountain streams tinkled like crystal during the day, and the snow was now covered by a porous crust.

At night, however, the frost still held sway. Everything grew still but the air, which turned prickly and burned the lungs.

Salang's wolfish fangs were still bared at the sky. But now it resembled the moribund scowl of an injured animal. A week after the fighting, the mountains hadn't yet cooled down. The harsh odor of freshly spilled blood hung in the air. Where the fighting had been the heaviest, the charred ruins of *kishlak* huts lined both sides of the road. Almost everyone in South Salang had left their native villages. They'd gone into the mountains or toward Charikar. Only a few hesitant and puny plumes of smoke rose from the stoves of the mud houses.

The fighting broke out at half past six in the morning near a thirty-five-kilometer stretch of the road from Jabal os Siraj to the southern approaches to the Salang Tunnel. The Soviet division stationed on the road was firing all of its weapons. The 82-millimeter automatic mortars were choking and coughing. The artillery was pounding the mountain paths in an effort to trigger avalanches that would prevent additional rebel detachments from reaching the road.

The SU-17 and -24 fighter-bombers, SU-25 fighters, and MiGs were launching an assault north of Charikar, in the gorges of Panjshir, Garband, Shutul, Margi, Arzu, and Katlomi. The ground was torn up and shaking. The cliffs were crumbling.

The guerrillas shot at us sporadically from the *kishlaks*, hitting our installations and sentry posts and moving machinery with sparse bursts of machine-gun fire. By ten o'clock in the morning the first reports of casualties had reached Kabul.

Soon after the battle broke out, peaceful civilians in the villages began to hang white flags out of their windows. At the same time, however, snipers continued to fire on us from neighboring houses. Our APC gunner didn't have time to find out who was who; he demolished everything in sight. At this point women, children, and old men started coming down to the road with their arms raised in the air. Behind them others carried the wounded and the dead, placing their bodies in stacks along the road. The dark-skinned faces of the dead grew even darker in the sun. For the first time our soldiers welcomed the cold.

At Chaugan we set up a little city of heated tents for Afghans who needed medical attention, food, and shelter. Many of the wounded women, however, wouldn't let the Soviet soldiers treat them; they would rather die, apparently, than be touched by infidels.

That day the clear mountain streams turned crimson. The snow swelled up and turned soft and gray from the thousands of explosions and the thick gunpowder fumes.

That day the sign of Aquarius rose slowly in the east.

The heaviest fighting took place eighty meters from the Forty-second Post, near the *kishlak* of Kalatak. It was there, according to intelligence reports, that Karim's detachment—only 120 or so rebels—had dug in. They had submachine guns, a mountain cannon, a recoilless gun, and DShKs. A sniper fired from behind a *duval* [a mud fortification]. Our artillery fired a return volley that planted ten shells around his place of cover. The sniper grew quiet.

Major Urasov, the chief of headquarters of the Second Airborne Battalion, surrounded the *kishlak* with a detachment of soldiers. He knew that there were a lot of civilians in the village and offered Karim a chance to surrender. But Karim and his band of rebels started to retreat to the mountains, using some of the peaceful villagers for cover. Urasov, trying to cut the guerrillas off from the civilians, requested some reserve troops from the battalion's command post. At that moment, however, a spray of machine-gun fire came from the *kishlak*, hitting Urasov in the thigh and groin and puncturing his femoral artery. Grasping at the air with his hands, he flapped his arms helplessly and slowly fell into the snow.

Private Shapalov rushed toward Urasov. Another spray of machine-gun fire. Shapalov's *ushanka* [a Russian fur cap with earflaps] had been blown off his head, but he continued to crawl, pressing his entire body into the snow. His face grew very pale. Karim's machine gunner was showered with grenades.

When they got to Urasov, he was lying on the ground with his arms spread wide. He was bleeding profusely.

Within fifteen minutes he was gone.

Karim's men and the villagers behind whom they hid no longer were treated with kid gloves; all of them were shot point-blank.

Urasov's body was brought to the battalion's command post. A doctor washed him, clothed him in a fresh uniform, and tied together his ice-cold arms, which were beginning to grow rigid. The corpse was wrapped in an OZK [rubberized gear for use in chemical warfare], covered with a waterproof cape, and put in an APC.

Urasov had a wife and two daughters in Kastroma. He'd planned to apply to the Frunze Military Academy in the fall. The day after his death, a letter from Kastroma addressed to him reached the battalion. His wife wrote:

Hello, our dear daddy!
Everything here is more or less the same. We can't wait for the final withdrawal.

It's warm outside. Instead of the January frosts, it's thawing.

On Saturday we are expecting Grandpa Vanya.

Burov is staying in the hospital until the end of January. After that we'll have to see.

Anya is next to me, drawing.

Katya has begun an everyday working life; that math teacher of hers is going to drive me crazy.

My head is empty right now.

The TV is acting weird again. I have a feeling that soon there'll be more running around the shops to get it fixed again.

Anya hates washing up. Every day I have to fight to make her do it. She almost never goes on her own.

Detergent and soap will now be sold every four months by special coupons.

Well, that's it.

I wrote you a little bit about everything.

Good-bye. Big kiss.

Lena
1/18/89

After the shooting ended for the first time on January 23, the dead and wounded were sent south. The wailing of the women along the road rose above the roar of machinery.

"Yes, it was a grim day," Valera Semakhin, an APC gunner, told me. "Something collapsed inside of me. I'll remember it for the rest of my life. I was up at four-thirty A.M. I started getting the vehicle ready for battle. I checked over the gun to see how well it could be turned and raised. The day before I'd taken it apart and cleaned it, so that it wouldn't get jammed. At five-thirty A.M. my vehicle was completely ready for action. Lieutenant Colonel Ushakov, the commander of the battalion, gave orders to fire only at the *dukhi*, not the peaceful civilians. But I didn't see any *dukhi*. I fired only at the houses where I thought they were hiding. I was given a reference point and a sector of firing. I fired from six-thirty A.M. to twelve-thirty P.M. When it was over, the first company began evacuating the dead and the wounded. They were transported by *barbukhaiki* [buses]."

"I was given a sector—several windows in the *kishlak*," recalled Semakhin's friend, who was in another APC a few hundred meters down the same road. "We tried to shoot above people's heads so we wouldn't hit them. It's one thing just to be banging at the *kishlak* walls. That's not so bad. But firing at people? No, I'm not ready for something like that. I swear, I'm not ready. The civilians come down to the road and want to kiss you because you didn't finish them off. Strange people. They should hate us, but instead they are grateful.

Life is worth very little here: two sacks of peas and a sack of rice. I couldn't look them in the eyes. You wouldn't have been able to, either. I killed something in me that day. Naturally, all of us—right down to the last man—received medals so we'd keep our mouths shut. But that didn't make it any easier."

The fighting continued from January 23 to January 25. It would begin early in the morning and go on until the first signs of sunset. It was like that for three days.

Our soldiers and officers cursed the war, their orders, themselves, and Afghanistan.

On January 24, Afghanistan radio and television broadcast a statement from the high command of the armed forces, which said, in part: "For the last year and a half Ahmad Shah has refused to negotiate with the government. Armed bands under his leadership continued to hinder the safe passage of vehicles in the Salang Tunnel section of the Kairaton-Kabul road. The armed forces of the Republic of Afghanistan were forced to conduct a military operation. As a result, three hundred and seventy-seven extremists were eliminated, as well as three ammunition depots and four vehicles. We urge the opposition not to interfere with the passage of vehicles on this road. Otherwise, it shall have to accept full responsibility for the consequences."

The Soviet military command explained the events in South Salang as follows: "On the twenty-third of this month Afghan troops began to install checkpoints and sentry posts in the Tadzhikan area. They were fired upon. As a result, the bands of Ahmad Shah Massoud initiated a confrontation. The fighting, which continued along the entire South Salang area, was directed not only against the Afghan subdivisions but against the Soviet troops as well."

The Soviet command also reported that, from January 23 to January 31, subdivisions of the Fortieth Army in the South Salang area had suffered four dead and eleven wounded.

Ahmad Shah Massoud was said to have described the January fighting at Salang as one of the war's most brutal military operations.

Several days after the January operation, our political supervisor in Kabul asked me what I knew about it; someone had told him that I'd been there. Before I could answer, however, he gave me some friendly advice. "Even if you do know something, you have forgotten it all already," he said. "Right?"

22

The men of Lieutenant Colonel Ushakov's post had sunken and somehow aged.

I heard no soldiers laughing, no lieutenants barking orders. They went about their business in silence, only rarely exchanging brief words. Although no one at the post had been injured during the last operation, it seemed as if I were in a house where someone had died the day before.

It was there, on the evening of January 23, that the commander of the battalion collapsed on top of his cot and wept, hiding his face in his pillow.

"Now he's come around a bit," Slava Adliukov, the assistant commander of the mortar battery, told me in confidence. "But a week ago it was dangerous to come near him. Actually, we've all had an awful feeling in our hearts since that day. Soon after the operation, our battalion commander had a falling out with Antonenko, the deputy division commander. So we've got a whole slew of troubles here. Come in, take your jacket off."

Ushakov was in his little room, hunched near the window. Resting his elbows on his knees, he was squeezing his head with the palms of his huge hands and quietly whistling something into his mustache. He seemed beaten.

Outside there was a snowstorm. A chilly wind knocked at the window.

Without lifting his head, Ushakov cursed Adliukov. "Damn you! Keep the door closed, Slavka. There's a draft!"

Adliukov tugged at my sleeve and we went into his room, which was on the other side of a wooden partition. After settling comfortably into a KamAZ seat on the floor, Slavka turned to me and said, "One time the battalion commander went to see the *osobits* [in the army KGC]. But there was an avalanche on the road, and he was delayed. That's the day Colonel Antonenko paid us a visit. He started telling us what we were after in the upcoming operation and how we were going to do it. 'Comrade Colonel, what should we do about the peaceful civilians?' I asked. 'Kill them all,' he replied."

Slavka loosened his collar, twirled a cigarette in his fingers, and then lit it.

"During the fighting," he said, blowing a stream of smoke toward the ceiling, "Antonenko personally shot several dozen civilians, even though he was responsible only for being in charge. Shooting at people with a submachine gun wasn't part of his job.

"Later on, I heard an account of Colonel Antonenko's behavior on January twenty-third from many eyewitnesses. After reaching a group of landing troops near the Forty-second Post, they said, he grabbed an AK and, holding it at his hip, began cutting down the women, children, and old men who were coming down to the road. I heard that an *osobist*, Captain Morozov, ran up to him, screaming at the top of his lungs, 'Comrade Colonel! Why the women and children?' Antonenko apparently pushed him aside and snapped, 'What about Urasov? Did they spare Urasov? Why should I spare them now?' "

Slavka's voice dropped to a whisper.

"You'd have thought that Antonenko held Urasov closer and dearer than Captain Morozov. As if Urasov's death meant more to him than it did to all of us. Some ace demagogue. Here, in Salang, they even nicknamed Antonenko 'our Rambo.' He is some Tarzan. But he did rub the number off of his armored carrier so that the *dukhi* wouldn't be able to identify him. The reason he hates Ushakov is that he gave our battalion orders to shoot only at the *dukhi*, not at the peaceful civilians. And sure enough, in the zone that Ushakov's battalion was responsible for, the *kishlaki* were all undamaged. None of the civilians were hurt. Antonenko didn't want Ushakov to come out of this massacre clean."

There were persistent rumors throughout South Salang that Antonenko had ordered one of his subordinates to videotape him killing civilians. To keep his memory green. But I didn't—I couldn't—believe it.

Ushakov was called to the division command post in the first days of February. When he arrived, Antonenko was already there.

Antonenko addressed him formally, dispensing with the usual "Comrade Lieutenant Colonel." (After January there could be no friendship between them.) "Why did you fail to comply with your orders?" he asked Ushakov sharply. "Why were the *kishlaki* barely damaged, not entirely destroyed, in the zone that your battalion was responsible for? You reported to me that your men fired from three to five units of ammunition apiece, but, judging by the looks of the place, that's not so. My guess is that you were firing in the air and at the mountains—not at the targets you were given."

As he replied, Ushakov struggled to keep his voice from trembling. "Lieutenant Colonel Liashenko, the deputy commander of the regiment, was at my post on the twenty-third, and he can c-c-confirm that we did exactly what we were supposed to. Yes, it's true that there was no butchery or unnecessary destruction in the zone that my battalion was responsible for. We fired only to the extent that it was called for. We didn't erase a single *kishlak* from the face of the earth; we saw n-n-no need for it. We were firing only at the spots where the band leaders were hiding and at the ammunition depots. The enemy didn't reciprocate because we'd eliminated all the leaders and destroyed all the ammunition dumps. So there was no resistance. As for destruction for the sake of destruction, just for pleasure, I wouldn't allow it. Besides, I tried to avoid unnecessary casualties among the civilian population. How can you even try to accuse my soldiers of shooting in the air? Or of failing to follow orders?"

"I'm tired of talking to weak-minded imbeciles," Antonenko snapped.

"And I'm tired of having fools as my superiors," Ushakov blurted out.

Antonenko called Lieutenant Colonel Kuznetsov, the commander of the regiment, and ordered him to draw up a statement regarding the battalion's failure to carry out its mission in the course of a military operation.

Back at the sentry post, Ushakov found Liashenko. Because of his nervousness, he was stammering more than usual.

"Look, C-C-Comrade Lieutenant Colonel, go to the DKP [division command post] and explain to them how my b-b-battalion was fighting on the twenty-third," he said. "Otherwise, it looks like we sabotaged our orders. And what am I supposed to do now—go before a t-t-tribunal?"

The relationship between Antonenko and Ushakov had become tense in the extreme. Anything could happen.

Ushakov's friends were all telling him: "Don't push it, commander. So you clashed—enough is enough. Antonenko's connections go very deep, even as far as Moscow. He calls all the shots there. There's no point in marching on a tank with your shirt ripped open. If there's as much as one shot fired at our troops during our withdrawal in your zone, he really will have you go before a tribunal."

Ushakov would turn away, his eyes hidden by his dark eyebrows, and stubbornly reply, "The *dukhi* will be shooting at us for sure. But it will happen where we put down the most civilians—where Antonenko was firing—and not in my zone. The *dukhi* will not let this go. Just remember my words. There will definitely be casualties."

These were chilling words. The end of the war wasn't too far off. But no one knew what it would be like—the end, that is—and most people tried not to think about it.

Late one night, some officers gathered in Ushakov's room. They were drinking strong Georgian tea, crunching cookies and cubes of sugar, and smoking pungent tobacco. A bluish haze hung in the air. Damp wood crackled in the stove. A CB radio hissed in the corner. Ushakov was curled up on his cot.

"Antonenko is covered in blood up to his elbows," Ushakov said. "He won't be able to get away with it. I w-w-will not allow it. He's up for a decoration; they're pushing him into the General Staff Academy. If people like him will be in charge, it would be better to have the whole army disbanded. What kind of an example is he for the young people? Take Slavka Adliukov, a nice guy and a good lieutenant. He's decided to leave the army. That's really too bad."

Liashenko interrupted him. "Calm down, Commander, calm down."

"I'm not going to," Ushakov said, challenging the lieutenant colonel's stare. "When we found out about the executions during the latest combat, I reported it to Yakubovsky, the chief of the operations group, to the *osobists* of the airborne paratrooper regiment, and to Colonel Vostrotin."

"Did you report to Vostrotin about Antonenko?" I asked.

"N-n-no, I informed Vostrotin about the actions of his landing troops," Ushakov replied. "They were having a field day, too."

"Did Vostrotin take action?"

"That doesn't concern me. I told him as one communist to another. We aren't connected workwise. B-B-Besides, I found it necessary to inform my superiors not only about the carnage conducted by Antonenko, but also that he is given to money-grubbing to an extreme degree. Even b-b-by local standards. Naturally, Antonenko found out about it. He began picking on me about all kinds of little things. But that's nothing new."

Ushakov flashed a bleak smile and lit a cigarette.

It was still snowing outside. The wind was ripping the snow off the mountains and throwing it onto the sentry post. Pellets of ice clinked on the rocks.

Ushakov continued. "Before he left the post of commander of the regiment to become the deputy commander of the division, Antonenko took up a collection among the officers and ensigns for his own present. To the beloved commander from his loving subordinates, you might say. The political deputy of the Second Battalion, Captain Shavlai, can confirm all this. The money was collected and submitted to regiment headquarters. They bought a VCR and gave it to Antonenko. He sold it to someone else and made a bundle on it. Sh-Shavlai knew too much about Antonenko's activities. And this almost cost him his life."

"His *life*?" I asked in disbelief.

"That's right, his l-l-life. Fifteen minutes before the January twenty-third operation commenced, Colonel Antonenko ordered Captain Shavlai to drive down the road with one measly armored carrier to check out the situation. As a rule we usually take at least two vehicles for safety reasons. 'How am I supposed to take only one carrier?' Shavlai asked. 'You are a political deputy,' Antonenko replied. 'You should go and talk to the people.' They say that when Shavlai came back, still alive by some miracle, Antonenko was m-m-mighty unhappy."

"Yep, Shavlai really aggravated the colonel by staying alive," one of the officers remarked.

"He used to have this habit," another officer said. "Whenever he met a soldier on the road, he would stop him and tell him, 'All right, let's see what's in your pockets.' If the soldier had more than fifty checks [a form of Soviet currency issued to citizens abroad], he would take them away, and there would be no way to get the money back. In case there was any problem, he had a great excuse: a soldier cannot have more than fifty checks, he would say, and if he does, that means he stole them. It's foolproof."

23

Suddenly we heard loud, self-assured footsteps. The door opened with a bang.

Colonel Antonenko stood on the doorstep. With an abrupt motion of his hand, he brushed the frost from his mustache.

The dark-skinned face of Colonel Dolin, the chief of the division headquarters, appeared behind him. We heard a woman's deep-chested laughter. A moment later she stuck her head through the door.

"Hey, boys, it's us," she said flirtatiously. "You weren't expecting us, were you?"

She, too, was dressed in a military uniform. Locks of light hair escaped from her little hand-knit woolen hat, and an exotic aroma—the scent of perfume—floated into the room.

Everyone got up from the cots. There was an awkward silence. Ushakov nervously shifted from one foot to the other. He had no shoes on, just a pair of coarse woolen socks.

Antonenko went to the table and picked up the telephone receiver. Cradling it between his cheek and shoulder, he glanced at his watch. For ten seconds or so he waited for a connection.

"Hello, Pereval? Pereval, give me Courier! What's the story at the Forty-second? All right then, report in ten minutes."

Unfastening the collar of his *bushlat*, Antonenko sank wearily onto Ushakov's cot.

He drilled the floorboards with his eyes and addressed Ushakov. "Make some tea and get together some snacks," he said. "And hurry."

The woman and Colonel Dolin sat down next to Antonenko.

"It's nice and warm here," Colonel Dolin said with a smile, rubbing his hands together.

The woman gave Ushakov a wink. "*Kombatushka* [Little Commander], why are you taking so long with the tea? Can't you see that we are cold? We've been on the road. We're tired."

Ushakov put on his shoes and went out of the room. I heard his hoarse voice behind the partition; he was saying something to Senior Lieutenant Klimov, the commander of the mortar battery. In a few minutes he returned.

"You'll have your tea soon," he said, averting his eyes.

"Good boy!" the woman said with a laugh.

Only six people remained in the room: the woman, Antonenko, Colonel Dolin, Ushakov, Liashenko, and me. All the others had left while Antonenko was waiting for Courier.

The telephone rang. Antonenko picked up the receiver and listened in silence to the report.

Ushakov sat down on my cot. He picked up the December 1988 issue of *Unost* magazine from his night table and started to read. I took out a pack of cigarettes and lit one up.

Senior Lieutenant Klimov came back into the room with a towel, a teakettle, and six metal mugs. He put them down on a low table between the two cots and filled each mug to the brim with very strong tea. After wiping a few drops of tea from the table, he left the room, returning with a bowl of greasy but fragrant pork pilaf and a dish of leftover rice.

I tried not to look in Klimov's eyes. I felt awkward because the senior lieutenant had been turned into a waiter. Klimov himself was staring at the floor.

"*Kombatushka*," the woman called. "Come on, *Kombatushka*."

"What is it?" Ushakov asked without looking up from the magazine.

"*Kombatushka*, what are you reading there?" she asked, deftly crossing one leg over the other.

"Is it important for you to know?" he asked in return.

The woman seemed to be a bit offended. She studied the glowing tip of her cigarette and said, "The commander is so gloomy and unfriendly today, isn't he?"

Colonel Dolin interrupted as amicably as possible. "Yes, really, what's so interesting in your magazine that you keep staring and staring at it?" he asked. "You can't tear yourself away from it, can you? We've got a beautiful woman sitting here, and you're paying zero attention. Shame on you!"

"I'm reading an excerpt from Anton Antonov-Ovseenko's book, *Beria*," Ushakov replied, trying to speak as calmly as possible.

"So tell us," the woman said, putting out her lipstick-stained cigarette in an empty can. "What does this 'Fseenko' of yours write about?"

"About Stalin's mafia," Ushakov replied. "I could read some of it to you."

"Go ahead and read," Colonel Dolin said, glancing at Antonenko and smiling warily. "It'll be all the merrier."

Resting his back against the wall and fixing his gaze on Ushakov, Antonenko placed his hands behind his head. He was smoking, moving his cigarette from one corner of his mouth to the other.

Ushakov started reading: " 'All clans presuppose the existence of familial ties. These were absent both from the Beria-Malenkov camp and from Zhdanov's group. Each clan operated on the healthy basis of a fellowship of bandits, in which all the accomplices were united by a common goal as well as a common danger of dying at the hand of a rival.' Sh-Should I keep reading, or have you had enough?"

"Don't," Antonenko said, waving his arm imperiously. "They're letting the press get away with too much—they write whatever they want now. They've covered our whole history with dung. Nothing is sacred any more. It's one abomination after another."

He looked angrily in my direction.

"They were completely right in unbolting the mouth of the press," Ushakov said, lifting his eyes from the page and challenging the colonel's cloudy stare. "Otherwise, the mafia would keep flourishing."

"Why is the mafia any weaker now that every rag is writing about it?" Colonel Dolin asked. "Are there any fewer of them now than in the times of suppression?"

"No, there aren't," Ushakov said through his teeth. "And do you know why?"

"Why?"

"Because the mafia has penetrated everything. It's even sitting in th-th-this room."

From somewhere behind the mountain, a recoilless gun coughed several times. Colonel Dolin nervously grabbed a sugar cube from the table. Tossing it into his mouth, he crunched down on it several times.

"What mafia are you referring to exactly?" he asked. "Be specific."

"You bet," Ushakov snapped, jumping up from his cot. He told of the Afghan KamAZs that had gone to Panjshir, accompanied by armored carrier #209 and a numberless APC; both vehicles were stationed permanently at Lieutenant Colonel Abramov's command post.

"When they were heading to Panjshir, to Ahmad Shah, the vehicles were loaded to the top," Ushakov exclaimed hoarsely. "But when they returned, they were empty. And one KamAZ was sent as a baksheesh to the senior chief."

At that point Colonel Dolin interrupted him, his eyes flashing wildly. "Comrade Lieutenant Colonel, you have just insulted all of us!" he shouted. "Your accusations are unfounded. And therefore, Comrade Lieutenant Colonel, get out of this room immediately! Immediately! Do you understand me?"

"Yes," Ushakov replied, "I do." He threw up his arms, grabbed the copy of *Unost*, and left the room, slamming the door as he went.

A thick silence fell over the room. Liashenko was chain-smoking. For no reason at all, Colonel Dolin untied a shoelace and then tied it again. Antonenko stretched, cracking his shoulder blades.

Breaking the silence, the woman turned to me and said, "You know, our *kombatushka* has had a concussion. And he's been in the nuthouse more than once. He's got very bad nerves. But we won't tell anyone about that, will we?"

She gave me a tender smile, slightly lowering her eyelashes.

"He's a nut, no two ways about it," Antonenko said grimly but quietly, as if he were speaking to himself. "He is accusing Lieutenant Colonel Abramov of robbery and me of executing peaceful civilians.

A nut. Well, enough about him—he's hardly worth it. You know, I just got back from Termez. I went there to see what kind of town is waiting for our division. And I got to see my brother at the same time."

Colonel Dolin was drumming his fingers on a stool.

Antonenko reached into his bag and took out some bologna, a bottle of whiskey, several bottles of beer, and some smoked bream.

"You can find some excellent bream in the Termez lakes," he said, smiling with the corner of his mouth. "As soon as we cross the border, I'll invite you to go fishing."

"I appreciate it," I said.

Antonenko started cutting the fish into several pieces. "You see, certain crazies, like this battalion commander, are trying to make me into a scapegoat—a kind of Soviet Lieutenant Calley. Calley is no criminal! In wartime you either kill or get killed. Those are the only alternatives."

Colonel Dolin stared at the light bulb through a fish scale. "Beautiful," he said with a smile.

Antonenko poured beer into the mugs, blew the foam from his, and, after a brief pause, continued. "Ushakov, for instance, didn't fire at the *kishlaki* during the last operation. That's criminal. Now, at any time, the *dukhi* in his zone can start firing at our troops without any risk."

He emptied his mug to the last drop and shook the yellow drops off his mustache.

"What was I supposed to do when all these *kishlak* women started coming down toward our sentry post? How was I supposed to know who was hiding underneath the yashmaks? It might easily have been the *dukhi* in women's clothes. They could have come right up to the post and shot all of us, knocking everybody out. The soldiers, those curs, would be dead before they could give out so much as a squeak. So I was forced to open fire. Well, at first I did fire a round above their heads. But they kept coming down. I had no alternative. Incidentally, my orders were to open fire. So I was following orders. Battalion Commander Ushakov wasn't. If the *dukhi* take cover in his zone and start shooting at our rear guard, Ushakov will be the only one responsible. He committed a crime. There's no doubt about it."

I looked deep into Antonenko's eyes. He was sheltered securely underneath the invincible armor of good intentions.

"You tell me," Antonenko said, meeting my stare and narrowing his eyes a little. "What's more important for a Soviet commanding officer: to eliminate the *dukhi* and kill some women along with them to save your own soldiers or to remain passive and allow the destruction of a Soviet sentry post? I really think that any officer in his right mind would choose the former. And besides, did they spare Urasov? We had to avenge him. There are no saints anymore, and it seems as if there won't ever be any again. Let's drink to everything that's good in the world."

There's a certain kind of varnish that's impossible to scratch, even if you scrape it with a nail. Antonenko was apparently coated with it.

"Hey, boys," the woman suddenly exclaimed, letting a hint of sadness touch her smile. "What will you do when the war is over? What will you be doing when you return? What would you do without the war, my little ones? Without Afghanistan. My poor, poor dears."

"Let's drink to the General Staff Academy," Colonel Dolin suggested. He embraced Antonenko and kissed him on the lips.

The woman stretched out her hand to turn on the radio that sat on the table. We heard the faraway voice of Sofia Rotaru.

"Sofia is experiencing a second youth," Antonenko said as he listened with a dreamy expression. "She's really ripened to maturity."

"It would be a perfect time, wouldn't it?" Colonel Dolin said. Winking at me, he used his hands to outline the shape of a woman's hips.

"Yeah, but Gurchenko is starting to show the signs of her age," Antonenko said after a pause. His voice seemed full of regret.

The woman was clearly unhappy at the turn the conversation had taken. "Hey boys," she said, throwing up her hands, "do you think it will be cold in Termez again?"

"Don't worry," Colonel Dolin replied. "You and I will be warm."

"And maybe even hot," Antonenko added.

"Let's drink to the women we love!" Colonel Dolin exclaimed, his eyes glittering. "Let's drink standing up."

He pressed the glass between his left cheek and the edge of his right hand, sticking out his elbow. With an abrupt motion of his hand, the glass pivoted toward his mouth. He threw back his head and emptied the glass, stamping his foot softly on the floor.

There was a knock on the door, and Klimov entered the room. After collecting the dirty dishes, he disappeared without a word. Antonenko's eyes followed him. Then he pulled out a color photograph of his wife and children and said, "Here's my family."

They were exceptionally beautiful. I meant to say this to him, but I suddenly remembered January 23 and kept silent.

"I just bought a GAZ-24," Antonenko added for some reason.

Colonel Dolin embraced him tightly once again and planted another wet kiss on his cheek. Then he suddenly recoiled and asked me, "Would you like us to present you with a VCR?"

"Thank you," I replied, "but I hope that some day I can make enough money to afford that stuff."

"He is poor but proud," Antonenko said, laughing.

Colonel Dolin wouldn't leave me alone. "Are you taking home any weapons?" he asked.

"I'd love to," I replied, "but we might get quite a shakedown at the customs in Khairaton."

"He is poor, proud—and naive, too," Colonel Dolin said, falling into a hearty laugh.

"Colonel Dolin wants to joke," Antonenko said, drawing his eyebrows together. "But you are quite right. There is customs at Khairaton, and it's better not to risk it. It would make a lot of sense to catch some z's for a few hours right now, don't you think?"

24

The next day I was up early, awakened by the rattling of the laundry I'd washed the day before. It had frozen during the night.

"Wow, it's freezing." The sound of my own voice came from a distance.

Slavka Adliukov ran into the room.

"So," he said with a smile, his eyes darting around the room, "get your stuff together and off we go into the mountains."

At seven in the morning we were supposed to climb up to Tulip, a sentry post in the mountains. As Ushakov put it, it was absolutely the last ascent of the war.

As soon as I had shaved, the caravan was ready to go. We stuffed our backpacks with wood, coal, submachine guns, ammunition for the grenade launchers and the mortars, plus rice, butter, sugar, and tobacco and neatly stacked them all next to Adliukov's quarters.

"Maintain a d-d-distance of no less than ten steps," Ushakov reminded us. "The sapper will go first. The caravan will be walking twenty steps behind him. Walk in each other's tracks; don't forget about the mines. If you get shot at and need help from below, let off a red s-s-skyrocket. Any questions?"

I wore two sweaters, a *bushlat*, and padded pants and had put leggings on top of my mountain boots to keep my feet from getting wet. An MT-LB [multipurpose tracked vehicle] gave us a lift to the point of departure, and we started walking.

The mountains arched underneath the heavy snow. We were buried in snow up to our hips. The wind and the sun were, in their own way, worse than tear gas; the tears rolling from our blinded eyes turned into icicles on our cheeks.

We were moving along the bottom of a gorge like ants in the hollow of a human spine, ascending the dazzling, sugar-white ridge step by step.

The road below now resembled a tiny snake; the MT-LB was just a dot. Knowing that it was equipped with a Cornflower [an automatic mortar] had something of a calming effect on us.

The wind blew right through my woolen hat, and my wet hair gradually hardened into a shell of ice. I unfastened the helmet from my belt, put it on, and heard the snowstorm drumming against the metal.

Soon we passed a deserted, dilapidated *kishlak*. We could see charred walls and shell holes in the roofs; the contents of the huts were strewn about outside.

Competing with the howling of the blizzard, Adliukov shouted to Sergeant Pakhimov to keep his eyes on the *kishlak* as we passed it.

Far away, on the other side of the road, our aircraft were working hard. The mountains sighed but stoically withstood the attack, and from time to time the wind brought us their hollow moan: "Ohhh . . . uhhh . . . ohhh . . . uhhh . . ."

The endless ridges formed an elaborate pneumatic system, much like a church organ, complete with its own air pipes and amplifiers. The wind from Panjshir, the spirit of the nine-year war, gave us a concert as it raced through the mountains. It held the bass notes of grief and melancholy for a long time, accompanying our small detachment as we stubbornly climbed upward.

The higher and steeper the slope, the less snow there was. We made our way across a crust of ice that was many meters thick, crawling on our hands and knees under the weight of our backpacks. The knit lining of my helmet kept falling on my face. My eyes were full of snow and nearly frozen shut. Ahead of us, the sapper pointlessly tapped the ice with a ramrod. The MT-LB below was no longer visible; neither was the sentry post above. Somewhere in the unthinkable heights of the sky, we could see the white summits of the mountains. The Afghan sun broke through their powdered snow halos.

Suddenly and menacingly, a gigantic boulder appeared in front of us, right above our heads. I contemplated the delicate balance of good and evil. What if someone had fired a single shot? What if we'd committed one too many sins in our lives? Would the boulder have come tumbling down, crushing us in its path? Some unknown and saving grace, however, kept it from falling.

A gaunt bird with a hooked beak circled above our heads. He seemed to be looking down on the detachment in a happy state of anticipation. Without even bothering to aim, the soldier in front of me fired several shots at it. "What a bastard," he wheezed, wiping his forehead with the back of his sleeve. It was easy to imagine the bird pecking at our corpses.

My eyelashes had frozen together completely. It would take an ice pick, it seemed, to pry them apart. But I managed to scrape the ice from my eyes with my rough canvas gloves, and then I saw Tulip, the mobile sentry post.

The soldiers who served here, at an altitude of forty-seven hundred meters, had seen nothing but mountains for more than a year. Only once in a while would they go down to Ushakov's post to take a bath, cure their hearts of alpine fever, pick up their mail, and grab some ammunition before heading back up to Tulip.

The senior lieutenant who served as the post's commander had spent nearly two years in the mountains. "I've struck them from my life," he told me impassively, putting his feet up on a stool and nodding at the window, where the sun was getting ready to set. "And so, the continuation of *Mountains*, the multipart film produced at the Afghan Studio. Part five hundred and six—'Evening.' Take your seat. We'll watch it together."

I remembered Sergeant Saigakov, who, in the summer of 1986, had gone AWOL just so he'd be sent to the real war as punishment. The fear of death, he said, was easier to endure than the impenetrable boredom of keeping watch.

Here at Tulip, however, life and war occasionally provided the soldiers with some excitement.

Once, a couple of them went to the spring, which wasn't more than four hundred meters from the post. At a prearranged time every week, under a longstanding agreement, some Afghan children would bring *chars*,* which they would trade for cartridges. One of the *bachata* asked the soldiers if he could play with a rifle—just for laughs. They innocently handed him an AK. The *bachonok*, continuing to laugh, twisted the safety off and changed the switch to automatic fire.

"Hey, *bacha*, stop kidding around," one of the soldiers said.

But the kid, flashing one more smile at the soldier, pressed the trigger and gunned him to the ground with a short burst of fire. The other soldier managed to flee to safety.

This was just one of the many stories I was told by the soldiers at Tulip. They bombarded me with the most unexpected questions, and I wound up doing most of the talking. We spent about an hour and a half at the sentry post, resting, drinking hot tea, and warming our hands and feet. Then, emptying our backpacks, we started to prepare for the descent.

"And now," Adliukov said, "it's time to sled."

He sat down on his empty backpack. Putting his gun in his lap and kicking up some snow, he raced downward, as if into his own childhood. Everyone else followed suit.

We really were children—children of the war.

---

*A homemade opiate consisting of opium, horse sweat, and horse manure.

25

Two days later the battalion was up at dawn.

Our armored carriers lined up along the road as the last of the darkness was melting away.

Ushakov came out onto the road and looked the battalion over. Eleven vehicles—almost a whole company—were missing. Six had left earlier with the commander of the regiment. The rest he'd passed on to the greens.

A red flag flapped on the antenna of the second armored carrier from Mokasiy's company. It resembled the wing of a *podranok* [a Russian bird].

"Stick the flag up your butt, soldier!" Ushakov shouted angrily. "This isn't a parade. Better take all the rubbish off the car. If something happens, you won't be able to turn your gun."

The soldier wanted to answer, but the commander of the company quickly warned him to keep his mouth shut.

A political deputy from another battalion attempted to intervene. "I'm counting this as—" he began, but Ushakov abruptly interrupted him.

"Why don't you count to a hundred," Ushakov said. "I'm going to act the way I see fit."

The company commander backed Ushakov up. "Instead of the flag, we'll stick the political deputy's head on the car with bows in his hair," he said. "The journalists in Termez will piss in their pants."

Klimov's mortar battery had gotten held up on its way out of the post; a broken-down armored carrier blocked the exit. Adliukov had been unsuccessfully poking around in the engine for two hours.

Ushakov ran around the paralyzed vehicle, muttering and cursing as he went. "Stupid pups. You wouldn't listen to the battalion commander, who's been around. Didn't I tell you to check the cars the night before?"

But the armored carrier couldn't be started. So they dumped two buckets of diesel fuel on it and used a rocket gun to set it on fire. A single flare went up in the air with a blaze.

The metal joints of the battalion cracked in unison, and it slowly started to climb up the mountain.

The engines roared madly and filled the air with exhaust fumes. Then the treads began to turn, tossing back dirty wads of snow with each forward lunge.

Soon the column disappeared behind a mountain. Two kilometers below, the Second Airborne Battalion was climbing toward the Salang Tunnel.

The third platoon was accompanied by APC #427. A bunch of soldiers were huddled together, clinging to its tower. Andrei Lanshenkov, Sergei Protapenko, and Igor Liakhovich sat in the back. They all wore bulletproof jackets.

That evening, a little after seven o'clock, the battalion stopped at the Forty-second Post, near the *kishlak* of Kalatak. This was the place where Major Urasov had died, and where he had been so harshly avenged by Colonel Antonenko.

The black of the night spread through the sky like ink on a blotter.

The commander of the battalion ordered the marking lights of all the cars to be turned off.

"Another twenty-four hours and we'll be at the border," Liakhovich said. "It's hard to believe."

"If the troops don't get jammed up at the pass," Lanshenkov replied, "we will."

"God willing," Protapenko added.

Liakhovich had served in the sapper company, where he'd been nicknamed "Sapper." He was later transferred to Senior Lieutenant

Ovchinikova's special intelligence platoon, but the nickname stuck with him.

Sapper had arrived at the Fortieth Post in December of the past year. His job was to sweep for mines, thus ensuring that blockades could be set up safely.

During the entire year the platoon hadn't suffered any casualties.

It was getting colder by the minute. The driver started the engine, and soon the soldiers were inhaling hot exhaust.

In a few minutes the entire battalion was roaring, but no one moved.

The technical deputy's Ural refused to start. He opened the hood and checked the starter.

Major Dubovsky came up to APC #427 and grabbed a crescent wrench, but the driver needed a tetrahedral wrench.

"I need a number seventeen," the driver said.

Suddenly a GAZIK pulled up to the Ural. The commander of the division stuck his head out the window.

"Hey, you son of an inferior nation," he shouted through a loudspeaker. "What are you doing? Don't switch the gears. Start the car up and let's go."

The driver probably didn't understand him. He didn't respond and continued fussing with the engine. The GAZIK sped away.

At regular intervals a compressor kicked air into the tires of the armored carrier.

The commander of the company and the major returned with the right wrench and gave it to the driver. Then they climbed back into the APC to get warm. One by one, eight lights appeared inside. The soldiers were smoking, warming their bluish lips and fingers with cigarette smoke.

"Nice," Sapper said to Lanshenkov as he took a deep puff.

He was going to say something else, but suddenly a spray of submachine-gun fire cut across the road. The red dotted lines of tracers pierced the darkness.

The shots came from the post, which had just been handed over to the greens.

The armored carrier up ahead fired a warning round into the

sky. The rest were silent. Apparently the commander of the battalion had decided not to get involved in the shooting.

Lanshenkov heard Sapper wheezing something into his ear. Turning toward him, he saw Sapper helplessly sucking air into his mouth.

"What?" Lanshenkov asked. "What?"

Sapper remained sitting in the same position. Then his head fell back; he was looking at the sky.

"Sapper!" Lanshenkov shouted. "What's wrong?"

Sapper didn't answer.

The company commander ran up to the APC. Shaking Sapper on the shoulder, he yelled to the driver: "Turn your lights on! Where did he get hit?"

Sapper was carefully lowered from the vehicle and placed on the ground, where he was enveloped in a yellow circle of electric light. A little red stream of blood trickled its way over the ice toward the curb.

"A neck wound," the company commander said, getting up from his knees. "The bullet went right through and came out the back of his head. Damn it!"

An ensign squatted next to Sapper, feeling his left wrist.

"He still has a pulse," he said.

Two soldiers cut off the sleeve of Sapper's *bushlat*. The medical supervisor injected Promedol into his gray arm, which was already growing cold. He made a tourniquet, waited for the vein to swell, and inserted an IV.

"There it goes," Lanshenkov said.

The company commander radioed the battalion commander and yelled into the mike: "I've got a three hundred or a twenty-one. Do you read me?"

"Take him to the Forty-sixth," came the reply.

There was a first-aid station at the post.

Sapper was put on the APC. The driver started the vehicle. With a sudden jerk, it began to move up the mountain.

"Put in a second IV!" the company commander shouted.

The medical supervisor put it in, but the liquid wouldn't flow. It was frozen.

"Fuck!" the company commander cursed. He took someone's

bushlat and used it to cover Sapper, who was lying on the silvery surface of the APC's sharklike snout, looking up at the stars.

The crescent moon resembled a lifeboat in the sky.

"Fuck!" the company commander cursed again. A grimace twisted his face.

We reached the Forty-sixth Post. Sapper was wrapped in a blanket and carried to the doctor. The doctor fussed over him for about five minutes, listening to his pulse and examining his wound.

Finally the doctor opened the door and came outside. "That's it," he said. "The bullet went through his vertebrae. There's damage to the base of the skull, a hemorrhage of the brain. That's it."

They carried Sapper into the fresh air and put him back on the APC.

The moonlit sky illuminated Sapper's face.

His skin had come to look like waxed paper. Blood still streamed from his nose and ears. The reflection of the night sky was in his eyes, just as it had been twenty minutes ago.

"Shut his eyes and cover his face," somebody said.

Sapper's body was wrapped in a blanket and placed on the stretcher.

Five minutes later the blanket was covered with snow.

The soldiers gathered around the APC.

In the eyes of one was the question "Sapper, why you?"

In the eyes of another, "Good-bye."

In the eyes of a third, "Better you than me."

In the eyes of a fourth, "If I'm not lucky, we'll meet soon."

In the eyes of a fifth, "Fuck!"

In the eyes of the company commander, tears.

Not a single one of them wished to become the *last Soviet soldier to be killed in Afghanistan.*

So Sapper had taken it upon himself, saving the several thousand Soviet soldiers who still remained.

He'd also put the period at the end of the war.

EPILOGUE

The Moscow magazine *Ogonyok*, where I have been working now for almost ten years and which sent me on a number of occasions to Afghanistan to cover the war, recently finished publishing extracts from my book *The Hidden War*.

The path taken by *The Hidden War* onto the pages of the magazine was not smooth. When I got the manuscript back from the military censor I discovered more than two hundred serious deletions, distortions, additions, and corrections made by the heavy hand of the colonel-censor.

I could not agree to such changes.

A long battle began between *Ogonyok* and the censor. It lasted over three months. Both of the contesting sides employed powerful forces from their reserves in the rear.

On our side was glasnost and the conviction that the country needed to know the truth about the Afghan war. On their side was something more material: power.

But the circumstances surrounding the unpublished story became, thanks to glasnost, a cause célèbre. People began to speak and even to write about it.

And the military retreated.

But only so as to quickly inflict a series of answering blows. They rained down from the right in the form of articles and reviews published in brief intervals in the military and conservative civilian press. These pieces had titles like "The Half-Truth, or How They Are Feeding the Public What It Wants to Hear About Afghanistan," "What Artyom Borovik Neglects to Say," "The Hidden Heroism," "The Truth Does Not Tremble Before the Real State of Affairs," and so on.

They accused me of all sorts of mortal sins: that in reality I had never been in Afghanistan and therefore all my descriptions were sheer fabrications; that I was a traitor and a literary impotent (this for my remark that, by the end, the war reminded me more and more of the sexual act of the impotent); that I deliberately hid from the public information that I was very familiar with, information about how it was actually the Jews who had induced Brezhnev to send troops into Afghanistan. Even President Najibullah became irate: he forced the Afghan Union of Journalists to come out with an official damnation of me in the journal *Paiam*. They did not, of course, sentence me to death, as the Iranians under Khomeini did to the British novelist Salman Rushdie for his book *The Satanic Verses*. No, nothing like that. But they didn't give me a visa for my last trip to Afghanistan. And in a noisy ceremony, the Writers' Union of the USSR solemnly refused to elect me into their ranks, having declared that I had shamed the Soviet corps of generals.

Until that point I had diligently answered any attack on me, but then I stopped. In the first place, I understood that I would otherwise waste my whole life in polemics with the generals. Moreover, argument gives birth not so much to the truth as to mutual hatred. And we have more than enough of this in my country to begin with.

In concluding this book, I would like to cite several letters from the huge number that have been sent me since the extracts from *The Hidden War* appeared in *Ogonyok*.

Esteemed Comrade Borovik!

I read and reread with great interest and emotion your story *The Hidden War*, which was published in the magazine

Ogonyok in November 1989, or more precisely, as published in
Ogonyok no. 46. . . . I completely agree that the introduction
of Soviet forces into the DRA [the Democratic Republic of
Afghanistan] was a tragic mistake! I only want to say that
I consider the official figure of 15,000 dead *a great underestimate*.

As early as February 1981 an officer in the forces of the
USSR Interior Ministry told me that in January 1981 losses
already came to 15,000 officers and soldiers. And there were
20,000 dead by May 1981—this figure was given me by a worker
in the Komsomol [the Communist Youth League]. It is impossible to believe that our expeditionary force of some 100,000 to
120,000 men had such "small" losses!

Esteemed Artem Genrikhovich, why did our new, "re-
structured" leadership in March or April 1985 not order a
withdrawal of forces from the "Afghan" quagmire?! So many
lives could have been saved!!!

You write that the principal perpetrators have been laid to
rest: Brezhnev, Suslov, Ustinov, Andropov.

But what of those still alive and now on pension, the
former members of the Politburo of the Central Committee of
the CPSU: Kirilenko, Grishin, Tikhonov, Romanov, Kunaev?!
And what of the yet living Academician B. N. Ponomarev,
who from 1961 to 1986 was a Secretary of the CPSU Central
Committee and from 1972 a candidate member of the Central
Committee Politburo—for all these years Boris Nikolaevich was
in charge of the international communist workers' movement
and knew what was going on. Indeed, all these people must
have known about the tragedy that had "broken out" in Afghanistan.

But they knew and . . . they remained silent!

Why, even now, are figures not being published: the dead,
wounded, and missing in action in the fulfillment of "internationalist duty" in East Germany (1953), in Hungary and Poland
(1956), and in Czechoslovakia in August 1968?

No doubt you, Artem Genrikhovich, know that our
military and civilian allies died in Angola, in Lebanon, in the
Republic of Cuba, in Syria, in Egypt, in Mozambique. Unfortunately, nothing is known about our human casualties in the

socialist countries of Europe and in the countries of the Third World. Alas, comrade Borovik, it would have been very desirable if *The Hidden War* had been published as a separate book so that it would not be forgotten. In my view, your story, written in a sharp, vital, and rich language, and based on a wealth of factual material, deserves to be published as a separate book.

. . . It seems to me that the misfortune was the result not of the senility of Leonid Ilyich [Brezhnev] and his "comrades-in-arms" on the Politburo, but rather of the very *system* that gave birth to those *sorry politicians* who were unaccountable either to the LAW or to their OWN PEOPLE. I have in mind the notorious duty of the "military-internationalist."

I am writing you, Artem Genrikhovich, this letter and I think that you know about all this better than I, that is, about the SYSTEM OF POWER!

I conclude with this.

Respectfully yours,
Dmitrii Khimich.

Greetings, esteemed Artem!

Please allow me to call you this.

Artem! I thought for a long time before deciding to send you this letter. It seems to me that I have suffered a great misfortune and that only you can understand me.

I followed your reports about Afghanistan, saw you with our children there—on that hot ground. Indeed, nobody other than you, it seems to me, can understand me. And so I am writing you.

My son Vadim was drafted into the Soviet Army in 1986 and ended up almost immediately in Afghanistan (after three months of training in Termez, of course). He served in the special forces (Spetsnaz) in Baraki. Initially he drove an armored car, and later was sent to Kabul.

What we went through those two years I do not need to tell you. You yourself know. I can say only one thing: I was raised without parents and, like many children of war, I had to live however and with whomever I could, and therefore my family and my children are everything to me. I tried to be a good mother.

For the two years of my son's service I lived in constant fear, waiting for months for his letters (although he wrote often). I had the feeling that something had happened to him: when he twice ended up in the hospital, again when some great danger threatened him, and at other times as well. My body did not endure it, and I fell apart and became very ill—I received the official designation of an invalid.

But, thank God, as they say in Russian, in December 1988 my son returned home from a Tashkent hospital.

It is hard to relate, Artem, what kind of shape he was in.

He went into the army weighing 80 kilograms at a height of 1 meter 80 centimeters, a hardened, strong, young sportsman (he was wild about hiking). But he returned weighing 54 kilograms, yellow, black, emaciated. And his eyes . . . they were not his eyes. Something was absent, they lacked understanding. I look at him—and he is not himself. I don't recognize him.

At first he was completely depressed, ate and slept badly, went nowhere. He just stayed in bed.

Gradually, he began to become himself again. He took preparatory courses at an institute; he got a job. But he began to complain about gaps in his memory. I too noticed it. He began to get nervous, to fall apart, and to cry out in his sleep.

It was terrible to hear him "do battle" at night. An extraordinary excitability seized him.

I did not know what to do. I ran to different doctors, made herbal remedies and potions. But still: he would suddenly in the course of a conversation withdraw and begin to stare at a single point. It was awful to watch him.

The withdrawal of our forces began. Some young men came to stay with us, and then Vadim revived, and then things at home grew less alarming. Even the condition of my soul became less alarming.

But what I want to mention, Artem, is that the young

men did not drink at all, even though they lived with us for several days.

But an unfortunate thing occurred nonetheless. I began to feel poorly. I had to go and stay at a hospital, but I was afraid to leave him in such a condition. But illnesses do not wait. Vadim on several occasions at night had to summon ambulances for me. It was already March.

Suddenly a brother-soldier came to see him, Volodia from Leningrad, with his brothers and sisters. They brought alcohol with them. I was bedridden at the time. In the morning they were going to take me off to the hospital.

They had a fair amount to drink (as I later found out) and left to accompany a friend, but on the bus they picked a fight with some young people and assaulted two of them. They were taken in by the militia. Thus began an affair that has already lasted twelve months.

For all of us, and for him particularly, this was a terrible, unexpected shock.

Artem! I have been unable to understand how this could have happened. How could our children, who have gone through such a "cauldron," do such a thing, thereby lowering our human dignity.

This understandably will remain on Vadim's conscience for the rest of his life, and on mine as well, since I have always believed that parents too must answer for all the mistakes of their children.

To live with this has become difficult.

And it's difficult for Vadim as well.

But time heals all. Eventually things got a bit easier for him. With great difficulty he transferred to the Kashenko hospital, where he stayed for a month for medical examination; the court, which convened on November 20, 1989, sentenced him to two years of working off his sentence in the chemical construction industry. After the sentence, we appealed to the Moscow City court.

You know, Artem, Vadim did not understand what was happening to him, because in September he suddenly confessed to me: "Mama, something has left my soul—something heavy, a fire. It has become easier for me to breathe." And in September, he cried out for the last time in his sleep.

Dear Artem, I am so afraid for him. I know very well that it is impossible for him now to leave his home, his family, his collective. I understand that he must pay for what he has done. But I am terribly tired. Who will pay me for the loss of his health? For all my losses? For the well-being of my family?

I am not justifying his actions in any way, but I can't understand why they didn't take at least into partial consideration in sentencing him his positive characteristics.

Now my son is in a special commandant's office [spetskomendatura] in the city of Kolomna. As I surmised, he cannot survive this term. During a visit to him I saw how much he had changed. Again a psychosis has begun inside him. He told me: "Mama, I am afraid of falling apart. I can't survive again for two years."

Yes, I agree, and I too will not be able to survive.

And my son, to prevent something from happening to him, put himself voluntarily into the psychiatric hospital. He is simply afraid to live, afraid of falling apart.

What is to be done? What is to be done?

I understand that he is guilty, and he too understands this well. Is there really no way he could have been punished differently?

If he could live at home and work at his collective, he would be able finally to return to normal, to adapt. But now I am full of doubts.

Tell me, please, what to do, how to help him, how to save him. He is so terribly upset and overwrought, believes in nothing, is so embittered.

Respectfully,
Kirukova, I. A.

Greetings, esteemed Artem!

The Afghan veteran Sergei Petrovich Chekushkin is

writing you. I have wanted to write you for a long time because I consider you one of those people who write the truth about Afghanistan. I have written to *Pravda*, to *Komsomolskaya Pravda*, to the T.V. show *Vzgliad*, but I have received a reply only from *Komsomolskaya Pravda*: "We understand your feelings. We will be writing about this in the paper. Direct your inquiries to the Decoration Department of the Defense Ministry." And that was that. On the pages of *Komsomolskaya Pravda* not a line from my letter was published.

I will try with utmost brevity (although this is very difficult) to express my thoughts about Afghanistan, although not from the "high" position of an adviser to Major-General Tsagolev (I read his article in one of the issues of *Aif* and saw his appearance on *Vzgliad*—by the way, I do not agree with Tsagolev) but "from below," if one can put it that way, from the very "rank and file" of the officer corps, i.e., from a platoon leader.

I served (and I stress served) in Afghanistan (I did not fulfill my internationalist duty but rather what we called our "inter-needless duty") from June 1987 to June 1988 in the 191st Corps of the Gazninsky Infantry Division in Gazny Province as the commander of a tank platoon. I have seldom found the truth about the Afghan War written in the press.

Why do we deceive the people in our country? Let them know the truth, even the bitter truth about how we fought there, how we received decorations, lived a garrison life in all its purity and filth, the consequences of which (judging by the Garrison Regiment and by the 56th Corps of the Airborne Ranger Brigade of which I was the commander for two months in Gardez, Paktiia Province) were great. If we judge by the Fortieth Army, then such a huge pile of muck will be turned up. I can write a great deal to you about all this, but doing so would, to put it bluntly, waste time and sully the page. Write me several lines and I will send you a letter with all the details about how some there "did battle," received and then were deprived of battle decorations, falsified the lists of those who would receive decorations, redistributed equipment and personal gear, about what our superiors drank, what the higher-ups had for dinner and what the majority ate, where goods for the Afghan population disappeared to, how the officers made cripples of their soldiers and ignored murders and suicides, about the tragic events in battle that were committed with the full knowledge and under the orders of high officials, how we lived and how they, the "regimental elite," lived, about how lists of those decorated were not issued according to the rules because of the personal enmity of superiors to their subordinates, how housekeepers, bathhouse attendants, and gardeners were rewarded, and in general about anything and everything. I will include dates, circumstances, names—I have many friends who can confirm every one of my words. I will be waiting for a response.

Don't ignore my letter and you will receive a huge amount of information.

With respect,
Senior Lieutenant in the Reserves,
Sergei Petrovich Chekushkin.

Greetings, Artem!
When will your book about the Afghan War appear. I read that you will be published in *Ogonyok*, but I have been unable to find a copy. I have read that you wrote an essay about a fellow from Tomsk. Who is this person and when will we read it? It will be of great interest to me. I am acquainted with the Afghan veterans of our city.

For several years in a row I have been seeing and treating in our stomological polyclinic participants from the war, the Afghan veterans as well as the relatives of those who perished. I am acquainted with mothers who have long had wet eyes. To see them . . . is horrible.

Artem, the war was indeed an evil gamble, but the lads

died heroically, they were convinced that they were defending the Fatherland. They were totally deceived.

We await your essays on the young men who loved their Homeland deeply, there, so far away.

With respect,
Doctor-Stomatologist,
T. I. Kuznetsova.